Kelli Crowe

Stepping Heavenward

Calvary Press
PUBLISHING
AMITYVILLE, NEW YORK 11701
1 800 789-8175

Stepping Heavenward

Elizabeth Prentiss

Calvary Press Publishing
P.O. Box 805
Amityville, NY 11701
U.S.A.
1 (800) 789-8175

ISBN   1-879737-29-9

Calvary Press can be found on the World Wide Web at:
calvarypress.com

Book and Cover Design by Michael Rotolo

Cover Photograph by Ken Druse from
The Natural Shade Garden
Clarkson Potter, NYC

Calvary Press Publishing P.O. Box 805 Amityville, NY 11701

Prentiss, Elizabeth, 1818-1878
   Stepping Heavenward
Recommended Dewey Decimal Classification: 234
Suggested Subject Headings:
1. Fiction—Christian—Women's Interest
2. Religion—Christian literature—Heaven
3. Christian literature—Devotional—Elizabeth Prentiss
I. Title

Manufactured in the United States of America
1 2 3 4 5 6 7 8 9 10   98 99 00 01

Foreword
by Elisabeth Elliot

This charming journal of a nineteenth century girl takes us from her sixteenth birthday ("How dreadfully old I am getting!") to her last entries when she was ill and in her forties, aware that she had very little time left. It is a story of the shaping of a soul— of her learning day by day, in the seemingly insignificant little events of ordinary life, that deep happiness is found, not in seeking fulfillment for oneself, but in a glad and free self-offering for the sake of others.

We follow her maturing to womanhood, we learn of her narrow escape from commitment to the wrong man, and of her engagement and marriage to the right one. But there was not as much "honey" on the honeymoon as her dreams had predicted. She had had no practice in giving up her own preferences in a day-to-day relationship with a man. She says to herself, at one point in her journal, "I would like to know if there is any reason on earth why a woman should learn self-forgetfulness which does not also apply to a man?"

When little Ernest is born she finds he has a passionate temper and a good deal of self-will, along with fine qualities. "I wish he had a better mother. I am so impatient with him when he is wayward and perverse!... Next to being a perfect wife I want to be a perfect mother. How mortifying, how dreadful in all things to come short of one's standards!" Having in-laws living with the family is another opportunity to "step heavenward," receiving grace to help as grace is continually needed.

This book is a treasure of godly and womanly wisdom, told with disarming candor and humility, yet revealing a deep heart's desire to know God. We need such intimate accounts, need them desperately when the word *commitment* is so little understood and so seldom practiced. We need to see that love for the Lord really does make a difference, not merely on Sunday, but from Monday through Saturday. We need to be able to enter this woman's life, her home, her kitchen, and see, as she so generously and honestly lets us do, just what the crucial difference is.

I have given a copy of *Stepping Heavenward* to my daughter and to a number of other young mothers. I do not hesitate to recommend it to men, who need to try to understand the wives they live with, and to any woman who wants to walk with God.

Magnolia, Massachusetts
February, 1992

Introductory Note

by George L. Prentiss

ELIZABETH PRENTISS was born at Portland, Me., on the 26th of October, 1818, and died, after a brief illness, at Dorset, Vt., on the 13th of August, 1878. She was the youngest daughter of the Rev. Edward Payson, D.D., a very eminent servant of Christ, whose praise is still in all the churches. At the age of sixteen she began to write for the press— the little volume entitled *Only a Dandelion*, consisting chiefly of her early contributions to "The Youth's Companion," of Boston. The works by which she is best known, are *Little Susy's Six Birthdays*, with its companions, and *Stepping Heavenward*. The latter was first published in 1869. It has passed through many editions in this country and has had a very wide circulation in Great Britain, Canada and Australia. It was also translated into French and German, and several editions in this country and several editions of it have been issued in those languages. Last year it appeared at Leipsic in Tauchnitz's "Collection of

British Authors." Among Mrs. Prentiss' other works, which have been widely circulated both at home and abroad, are *The Flower of the Family, Little Lou's Sayings and Doings, Henry and Bessie, Fred and Maria and Me, The Percys, Nidworth and His Three Magic Wands, The Story Lizzie Told, The Home at Greylock, Aunt Jane's Hero, Urbane and His Friends, Pemaquid,* and *Golden Hours; or Hymns and Songs of the Christian Life.* The aim of her writings, whether designed for young or old, is to incite to patience, fidelity, hope, and all goodness by showing how trust in God and loving obedience to His blessed will brighten the darkest paths and make a heaven upon earth.

Of her religious character the key-note is struck in her own hymn, "More Love to Thee, O Christ." That was her ruling passion in life and in death. Writing to a young friend from Dorset, in 1873, she says: "To love Christ more— this is the deepest need, the constant cry of my soul. Down in the bowling-alley, and out in the woods, and on my bed, and out driving, when I am happy and busy, and when I am sad and idle, the whisper keeps going up for more love, more love, more love!"

The following recollections of her by Mrs. Mary H. B. Field, now of San José, California, may fitly complete this sketch:

It was the first Sunday in September, 1866— a quiet, perfect day among the green hills of Vermont— a sacramental Sabbath— and we had come seven miles over the mountain to go up to the house of the Lord. I had brought my little two-months-old baby in my arms, intending to leave her during the service at our brother's home, which was near the church. I knew that Mrs. Prentiss was a "summer boarder" in this home, that she was the wife of a distinguished clergyman, and a literary woman of decided ability; but it was before the *Stepping Heavenward* epoch of her life, and I had no very deep interest in the prospect of meeting her. We went in at the hospitably open door, and meeting no one, sat down in the pleasant family living-room. It was about noon, and we could hear cheerful voices talking over the lunch-table in the dining room. Presently the door opened, and a slight, delicate-featured woman, with beautiful large dark eyes, came with rapid step into the room, going across the hall door; but her quick eye caught a glimpse of my little "bundle of flannel," and not pausing for an introduction or word of preparatory speech, she came towards me with a beaming face and outstretched hands—

"O, have you a baby there? How delightful! I haven't seen one for such an age! Please, may I take it? The darling tiny creature!— a girl? How lovely!"

She took the baby tenderly in her arms and went on in her eager, quick, informal way, but with a bright little blush and smile— "I'm not very polite— pray, let me introduce myself! I'm Mrs. Prentiss, and you are Mrs. Field, I know."

After a little more sweet, motherly comment and question over the baby— "a touch of nature" which at once made us "akin"— her whole beautiful character had revealed itself to me in that little interview— the quick perception, the wholly frank, unconventional manner, the

—

sweet motherliness, the cordial interest in even a stranger—
I was Mrs. Prentiss' warm friend for evermore.

For seven successive summers I saw more or less of
her in this "Earthly Paradise," as she used to call it, and
once I visited her in her city home. I have been favored
with many of her sparkling, vivacious letters, and have read
and re-read all her published writings; but that first meeting held in it for me the key-note of all her wonderfully
beautiful and symmetrical character.

She brought to that little hamlet among the hills a
sweet and wholesome and powerful influence. While her
time was too valuable to be wasted in a general sociability,
she yet found leisure for an extensive acquaintance, for a
kindly interest in all her neighbors, and for Christian work
of many kinds.

She had in a remarkable degree the lovely feminine
gift of *homemaking*. She was a true decorative artist. Her
room when she was boarding, and her home after it was
completed, were bowers of beauty. Every walk over hill and
dale, every ramble by brookside or through wildwood, gave
to her some fresh home-adornment. Some shy wildflower
or fern, or brilliant tinted leaf, a bit of moss, a curious li-
chen, a deserted bird's nest, a strange fragment of rock, a
shining pebble, would catch her passing glance and reveal
to her quick, artistic sense possibilities of use which were
quaint, original, characteristic. One saw from afar that hers
was a poet's home; and, if permitted to enter its gracious
portals, the first impression deepened into certainty. There
was as strong an individuality about her home, and

especially about her own little study, as there was about herself and her writings. A cheerful, sunny, hospitable Christian home! Far and wide its potent influences reached, and it was a beautiful thing to see how many another home, humble or stately, grew emulous and blossomed into a new loveliness.

Mrs. Prentiss was naturally a shy and reserved woman, and necessarily a preoccupied one. Therefore she was sometimes misunderstood. But those who knew her best, and were blest with her rare intimacy, knew her as a "perfect woman nobly planned." Her conversation was charming. Her close study of nature taught her a thousand happy symbols and illustrations, which made both what she said and wrote a mosaic of exquisite comparisons. Her studies of character were equally constant and penetrating. Nothing escaped her; no peculiarity of mind or manner failed of her quick observation, but it was always a kindly interest. She did not ridicule that which was simply ignorance or weakness, and she saw with keen pleasure all that was quaint, original or strong, even when it was hidden beneath the homeliest garb. She had the true artists's liking for that which was simple and *genre*. The common things of common life appealed to her sympathies and called out all her attention. It was real, hearty interest, too— not feigned, even in a sense generally thought praiseworthy. Indeed, no one ever had a more intense scorn of every sort of feigning. She was honest, truthful, genuine to the highest degree. It may have sometimes led her into seeming lack of courtesy, but even this was a failing which "leaned to virtue's side." I chanced to know of her once calling with a friend on a country neighbor, and finding the good house-wife busy over a rag-carpet, Mrs. Prentiss, who had never seen one of these bits of rural manufacture in its elementary processes, was full of questions and interest, thereby quite evidently pleasing the unassuming artist in assorted rags and home-made dyes. When the visitors were safely out-side the door, Mrs. Prentiss' friend turned to her with excla-mation, "What tact you have! She really thought you were interested in her work!" The quick blood sprang into Mrs. Prentiss' face, and she turned upon her friend a look of amazement and rebuke. "Tact!" she said, "I despise such tact! Do you think *I would look or act a lie?*"

She was an exceedingly practical woman, not a dreamer. A systematic, thorough housekeeper, with as ex-alted ideals in all the affairs which pertain to good house-wifery as in those matters which are generally thought to transcend these humble occupations. Like Solomon's virtuous woman she "looked well after the ways of her household."

Methodical, careful of minutes, simple in her tastes, temperate, and therefore enjoying evenly good health in spite of her delicate constitution— this is the secret of her accomplishing so much. Yet all this foundation of ex-actness and diligence was so "rounded with leafy graceful-ness" that she never seemed angular or unyielding.

With her children she was a model disciplinarian, ex-ceedingly strict, a wise law-maker; yet withal a tender, de-voted, self-sacrificing mother. I have never seen such exact obedience required and given, or a more idolized mother. "Mamma's" word was indeed law, but— O, happy combination!— it was also gospel.

How warm and true her friendship was! How little of selfishness in all her interaction with other women! How well she loved to be of service to her friends! How anxious that each should reach her highest possibilities of attainment! I record with deepest sense of obligation the cordial, generous, sympathetic assistance of many kinds extended toby her to me during our whole acquaintance. To every earnest worker in any field she gladly "lent a hand," rejoicing in all the successes of others as if they were her own.

But if weakness, or trouble, or sorrow of any sort or degree overtook one she straightway became as one of God's own ministering spirits— an angel of strength and consolation. Always more eager, however, that *souls should grow than that pain should cease.* Volumes could be made of her letters to friends in sorrow. One tender monotone steals through them all—

Come unto me, my kindred, I enfold you
In an embrace to sufferers only known;
Close to this heart I tenderly will hold you,
Suppress no sigh, keep back no tear, no moan.

Thou Man of Sorrows, teach my lips that often
Have told the sacred story of my woe,
To speak of Thee till stony griefs I soften,
Till hearts that know Thee not learn Thee to know.

Till peace takes place of storm and agitation,
Till lying on the current of Thy will
There shall be glorying in tribulation,
And Christ Himself each empty heart shall fill.

Few have the gift or the courage to deal faithfully yet lovingly with an erring soul, but she did not shrink back even from this service to those she loved. I can bear witness to the wisdom, penetration, skill and fidelity with which she probed a terribly wounded spirit, and then said with tender solemnity, *"I think you need a great deal of good praying."*

O, "vanished hand," still beckon to us from the Eternal Heights! O, "voice that is still," speak to us yet from the Shining Shore!

Still let thy mild rebuke stand
Between us and the wrong,
And thy dear memory serve to make
Our faith in goodness strong.

New York, New York
October 26, 1880

Stepping Westward

While my fellow-traveller and I were walking by the side of Loch Katrine one fine evening after sunset in our road to a hut where in the course of our tour we had been hospitably entertained some weeks before, we met, in one of the loneliest parts of that solitary region, two well-dressed women, one of whom said to us by way of greeting, "What, you are stepping westward?"

"What, you are stepping westward?" "Yea."
— 'Twould be a wildish destiny
If we, who thus together roam
In a strange land, and far from home,
Were in this place the guests of chance:
Yet who would stop, or fear to advance,
Though home or shelter he had none,
With such a sky to lead him on?
The dewy ground was dark and cold:
Behind, all gloomy to behold:
And stepping westward seemed to be
A kind of *heavenly* destiny:
I liked the greeting; 'twas a sound
Of something without place and bound,
And seemed to give me spiritual right
To travel through that region bright.
The voice was soft, and she who spake
Was walking by her native lake:
The salutation had to me
The very sound of courtesy:
Its power was felt; and while my eye
Was fixed upon the glowing sky,
The echo of the voice enwrought
A human sweetness with the thought
Of travelling through the world that lay
Before me in my endless way.

—WORDSWORTH

Chapter 1

January 15, 1831

How dreadfully old I am getting! Sixteen! Well, I don't see as I can help it. There it is in the big Bible in father's own writing— *Katherine, born January 15, 1815.*

I meant to get up early this morning, but it looked dismally cold out of doors, and felt delightfully warm in bed. So I covered myself up, and made ever so many good resolutions.

I determined, in the first place, to begin this Journal. To be sure, I have begun half a dozen, and gotten tired of them after a while. Not tired of writing them, but disgusted with what I had to say about myself. But this time I mean to go on, in spite of everything. It will do me good to read it over, and see what a creature I am.

Then I resolved to do more to please mother than I have done.

And I determined to make one more effort to conquer my hasty temper. I thought, too, I would be self-denying this winter, like the people one reads about in books. I fancied how surprised and pleased everybody would be to see me so much improved!

Time passed quickly amid these agreeable thoughts, and I was quite startled to hear the bell ring for prayers. I jumped up in a great flurry and dressed as quickly as I could. Everything conspired together to plague me. I could not find a clean collar, or a handkerchief. It is always just so. Susan is forever poking my things into out-of-the-way places! When at last I went down, they were all at breakfast.

"I hoped you would celebrate your birthday, dear, by coming down in good season," said mother.

I do hate to be found fault with, so I flared up in an instant.

"If people hide my things so that I can't find them, of course I have to be late," I said. And I rather think I said it in a very cross way, for mother sighed a little. I wish mother wouldn't sigh. I would rather be called names out and out.

The moment breakfast was over I had to hurry off to school. Just as I was going out mother said, "Have you your overshoes, dear?"

"Oh, mother, don't hinder me! I shall be late," I said. "I don't need overshoes."

"It snowed all night, and I think you do need them," mother said.

"I don't know where they are. I hate overshoes. Do let me go, mother," I cried. "I do wish I could ever have my own way."

"You shall have it now, my child," mother said, and went away.

Now what was the use of her calling me "my child" in such a tone, I would like to know.

I hurried off, and just as I got to the door of the schoolroom it flashed into my mind that I had not said my prayers! A nice way to begin on one's birthday, to be sure! Well, I had no time. And perhaps my good resolutions pleased God almost as much as one of my rambling stupid prayers could. For I must admit I can't make good prayers. I can't think of anything to say. I often wonder what mother finds to say when she is shut up by the hour in her prayer closet.

I had a pretty good time at school. My teachers praised me, and Amelia seemed so fond of me! She brought me a birthday present of a purse that she had knit for me herself, and a net for my hair. Nets are just coming into fashion. It will save a good deal of time my having this one. Instead of combing and combing and combing my old hair to get it glossy enough to suit mother, I can just give it one twist and one squeeze and the whole thing will be settled for the day.

Amelia wrote me a dear little note, with her presents. I really do believe she loves me dearly. It is so nice to have people love you!

When I got home mother called me into her room. She looked as if she had been crying. She said I gave her a great deal of pain by my self-will and ill temper and conceit.

"Conceit!" I screamed out. "Oh mother, if you only knew how horrid I think I am!"

Mother smiled a little. Then she went on with her list

till she made me out to be the worst creature in the world. I burst out crying, and was running off to my room, but she made me come back and hear the rest. She said my character would be essentially formed by the time I reached my twentieth year, and left it to me to say if I wished to be as a woman what I was now as a girl. I felt sulky, and would not answer. I was shocked to think I had only four years in which to improve, but after all a good deal could be done in that time. Of course I don't want to be always exactly what I am now.

Mother went on to say that I had in me the elements of a fine character if I would only conquer some of my faults. "You are frank and truthful," she said, "and in some things conscientious. I hope you are really a child of God, and are trying to please Him. And it is my daily prayer that you may become a lovely, loving, useful woman."

I made no answer. I wanted to say something, but my tongue wouldn't move. I was angry with mother, and angry with myself. At last everything came out all in a rush, mixed up with such floods of tears that I thought mother's heart would melt, and that she would take back what she had said.

"Amelia's mother never talks to her this way!" I said. "She praises her, and tells her what a comfort she is to her. But just as I am trying as hard as I can to be good, and making resolutions, and all that, you scold me and discourage me!"

Mother's voice was very soft and gentle as she asked, "Do you call this 'scolding,' my child?"

"And I don't like to be called conceited," I went on. "I know I am perfectly horrid, and I am just as unhappy as I can be."

"I am very sorry for you, dear," mother replied. "But you must bear with me. Other people will see your faults, but only your mother will have the courage to speak of them. Now go to your own room, and wipe away the traces of your tears that the rest of the family may not know that you have been crying on your birthday." She kissed me but I did not kiss her. I really believe Satan himself hindered me.

I ran across the hall to my room, slammed the door, and locked myself in. I was going to throw myself on the bed and cry till I was sick. Then I would look pale and tired, and they would all pity me. I do like so to be pitied! But on the table, by the window, I saw a beautiful new desk in place of the old clumsy thing I had been spattering and spoiling so many years. A little note, full of love, said it was from mother, and begged me to read and reflect every day of my life upon a few verses of a tastefully bound copy of the Bible which accompanied it. "A few verses," she said, "carefully read and pondered, instead of a chapter or two read for mere form's sake." I looked at my desk, which contained exactly what I wanted, plenty of paper, seals, wax and pens. I always use wax. Wafers are vulgar. Then I opened the Bible at random, and chanced upon these words: "Watch, therefore, for ye know not what hour your Lord doth come" (Matt. 24:42). There was nothing very cheering in that. I felt a real repugnance to be always on the watch, thinking I might die at any moment. I am sure I am not fit to die. Besides I want to have a good time, with nothing to worry me. I hope I shall live ever so long. Perhaps in the course of forty or fifty years I may get tired of this world and want to leave it. And I hope by that time I shall be a great deal better than I am now, and fit to go to heaven.

I wrote a note to mother on my new desk, and thanked her for it. I told her she was the best mother in the world, and that I was the worst daughter. When it was done I did not like it, and so I wrote another. Then I went down to dinner and felt better. We had such a nice dinner! Everything I liked best was on the table. Mother had not forgotten one of all the dainties I like. Amelia, was there too. Mother had invited her to give me a little surprise. It is bedtime now, and I must say my prayers and go to bed. I have gotten all chilled through, writing her in the cold. I believe I will say my prayers in bed, just for this once. I do not feel sleepy, but I am sure I ought not to sit up another moment.

January 30

Here I am at my desk once more. There is a fire in my room, and mother is sitting by it, reading. I can't see what book it is, but I have no doubt it is Thomas à Kempis.[1] How she can go on reading it so year after year, I cannot imagine. For my part I like something new. But I must go back to where I left off.

That night when I stopped writing, I hurried to bed as fast as I could, for I felt cold and tired. I remember saying,

"Oh, God, I am ashamed to pray," and then I began to think of all the things that had happened that day, and never knew another thing till the rising bell rang and I found it was morning. I am sure I did not mean to go to sleep. I think now it was wrong for me to be such a coward as to try to say my prayers in bed because of the cold. While I was writing I did not once think how I felt. Well, I jumped up as soon as I heard the bell, but found I had a dreadful pain in my side, and a cough. Susan says I coughed all night. I remembered then that I had just such a cough and just such a pain the last time I walked in the snow without overshoes. I crept back to bed feeling about as mean as I could. Mother sent up to know why I did not come down, and I had to admit that I was sick. She came up instantly looking so anxious! And here I have been shut up ever since; only today I am sitting up a little. Poor mother has had trouble enough with me; I know I have been cross and unreasonable, and it was all my fault that I was ill. The next time I will do as mother says.

January 31

How easy it is to make good resolutions, and how easy it is to break them! Just as I had gotten so far, yesterday, mother spoke for the third time about my exerting myself so much. And just at that moment I fainted away, and she had a great time all alone there with me. I did not realize how long I had been writing, nor how weak I was. I do wonder if I shall ever really learn that mother knows more than I do!

February 17

It is more than a month since I took that cold, and here I still am, shut up in the house. To be sure the doctor lets me go down stairs, but then he won't listen to a word about school. Oh, dear! All the girls will get ahead of me. This is Sunday, and everybody has gone to church. I thought I ought to make a good use of the time while they were gone, so I took the Memoir of Henry Martyn[2], and read a little in that.

I am afraid I am not much like him. Then I knelt down and tried to pray. But my mind was full of all sorts of things, so I thought I would wait till I was in a better frame of mind. At noon I disputed with James about the name of an apple. He was very provoking, and said he was thankful he had not gotten such a temper as I had. I cried, and mother reproved him for teasing me, saying my illness had left me nervous and irritable. James replied that it had left me where it found me, then. I cried a good while, lying on the sofa, and then I fell asleep. I don't see as I am any the better for this Sunday, it has only made me feel unhappy and out of sorts. I am sure I pray to God to make me better, and why doesn't He?

February 20

It has been quite a mild day for the season, and the doctor said I might drive outside. I enjoyed getting the air very much. I feel just as healthy as ever, and long to get back to school. I think God has been very good to me in making me healthy again, and wish I loved Him better. But, oh, I am not sure I do love Him! I hate to admit it to myself, and to write it down here, but I will. I do not love to pray. I am always eager to get it over with and out of the way so as to have leisure to enjoy myself. I mean that this is usually so. This morning I cried a good deal while I was on my knees, and felt sorry for my quick temper and all my bad ways. If I always felt so, perhaps praying would not be such a task. I wish I knew whether anybody exactly as bad as I am ever got to heaven at last. I have read ever so many memoirs, and they were all about people who were too good to live in this sinful world, and so died; or else went on a mission. I am not at all like any of them.

March 26

I have been so busy that I have not said much to you, you poor old journal, you, have I? Somehow I have been behaving quite nicely lately. Everything has gone on exactly to my mind. Mother has not found fault with me once, and father has praised my drawings and seemed proud of me. He says he shall not tell me what my teachers say of me lest it should make me vain. And once or twice when he has met me singing and frisking about the house he has kissed me and called me his dear little Flibbertigib-bet, if that's the way to spell it. When he says that, I know he is very fond of me. We are all very happy together when nothing goes wrong. In the long evenings we all sit around the table with our books and our work, and one of us reads aloud. Mother chooses the book and takes her turn in reading. She reads beautifully. Of course the readings do not begin till the lessons are all learned. As for me, my lessons just take no time at all. I have only to read them over once, and there they are. So I have a good deal of time to read, and I devour all the poetry I can get hold of. I would rather read Pollok's "Course of Time"[3] than nothing at all.

April 2

There are three of mother's friends living near us, each having lots of little children. It is perfectly ridiculous how much those creatures are sick. They send for mother if so much as a pimple comes out on one of their faces. When I have children I don't mean to have such goings on. I shall be careful about what they eat, and keep them from getting cold, and they will keep healthy of their own accord. Mrs. Jones has just sent for mother to see her Tommy. It was so provoking. I had coaxed her into letting me have a black silk apron; they are all the fashion now, embroidered in floss silk. I had drawn a lovely vine for mine entirely out of my own head, and mother was going to arrange the pattern for me when that message came, and she had to go. I don't believe anything ails the child! a great chubby thing!

April 3

Poor Mrs. Jones! Her dear little Tommy is dead! I stayed at home from school today and had all the other children here to get them out of their mother's way. How dreadfully she must feel! Mother cried when she told me how the dear little fellow suffered in his last moments. It reminded her of my two little bothers who died in the same way, just before I was born. Dear mother! I wonder how I ever forget what troubles she has had. Why am I not always sweet and loving? She has gone now, where she always goes when she feels sad, straight to God. Of course she did not say so, but I know mother.

April 25

I have not been down on time for prayers once this week. I have persuaded mother to let me read some of Scott's novels,[4] and have sat up late and been sleepy in the morning. I wish I could get along with mother as nicely as James does. He is late far more often than I am, but he never gets into such scrapes about it as I do. This is what happens. He comes down when it suits him.

Mother begins— "James, I am very much displeased with you."

James— "I should think you would be, mother."

Mother, mollified— "I don't think you deserve any breakfast."

James, hypocritically— "No, I don't think I do, mother."

Then mother hurries off and gets something extra for his breakfast. Now let us see how things go on when I am late.

Mother— "Katherine" (she always calls me Katherine when she is displeased, and spells it with a K), "Katherine, you are late again; how can you annoy your father so?"

Katherine— "Of course I don't do it to annoy father

or anybody else. But if I oversleep myself, it is not my fault."

Mother— "I would go to bed at eight o'clock rather than be late as often as you. How would you like it if I were not down for prayer?"

Katherine, muttering— "Of course that is very different. I don't see why I should be blamed for oversleeping any more than James. I get all the scoldings."

Mother sighs and goes off.

I prowl around and get what scraps of breakfast I can.

May 12

The weather is getting perfectly delicious. I am sitting with my window open, and my bird is singing with all his heart. I wish I was as merry as he is.

I have been thinking lately that it was about time to begin on some of those pieces of self-denial I resolved on upon my birthday. I could not think of anything great enough for a long time. At last an idea popped into my head. Half the girls at school envy me because Amelia is so fond of me, and Jane Underhill, in particular, is just crazy to get intimate with her. But I have kept Amelia all to myself. Today I said to her, "Amelia, Jane Underhill admires you above all things. I have a good mind to let you be as intimate with her as you are with me. It will be a great piece of self-denial, but I think it is my duty. She is a stranger, and nobody seems to like her much."

"You dear thing, you!" cried Amelia, kissing me. "I liked Jane Underhill the moment I saw her. She has such a sweet face and such pleasant manners. But you are so jealous that I never dared to show how I liked her. Don't be vexed, dearie; if you are jealous it is your own fault!"

She then rushed off, and I saw her kiss that girl exactly as she kissed me!

This was in recess. I went to my desk and made believe I was studying. Pretty soon Amelia came back.

"She is a sweet girl," she said, "and only to think! She writes poetry! Just hear this! It is a little poem addressed to me. Isn't it nice of her?"

I pretended not to hear her. I was as full of all sorts of horrid feelings as I could hold. It enraged me to think that Amelia, after all her professions of love to me, would snatch at the first chance of getting a new friend. Then I was mortified because I was enraged, and I could have torn myself to pieces for being such a fool as to let Amelia see how silly I was.

"I don't know what to make of you, Katy," she said, putting her arms around me. "Have I done anything to annoy you? Come, let us make up and be friends, whatever it is. I will read you these sweet verses which Jane wrote to me; I am sure you will like them."

She read them in her clear, pleasant voice.

"How can you have the vanity to read such stuff?" I cried.

Amelia blushed a little.

"You have said and written much more flattering things to me," she replied. "Perhaps it has turned my head, and made me too ready to believe what other people say."

She folded the paper, and put it into her pocket. We walked home together, after school, as usual, but neither of us spoke a word. And now here I sit, unhappy enough. All my resolutions fail. But I did not think Amelia would take me at my word, and rush after that stuck-up, smirking character!

May 20

I seem to have gotten back into all my bad ways again. Mother is quite out of patience with me. I have not prayed for a long time. It does not do any good.

May 21

It seems this Underhill thing is here for reasons of health, though she looks as well as any of us. She is an orphan, and has been adopted by a rich old uncle, who makes a perfect fool of her. Such dresses and such finery as she wears! Last night she had Amelia there to tea, without inviting me, though she knows I am her best friend. She gave her a bracelet made of her own hair. I wonder how Amelia's mother lets her accept presents from strangers. My mother would not let me. On the whole, there is nobody like one's own mother. Amelia has been cold and distant to me of late, but no matter what I do or say to my darling, precious mother, she is always kind and loving. She noticed how I moped about today, and begged me to tell her what was the matter. I was ashamed to do that. I told her that it was a little quarrel I had with Amelia.

"Dear child," she said, "how I pity you that you have

inherited my quick, irritable temper."

"*Yours*, mother!" I cried out; "what can you mean?"

Mother smiled a little at my surprise.

"It is even so," she said.

"Then how did you cure yourself of it? Tell me quick, mother, and let me cure myself of mine."

"My dear Katy," she said, "I wish I could make you see that God is just as willing, and just as able to sanctify, as He is to redeem us. It would save you so much weary, disappointing work. But God has opened my eyes at last."

"I wish He would open mine, then," I said, "for all I see now is that I am just as horrid as I can be, and that the more I pray the worse I continue to grow."

"That is not true, dear," she replied; "go on praying— pray without ceasing."

I sat pulling my handkerchief this way and that, and at last rolled it up into a ball and threw it across the room. I wished I could toss my bad feelings into a corner with it.

"I do wish I could make you love to pray, my darling child," mother went on. "If you only knew the strength, and the light, and the joy you might have for the simple asking. God attaches no conditions to His gifts. He only says, '*Ask!*'".

"This may be true, but it is hard work to pray. It tires me. And I do wish there was some easy way of growing good. In fact I would like to have God send a sweet temper to me just as He sent bread and meat to Elijah. I don't believe Elijah had to kneel down and pray for them like I do."

Chapter 2

June 1

Last Sunday Dr. Cabot preached to the young people. He first addressed those who *knew* they did not love God. It did not seem to me that I belonged to that class. Then he spoke to those who knew they did. I felt sure I was not one of those. Last of all he spoke affectionately to those who did not know what to think, and I was frightened and ashamed to feel tears running down my cheeks, when he said that he believed that most of his hearers who were in this doubtful state really did love their Master, only their love was something as new and as tender and perhaps as unobserved as the tiny point of green that, forcing its way through the earth, is yet unconscious of its own existence, but promises a thrifty plant. I don't suppose I express it very well, but I know what he meant. He then invited those belonging to each class to meet him on three successive Saturday afternoons. I shall certainly go.

July 19

I went to the meeting, and so did Amelia. A great many young people were there and a few children. Dr. Cabot went about from seat to seat, speaking to each one separately. When he came to us I expected he would say something about the way in which I had been brought up, and reproach me for not profiting more by the instructions and example I had at home. Instead of that he said, in a cheerful voice,

"Well, my dear, I cannot see into your heart and positively tell whether there is love to God there or not. But I suppose you have come here today in order to let me help you to find out?"

I said, "Yes"; that was all I could get out.

"Let me see, then," he went on. "Do you love your mother?"

I said "Yes," once more.

"But prove to me that you do. How do you know it?"

I tried to think. Then I said, "I *feel* that I love her. I love to love her, I like to be with her. I like to hear people praise her. And I try sometimes at least— to do things to please her. But I don't try half as hard as I ought, and I do and say a great many things to displease her."

"Yes, yes," he said, "I know."

"Has mother told you?" I cried out.

"No, dear, no indeed. But I know what human nature is after having one of my own for fifty years, in addition to six of my children's to encounter."

Somehow I felt more courage after he said that.

"In the first place, then, you *feel* that you love your mother? But you never feel that you love your God and Savior?"

"I often try, and try, but I never do," I said.

"Love won't be forced, " he said, quickly.

"Then what *shall* I do?"

"In the second place, you like to be with your mother. But you never like to be with the Friend who loves you so much better than she does?"

"I don't know, I never was with Him. Sometimes I think that when Mary sat at His feet and heard Him talk, she must have been very happy."

"We come to the third test, then. You like to hear people praise your mother. And have you never rejoiced to hear the Lord magnified?"

I shook my head sorrowfully enough.

"Let us then try the last test. You know you love your mother because you try to do things to please her. That is to do what you know she wishes you to do? Very well. Have you never tried to do anything God wishes you to do?"

"Oh yes; often. But not so often as I ought."

"Of course not. No one does that. But come now, *why* do you try to do what you think will please Him? Because it is easy? Because you like to do what He likes rather than what you like yourself?"

I tried to think, and got puzzled.

"Never mind," said Dr. Cabot, "I have come now to the point I was aiming at. You cannot prove to yourself that you love God by examining your feelings towards Him.

They are indefinite and they fluctuate. But just as far as you obey Him, just so far, depend upon it, you love Him. It is not natural to us sinful, ungrateful human beings to prefer His pleasure to our own, or to follow His way instead of our own way, and nothing, nothing but love to Him can or does make us obedient to Him."

"Couldn't we obey Him from fear?" Amelia now asked. She had been listening all this time in silence.

"Yes; and so you might obey your mother from fear, but only for a season. If you had no real love for her, you would gradually cease to dread her displeasure; whereas it is in the very nature of love to grow stronger and more influential every hour."

"You mean, then, that if we want to know whether we love God, we must find out whether we are obeying Him?" Amelia asked.

"I mean exactly that. "He that keepeth my commandments he it is that loveth me" (John 14:21). But I cannot talk with you any longer now. There are many others still waiting. You can come to see me someday next week, if you have any more questions to ask."

When we got out into the street, Amelia and I got hold of each other's hands. We did not speak a word till we reached the door, but we knew that we were as good friends as ever.

"I understand all Dr. Cabot said," Amelia whispered, as we separated. But I felt like one in a fog. I cannot see how it is possible to love God, and yet feel as stupid as I do when I think of Him. Still, I am determined to do one thing, and that is to pray regularly instead of now and then, as I have gotten into the habit of doing lately.

July 25

School has closed for the season. I took the first prize for drawing, and my composition was read aloud on examination day, and everybody praised it. Mother could not possibly help showing, in her face, that she was very much pleased. I am pleased myself. We are now getting ready to take a journey. I do not think I shall go to see Dr. Cabot again. My head is so full of other things, and there is so much to do before we go. I am having four new dresses made, and I can't imagine how to have them trimmed. I mean to run down to Amelia's and ask her.

July 27

I was rushing through the hall just after I wrote that, and met mother.

"I am going to Amelia's," I said, hurrying past her.

"Stop one minute, dear. Dr. Cabot is downstairs. He says he has been expecting a visit from you, and that as you did not come to him, he has come to you."

"I wish he would mind his own business," I said.

"I think he *is* minding it, dear," mother answered. "His Master's business is his, and that has brought him here. Go to him, my darling child; I am sure you crave something better than prizes and compliments and new dresses and journeys."

If anybody but mother had said that, my heart would

have melted at once, and I would have gone right down to Dr. Cabot to be molded in his hands to almost any shape. But as it was I brushed past her, ran into my room, and locked my door. Oh, what makes me act so! I hate myself for it, I don't want to do it!

Last week I dined with Mrs. Jones. Her little Tommy was very fond of me, and that, I suppose, makes her have me there so often. Lucy was at the table, and very cranky. She cried first for one thing and then for another. At last her mother in a gentle, but very decided way put her down from the table. Then she cried louder than ever. But when her mother offered to take her back if she would be good, she screamed yet more. She wanted to come and *wouldn't let herself come*. I almost hated her when I saw her act so, and now I am behaving ten times worse and I am just as miserable as I can be.

July 29

Amelia has been here. She has had another talk with Dr. Cabot and is perfectly happy. She says it is so easy to be a Christian! It may be easy for her; everything is. She never has any of my dreadful feelings, and does not understand them when I try to explain them to her. Well, if I am destined to be miserable, I must try to bear it.

October 3

Summer is over, school has begun again, and I am so busy that I have not much time to think, or to be low spirited. We had a delightful journey, and I feel healthy and bright, and ever so happy. I never enjoyed my studies as I do those of this year. Everything goes on pleasantly here at home. But James has gone away to school, and we miss him sadly. I do wish I had a sister. Though I dare say I would quarrel with her, if I had one.

October 23

I am so glad that my studies are harder this year, as I am never happy except when every moment is occupied. However, I do not study all the time, by any means. Mrs. Gordon grows more and more fond of me, and has me there to dinner or to tea continually. She has a much higher opinion of me than mother has, and is always saying the sort of things that make you feel nice. She holds me up to Amelia as an example, begging her to imitate me in my fidelity about my lessons, and declaring there is nothing she so much desires as to have a daughter bright and original like me. Amelia only laughs and goes and purrs in her mother's ears, when she hears such talk. It costs her nothing to be pleasant. She was born so. For my part, I think myself lucky to have such a friend. She gets along with my odd, hateful ways better than any one else does. Mother, when I boast of this, says she has no penetration into character, and that she would be fond of almost any one fond of her; and that the fury with which I love her deserves some response. I really don't know what to make of mother. Most people are proud of their children when they see others admire them; but she does say such pokey things! Of course I know that having a gift for music, and a taste for drawing, and a reputation for saying witty, bright things isn't enough. But when she doesn't find fault with me, and nothing happens to keep me down, I am the happiest creature on earth. I do love to get with a lot of nice girls, and carry on! I have got enough fun in me to keep a houseful merry. And mother needn't say anything. I inherited it from her.

Evening

I knew it was coming! Mother has been in to see what I was about, and to give me a bit of her mind. She says she loves to see me merry and cheerful, as is natural at my age, but that levity quite upsets and disorders the mind, indisposing it for serious thoughts.

"But, mother," I said, "didn't you carry on when you were a young girl like me?"

"Of course I did," she said, smiling, "But I do not think I was quite so thoughtless as you are."

"Thoughtless" indeed! I wish I were! But am I not always full of uneasy, reproachful thoughts when the moment of excitement is over? Other girls, who seem less trifling than I, are really more so. Their heads are full of dresses and parties and boys, and all that sort of nonsense. I wonder if that ever worries their mothers, or whether mine is the only one who weeps in secret? Well, I shall be young but once, and while I am, do let me have a good time!

November 20, Sunday

Oh, the difference between this day and the day I wrote that! There are no good times in this dreadful world.

I have hardly courage or strength to write down the history of the past few weeks. The day after I had deliberately made up my mind to enjoy myself, cost what it might, my dear father called me to him, kissed me, pulled my ears a little, and gave me some money.

"We have had to keep you rather low in funds," he said laughing. "But I recovered this amount yesterday, and as it was a little debt I had given up, I can spare it to you. For girls like spending money, I know, and you may use this just as you please."

I was delighted. I want to take more drawing lessons, but did not feel sure he could afford it. Besides— I am a little ashamed to write it down— I knew somebody had been praising me or father would not have seemed so fond of me. I wondered who it was, and felt a good deal puffed up. "After all," I said to myself, "*some* people like me even if I have got my faults." I threw my arms around his neck and kissed him, though that cost me a great effort. I never like to show what I feel. But, oh! how thankful I am for it now.

As to mother, I know father never goes out without kissing her good-bye.

I went out with her on a walk at three o'clock. We had just reached the corner of Orange Street, when I saw a carriage driving slowly towards us; it appeared to be full of sailors. Then I saw our friend, Mr. Freeman, among them. When he saw us he jumped out and came to us. I don't know what he said. I saw mother turn pale and catch at his arm as if she was afraid of falling. But she did not speak a word.

"Oh! Mr. Freeman, what is it?" I cried out. "Has anything happened to father? Is he hurt? Where is he?"

"He is in the carriage," he said. "We are taking him home. He has had a fall."

Then we went on in silence. The sailors were carrying father in as we reached the house. They laid him on the sofa, and we saw his poor head—

November 23

I will try to write the rest now. Father was alive but insensible. He had fallen down into the hold of the ship, and the sailors heard him groaning there. He lived three hours after they brought him home. Mr. Freeman and all our friends were very kind. But we like best to be alone, us three, mother and James and I. Poor mother looks twenty years older, but she is so patient, and so concerned for us, and has such a smile of welcome for every one that comes in, that it breaks my heart to see her.

November 25

Mother spoke to me very seriously today, about controlling myself more. She said she knew this was my first real sorrow, and how hard it was to bear it. But that she was afraid I would become insane some time, if I indulged myself in such passions of grief. And she said, too, that when friends came to see us, full of sympathy and eager to say or do something for our comfort, it was our duty to receive them with as much cheerfulness as possible.

I said none of them had anything to say that did not provoke me.

"It is always a trying task to visit the afflicted," mother

said, "and you make it doubly hard to your friends by putting on a gloomy, forbidding air, and by refusing to talk of your dear father, as if you were resolved to keep your sorrow all to yourself."

"I can't smile when I am so unhappy," I said.

A good many people have been here today. Mother has seen them all, though she looked ready to drop. Mrs. Bates said to me, in her little, weak, watery voice:

"Your mother is wonderfully sustained, dear. I hope you feel reconciled to God's will. Rebellion is most displeasing to Him, dear."

I made no answer. It is very easy for people to preach. Let me see how they behave when they take their turn to lose their friends.

Mrs. Morris said this was a very mysterious dispensation. But that she was happy to see that mother was meeting it with so much firmness. "As for myself," she went on, "I was quite broken down by my dear husband's death. I did not eat as much as would feed a bird, for nearly a week. But some people have so much feeling; then again other are so firm. Your mother is so busy talking with Mrs. March that I won't interrupt her to say good-bye. Well, I came prepared to suggest several things that I thought would comfort her, but perhaps she has thought of them herself."

I could have knocked her down. Firm, indeed! poor mother.

After they had all gone, I made her lie down, she looked so tired and worn out.

Then I could not help telling her what Mrs. Morris had said.

She only smiled a little, but said nothing.

"I wish you would ever flare up, mother," I said.

She smiled again, and said she had nothing to "flare up" about.

"Then I shall do it for you!" I cried. "To hear that namby-pamby woman, who is about as capable of understanding you as an old cat, talking about your being firm! You see what you get by being quiet and patient! People would like you much better if you refused to be comforted, and wore a sad countenance."

"Dear Katy," said mother, "it is not my first object in life to make people like me."

By this time she looked so pale that I was frightened. Though she is so cheerful, and things go on much as they did before, I believe she has taken her death-blow. If she has, then I hope I have gotten mine. And yet I am not fit to die. I wish I was, and I wish I could die. I have lost all interest in everything, and don't care what becomes of me anymore.

November 28

I believe I shall go crazy unless people stop coming here, hurling volleys of texts at mother and at me. When soldiers drop wounded on the battlefield, they are taken up tenderly and carried "to the rear," which means, I suppose, out of sight and sound. Is anybody mad enough to suppose it will do them any good to hear Scripture quoted and sermons launched at them before their open, bleeding wounds are even stanched?[5]

Mother assents, in a mild way, when I talk so and says, "Yes, yes, we are indeed lying wounded on the battle-field of life, and in no condition to listen to any words save those of pity. But, dear Katy, we must interpret aright all the well-meant attempts of our friends to comfort us. They mean sympathy, however awkwardly they may express it."

And then she sighed, with a long, deep sigh, that told how it all wearied her.

December 14

Mother keeps saying I spend too much time in brooding over my sorrow. As for her, she seems to live in heaven. Not that she has long prosaic talks about it, but little words that she lets drop now and then show where her thoughts are, and where she would like to be. She seems to think everybody is as eager to go there as she is. For my part, I am not eager at all. I can't make myself feel that it will be nice to sit in rows, all the time singing, fond as I am of music. And when I say to myself, "of course we shall not always sit in rows singing," then I fancy a multitude of shadowy, phantom-like beings, dressed in white, moving to and fro in golden streets, doing nothing in particular, and having a dreary time, without anything to look forward to.

I told mother so. She said earnestly, and yet in her sweetest, most tender way, "Oh, my darling Katy! What you need is such a living, personal love to Christ as shall make the thought of being where He is so delightful as to fill your mind with that single thought!"[6]

What is "personal love to Christ?"

Oh, dear, dear! Why need my father have been snatched away from me, when so many other girls have theirs spared to them? He loved me so! He indulged me so much! He was so proud of me! What have I done that I should have this dreadful thing happen to me? I shall never be as happy as I was before. Now I shall always be expecting trouble. Yes, I dare say, mother will go next. Why shouldn't I brood over this sorrow? I like to brood over it; I like to think how wretched I am; I like to have long, furious fits of crying, lying on my face on the bed.

January 1, 1832

People talk a great deal about the blessed effects of sorrow. But I do not see any good it has done me to lose my dear father, and as for mother, she was good enough before.

We are going to leave our pleasant home, where all of us children were born, and move into a house in an out-of-the-way street. By selling this, and renting a smaller one, mother hopes, with the saving, to be able to carry James through college. And I must go to Miss Higgins' school because it is less expensive than Mr. Stone's. Miss Higgins, indeed! I never could bear her! A few months ago, how I would have cried and stormed at the idea of her school. But the great sorrow swallows up the little trial.

I tried once more, this morning, as it is the first day of the year, to force myself to begin to love God.

I want to do it; I know I ought to do it; but I cannot.

I go through the form of saying something that I try to pass off as praying, every day now. But I take no pleasure in it, as good people say they do, and as I am sure mother does. Nobody could live in the house with her, and doubt that.

January 10

We are in our new home now, and it is quite a cozy little place. James is at home for the long vacation and we are together all the time I am out of school. We study and sing together, and now and then, when we forget that dear father has gone, we are as full of fun as ever. If it is so nice to have a brother, what must it be to have a sister! Dear old Jim! He is the most pleasant, dearest fellow in the world!

January 15

I have come to another birthday, and am seventeen. Mother has celebrated it just as usual, though I know all these anniversaries, which used to be so pleasant, must be sad days to her, now that my dear father has gone. She has been cheerful and loving, and entered into all my pleasures exactly as if nothing had happened. I wonder at myself that I do not enter more into her sorrows, but though at times the remembrance of our loss overwhelms me, my natural elasticity soon makes me rise above and forget it. And I am absorbed with these schooldays, that come one after another, in such quick succession that I am all the time running to keep up with them. And as long as I do that I forget that death has crossed our threshold, and may do it again. But tonight, I feel very sad, and as if I would give almost any thing to live in a world where nothing painful could happen. Somehow mother's pale face haunts and reproaches me. I believe I will go to bed and to sleep as quickly as possible, and try to forget everything.

Chapter 3

July 16

My schooldays are over! I have come off with flying colors, and mother is pleased at my success. I said to her today that I would now have time to draw and practice to my heart's content.

"You will not find your heart content with either," she said.

"Why, mother!" I cried, "I thought you liked to see me happy!"

"And so I do," she said, quietly. "But there is something better to get out of life than you have yet found."

"I am sure I hope so," I returned. "On the whole, I haven't gotten much so far."

Amelia is now on such terms with Jenny Underhill that I can hardly see one without seeing the other. After the way in which I have loved her, this seems rather hard. Sometimes I am angry about it, and sometimes grieved. However, I find Jenny quite nice. She buys all the new books and lends them to me. I wish I liked more solid reading; but I don't. And I wish I was not so fond of novels;

but I am. If it were not for mother I would read nothing else. And I am sure I often feel quite stirred up by a really good novel, and admire and want to imitate every high-minded, noble character it describes.

Jenny has a miniature of her brother "Charley" in a locket, which she always wears, and often shows me. According to her, he is exactly like the heroes I most admire in books. She says she knows he would like me if we should meet. But that is not probable. Very few like me. Amelia says it is because I say just what I think.

August 1, Wednesday

Mother pointed out to me this evening two lines from a book she was reading, with a significant smile that said they described me:

> "A frank, unchastened, generous creature,
> Whose faults and virtues stand in bold relief."

"Dear me!" I said, "so then I have some virtues after all!"

And I really think I must have, for Jenny's brother, who has come here for the sake of being near her, seems to like me very much. Nobody ever liked me so much before, not even Amelia. But how foolish to write that down!

August 2, Thursday

Jenny's brother has been here all the evening. He has the most perfect manners I ever saw. I am sure that mother, who thinks so much of such things, would be charmed with him. But she happened to be out, Mrs. Jones having sent for her to see about her baby. He gave me an account of his mother's death, and how he and Jenny nursed her day and night. He has a great deal of feeling. I was going to tell him about my father's death, sorrow seems to bring people together so, but I could not. Oh, if he had only had a sickness that needed our tender nursing, instead of being snatched from us in that sudden way!

August 5, Sunday

Jenny's brother has been at our church all day. He walked home with me this afternoon. Mother, after being up all night with Mrs. Jones and her baby, was not able to go out.

Dr. Cabot preaches as if we all were going to die pretty soon, or else have something almost as bad happen to us. How *can* old people always try to make young people feel uncomfortable, and as if things couldn't last?

August 25

Jenny says her brother is perfectly fascinated with me, and that I *must* try to like him in return. I suppose mother would say my head was turned by my good fortune, but it is not. I am getting quite sober and serious. It is a great thing to be— to be— well— *liked.* I have seen some verses of his composition today that show that he is all heart and soul, and would make any sacrifice for the one he loved. I could not like a man who did not possess such sentiments as his.

Perhaps mother would think I ought not to put such things into my journal.

Jenny has thought of such a *splendid* plan! What a dear little thing she is! She and her brother are so much alike! The plan is for us three girls Jenny, Amelia and I, to form ourselves into a little class to read and to study together. She says "Charley" will direct our readings and help us with our studies. It is perfectly delightful.

September 1

Somehow I forgot to tell mother that Mr. Underhill was to be our teacher. So when it came my turn to have the class meet here, she was not quite pleased. I told her she could stay in the room and watch us, and then she would see for herself that we all behave ourselves.

September 19

The class met at Amelia's tonight. Mother insisted on sending for me, though Mr. Underhill had proposed to see me home himself. So he stayed after I left. It was not quite the thing in him, for he must see that Amelia is absolutely crazy about him.

September 28

We met at Jenny's this evening. Amelia had a bad headache and could not come. Jenny idled over her lessons, and at last took a book and began to read. I studied awhile with Mr. Underhill. At last he said, scribbling something on a bit of paper:

"Here is a sentence I hope you can translate."

I took it, and read these words:

"You are the brightest, prettiest, most warmhearted little thing in the world. And I love you more than tongue can tell. You must love me in the same way."

I felt hot and then cold, and then glad and then sorry. But I pretended to laugh, and said I could not translate Greek. I shall have to tell mother, and what *will* she say?

September 29

This morning mother began thus:

"Kate, I do not like these lessons of yours. At your age, with your judgment quite unformed, it is not proper that you should spend so much time with a young man."

"Jenny is always there, and Amelia," I replied.

"That makes no difference. I want the whole thing stopped. I do not know what I have been thinking of to let it go on so long. Mrs. Gordon says—"

"Mrs. Gordon! Ha!" I burst out, "I knew Amelia was at the bottom of it! Amelia is in love with him up to her very ears, and because he does not entirely neglect me, she has put her mother up to coming here, meddling and making—"

"If what you say of Amelia is true, it is most ungenerous of you to tell of it. But I do not believe it. Amelia Gordon has too much good sense to be carried away by a handsome face and agreeable manners."

I began to cry.

"He likes me," I got out, "he likes me ever so much.

Nobody ever was so kind to me before. Nobody ever said such nice things to me. And I don't want such horrid things said about him."

"Has it really come to this!" said mother, quite shocked. "Oh, my poor child, how my selfish sorrow has made me neglect you."

I kept on crying.

"Is it possible," she went on, "that with your good sense, and the education you have had, you are captivated by this mere boy?"

"He is not a boy," I said. "He is a man. He is twenty years old; or at least he will be on the fifteenth of next October."

"The child actually keeps his birthdays!" cried mother. "Oh, my wicked, shameful carelessness."

"It's done now," I said, desperately. "It is too late to help it now."

"You don't mean that he has dared to say anything without consulting me?" asked mother. "And that you have allowed it! Oh, Katherine!"

By this time my mouth shut itself up, and no mortal force could open it. I stopped crying, and sat with folded arms. Mother said what she had to say, and then I came to you, my dear old Journal—

> *Yes, he likes me and I like him.*
> *Come now, let's out with it once for all.*
> *He loves me and I love him.*
> *You are just a little bit too late, mother.*

October 1

I never can write down all the things that have happened. The very day after I wrote Jenny that mother had forbidden my going to the class, Charley came to see her, and they had a regular fight together. He has told me about it since. Then, as he could not prevail, his uncle wrote, told her it would be the making of Charley to be settled down on one young lady instead of hovering from flower to flower, as he was doing now. Then Jenny came with her pretty ways, and cried, and told mother what a darling brother Charley was. She made a good deal, too, out of his having lost both father and mother, and needing my affection so much. Mother shut herself up, and I have no doubt prayed over it. I really believe she prays over every new dress she buys. Then she sent for me and talked beautifully, and I behaved abominably.

At last she said she would put us on one year's probation. Charley might spend one evening here every two weeks, when she would always be present. We were never to be seen together in public, nor would she allow us to correspond. If, at the end of the year, we were both as eager for it as we are now, she would consent to our engagement. Of course we shall be, so I consider myself as good as engaged now. Dear me! how funny it seems.

October 2

Charley is not at all pleased with mother's terms, but no one would guess it from his manner to her. His coming is always the signal for her trotting downstairs; he goes to meet her and offers her a chair, as if he was delighted to see her. We go on with the lessons, as this gives us a chance to sit pretty close together, and when I am writing my exercises and he corrects them, I rather think a few little things get on the paper that sound nicely to us, but would not strike mother very agreeably. For instance, last night Charley wrote:

"Is your mother never sick? A nice little headache or two would be so convenient to us!"

And I wrote back.

"You dear old horrid thing! How can you be so selfish?"

January 15, 1833

I have been trying to think whether I am any happier today than I was at this time a year ago. If I am not, I suppose it is the tantalizing way in which I am placed concerning Charley. We have so much to say to each other that we can't say before mother, and that we cannot say in writing, because a correspondence is one of the forbidden things. He says *he* entered into no contract not to write, and keeps slipping little notes into my hand; but I don't think that quite right. Mother hears us arguing and disputing about it, though she does not know the subject under discussion, and today she said to me:

"I would not argue with him, if I were you. He never will yield."

"But it is a case of conscience," I said, "and he ought to yield."

"There is no obstinacy like that of a f—," she began and then stopped short.

"Oh, you may as well finish it!" I cried. "I know that you think him a fool."

Then mother burst out.

"Oh, my child," she said, "before it is too late, do be persuaded by me to give up this whole thing. I shrink from paining or offending you, but it is my duty, as your mother, to warn you against a marriage that will make shipwreck of your happiness."

"*Marriage!*" I fairly shrieked out. That is the last thing I have ever thought of. I felt a chill creep over me. All I had wanted was to have Charley come here every day, take me out now and then, and care for nobody else.

"Yes, *marriage!*" Mother repeated. "For what is the meaning of an engagement if marriage is not to follow? How can you fail to see, what I see, oh! so plainly, that Charley Underhill can never, never meet the requirements of your soul. You are captivated by what girls of your age call beauty, regular features, a fair complexion and soft eyes. His flatteries delude, and his professions of affection gratify you. You do not see that he is shallow, and conceited, and selfish and—"

"Oh, mother! How can you be so unjust? His whole purpose seems to be to please others."

"*Seems* to be—that is true," she replied. "His ruling passion is love of admiration; the little pleasing acts that attract you are so many traps set to catch the attention and the favorable opinion of those about him. He has not one honest desire to please because it is right to be pleasing. Oh, my precious child, what a fatal mistake you are making in relying on your own judgment in this, the most important of earthly decisions!"

I felt very angry.

"I thought the Bible forbid back-biting." I said.

Mother made no reply, except by a look which said about a hundred and forty different things. And then I came up here and wrote some poetry, which was very good (for me), though I don't suppose she would think so.

October 1

The year of probation is over, and I have nothing to do now but to be happy. But being engaged is not half so nice as I expected it would be. I suppose it is owning to my being obliged to defy mother's judgment to gratify my own. People say she has great insight into character, and sees, at a glance, what others only learn after much study.

October 10

I have taken a dreadful cold. It is too bad. I dare say I shall be coughing all winter, and instead of going out with Charley, be shut up at home.

October 12

Charley says he did not know that I was subject to a cough, and that he hopes I am not consumptive, because his father and mother both died of consumption[7], and it makes him nervous to hear people cough. I nearly strangled myself all the evening trying not to annoy him with mine.

Chapter 4

I really think I am sick and going to die. Last night I raised a little blood. I dare not tell mother, it would distress her so, but I am sure it came from my lungs. Charley said last week he really must stay away till I got better, for my cough sounded like his mother's. I have been very lonely, and have shed some tears, but most of the time have been too sorrowful to cry. If we were married, and I had a cough, would he go and leave me, I wonder?

November 18th, Sunday

Poor mother is dreadfully anxious about me. But I don't see how she can love me so, after the way I have behaved. I wonder if, after all, mothers are not the best friends there are! I keep her awake with my cough all night, and am mopy and cross all day, but she is just as kind and affectionate as she can be.

November 25

The day I wrote that was Sunday. I could not go to church, and I felt very deserted and desolate. I tried to get some comfort by praying, but when I got on my knees I just burst out crying and could not say a word. For I have not seen Charley for ten days. As I knelt there I began to think myself a perfect monster of selfishness for wanting him to spend his evenings with me, now that I am so unhealthy and annoy him so with my cough, and I asked myself if I ought not to break off the engagement altogether, if I was really in a consumption, the very disease Charley dreaded most of all. It seemed such a proper sacrifice to make of myself. Then I prayed— yes, I am sure I really prayed as I had not done for more than a year, and the idea of self-sacrifice grew every moment more beautiful in my eyes, till at last I felt an almost joyful triumph in writing to poor Charley, and telling him what I had resolved to do.

This is my letter:

My Dear, Dear Charley—

I dare not tell you what it cost me to say what I am about to do; but I am sure you know me well enough by this time to believe that it is only because your happiness is far more precious to me than my own, that I have decided to write you this letter. When you first told me that you loved me, you said, and you have often said so since then, that it was my "brightness and gayety" that attracted you. I knew there was something underneath my gayety better worth your love, and was glad I could give you more than you asked for. I knew I was not a mere thoughtless, laughing girl, but that I had a heart as wide as the ocean to give you— as wide and as deep.

But now my "brightness and gayety" have gone; I am sick and perhaps am going to die. If this is so, it would be very sweet to have your love go with me to the very gates of death, and beautify and glorify my path thither. But what a weary task this would be to you, my poor Charley! And so, if you think it best, and it would relieve you of any care and pain, I will release you from our engagement and set you free.

—Your Little Katy

I did not sleep at all that night. Early on Monday I sent off my letter, and my heart beat so hard all day that I was tired and faint. Just at dark his answer came; I can copy it from memory—

Dear Kate—

What a generous, self-sacrificing little thing you are! I always thought so, but now you have given me a noble proof of it. I will admit that I have been disappointed to find your constitution so poor, and that it has been very dull sitting and hearing you cough, especially as I was reminded of the long and tedious illness through which poor Jenny and myself had to nurse our mother. I vowed then never to marry a consumptive woman, and I thank you for making it so easy for me to bring our engagement to an end. My bright hopes are blighted, and it will be long before I shall find another to fill your place. I need not say how much I sympathize with you in this disappointment. I hope the consolations of religion will now be yours. Your notes, the lock of your hair, etc., I return with this. I will not reproach you

for the pain you have cost me; I know it is not
your fault that your health has become so frail.
    I remain your sincere friend,
                Charles Underhill

January 1, 1834

Let me finish this story if I can.

My first impulse after reading his letter was to fly to mother, and hide away forever in her dear, loving arms.

But I restrained myself, and with my heart beating so that I could hardly hold my pen, I wrote this:

    Mr. Underhill, Sir—
        The scales have fallen from my eyes, and I see
you at last just as you are. Since my note to you on
Sunday last, I have had a consultation of physi-
cians, and they all agree that my disease is not of
an alarming character, and that I shall soon recover.
But I thank God that before it was too late, you
have been revealed to me just as you are— a
heartless, selfish, shallow creature, unworthy of the
love of a true-hearted woman, and unworthy even
of your own self-respect. I gave you an opportunity
to withdraw from our engagement in full faith, lov-
ing you so truly that I was ready to go trembling
to my grave alone if you shrank from sustaining me
to it. But I see now that I did not dream for one
moment that you would take me at my word and
leave me to my fate. I thought I loved a man, and
could lean on him when strength failed me. I know
now that I loved a mere creature of my imagina-
tion. Take back your letters; I loathe the sight of
them. Take back the ring, and find, if you can, a

woman who will never be sick, never out of spirits,
and who never will die. Thank heaven it is not...
—*Katherine Mortimer*

These lines came to me in reply:

"Thank God it is not Kate Mortimer. I want
an angel for my wife, not a vixen.
—*C.U."*

January 15

What a tempest-tossed creature this birthday finds me! But let me finish this wretched, disgraceful story, if I can, before I quite lose my senses.

I showed my mother the letters. She burst into tears and opened her arms, and I ran into them as a wounded bird flies into the ark. We cried together. Mother never said, never even looked,

"I told you so." All she did say was this:

"God has heard my prayers! He is reserving better things for my precious child!"

Dear mother's are not the only arms I have flown to. But it does not seem as if God *ought* to take me in because I am in trouble, when I would not go to Him when I was happy in something else. But even in the midst of my greatest rapture I had many and many a misgiving; many a season when my conscience upbraided me for my willful-ness towards my dear mother, and my whole soul yearned for something higher and better even than Charley's love, precious as it was.

January 26

I have shut myself up in my room today to think over things. The end of it is that I am full of mortification and confusion of face. If I had only had confidence in mother's judgment I would never have gotten entangled in this silly engagement. I see now that Charley never could have made me happy, and I know there is a good deal in my heart he never drew out. I wish, however, I had not written him when I was in such a passion. No wonder he is thankful that he has gotten free from such a vixen. But, oh! the provocation was terrible!

I have made up my mind never to tell a human soul about this affair. It will be so high-minded and honorable to shield him from the contempt he deserves. With all my faults I am glad that there is nothing mean or petty about me!

January 27

I can't bear to write it down, but I will. The ink was hardly dry yesterday on the above self-laudation when Amelia came. She had been out of town, and had only just learned what had happened. Of course she was curious to know the whole story.

And I told it to her, every word of it! Oh, Kate Mortimer, how "high-minded" you are! How free from all that is "mean and petty"! I could tear my hair out if it would do any good!

Amelia defended Charley, and I was thus led on to say every harsh thing of him I could think of. She said he was of so sensitive a nature, had so much sensibility, and such a constitutional aversion to seeing suffering, that for her part she could not blame him.

"It is such a pity you had not had your lungs examined before you wrote that first letter," she went on. "But you are so impulsive! If you had only waited you would still be engaged to Charley!"

"I am thankful I did not wait," I cried, angrily. "Do, Amelia, drop the subject forever. You and I shall never agree upon it. The truth is, you are two-thirds in love with him, and have been, all along."

She blushed, and laughed, and actually looked pleased. If anyone had made such an outrageous speech to me, I would have been furious.

"I suppose you know," said she, "that old Mr. Underhill has taken such a fancy to him that he has made him his heir; and he is as rich as can be."

"Indeed!" I said, dryly.

I wonder if mother knew it when she opposed our engagement so strenuously.

January 31

I have asked her, and she said she did. Mr. Underhill told her his intentions when he urged her consent to the engagement. Dear mother! How unworldly, how unselfish she is!

February 4

The name of Charley Underhill appears on these pages for the last time. He is engaged to Amelia! From this moment she is lost to me forever. How desolate, how mortified, how miserable I am! Who could have thought this of Amelia! She came to see me, radiant with joy. I concealed my disgust until she said that Charley felt now that he had never really loved me, but had preferred her all along. Then I burst out. What I said I do not know, and do not care. The whole thing is so disgraceful that I would have to be a block of wood or a stone not to resent it.

February 5

After yesterday's passion of grief, shame and anger, I feel perfectly stupid and weary. Oh, that I was prepared for a better world, and could fly to it and be at rest!

February 6

Now that it is all over, how ashamed I am of the fury I have been in, and which has given Amelia such advantage over me! I was beginning to believe that I was really living a feeble and fluttering, but *real* Christian life, and finding some satisfaction in it. But that is all over now. I am doomed to be a victim of my own unstable, passionate, wayward nature, and the sooner I settle down into that conviction, the better. And yet how my very soul craves the highest happiness, and refuses to be comforted while that is lacking.

February 7

After writing that, I do not know what made me go to see Dr. Cabot. He received me in that cheerful way of his that seems to promise the taking of one's burden right off one's back.

"I am very glad to see you, my dear child," he said.

I intended to be very dignified and cold. As if I was going to have any of Dr. Cabot's undertaking to sympathize with *me!* But those few kind words just upset me, and I began to cry.

"You would not speak so kindly," I got out at last, "if you knew what a dreadful creature I am. I am angry with myself, and angry with everybody, and angry with God. I can't be good two minutes at a time. I do everything I do not want to do, and do nothing I try and pray to do. Everybody plagues me and tempts me. And God does not answer any of my prayers, and I am just desperate."

"Poor child!" he said, in a low voice, as if to himself. "Poor, heart-sick, tired child, that cannot see what I can see, that its Father's loving arms are all about it?"

I stopped crying, to strain my ears and listen. He went on.

"Katy, all that you say may be true. I dare say it is. But God loves you. He loves you."

"He loves me," I repeated to myself. "He loves me! Oh, Dr. Cabot, if I could only believe that! If I could believe that, after all the promises I have broken, all the foolish, wrong things I have done, and shall always be doing, God perhaps still loves me!"

"You may be sure of it," he said solemnly. "I, His minister, bring the gospel to you today. Go home and say over and over to yourself, 'I am a wayward foolish child. But He loves me! I have disobeyed and grieved Him ten thousand times over. But He loves me! I have lost faith in some of my dearest friends and am very desolate. But He loves me! I do not love Him, I am very angry with Him! But He loves me!'"

I came away, and all the way home I fought this battle with myself, saying, "He loves me!" I knelt down to pray, and all my wasted, childish, wicked life came and stared me in the face. I looked at it and said with tears of joy, "But He loves me!" Never in my life did I feel so rested, so quieted, so sorrowful, and yet so satisfied.

February 10

What a beautiful world this is, and how full it is of truly kind, good people! Mrs. Morris was here this morning, and just one squeeze of that long, yellow old hand of hers seemed to speak a bookful! I wonder why I have always disliked her so, for she is really an excellent woman. I gave her a good kiss to pay her for the sympathy she had sense enough not to put into pious-sounding words, and if you will believe it, dear old Journal, the tears came into her eyes, and she said:

"You are one of the Lord's beloved ones, though perhaps you do not know it."

I repeated again to myself those sweet, mysterious words, and then I tried to think what I could do for Him. But I could not think of anything great or good enough. I went into mother's room and put my arms around her and told her how much I loved her. She looked surprised and pleased.

"Ah, I knew it would come!" she said, laying her hand on her Bible.

"Knew what would come, mother?"

"*Peace*," she said.

I came back here and wrote a little note to Amelia, telling her how ashamed and sorry I was that I could not control myself the other day. Then I wrote a long letter to James. I have been very careless about writing to him.

Then I began to hem those handkerchiefs mother asked me to finish a month ago. But I could not think of anything to do for God. I wish I could. It makes me so happy to think that all this time, while I was caring for nobody but myself, and fancying He must almost hate me, He was loving and pitying me.

February 15

I went to see Dr. Cabot again today. He came down from his study with his pen in his hand.

"How dare you come and spoil my sermon on Saturday?" he asked, good-humoredly.

Though he seemed full of loving kindness, I was ashamed of my thoughtlessness. Though I did not know he was particularly busy on Saturdays. If I were a minister I am sure I would get my sermons done early in the week.

"I only wanted to ask one thing," I said. "I want to do something for God. And I can't think of anything unless it is to go on a mission. And mother would never let me do that. She thinks girls with delicate health aren't fit for such work."

"At all events I would not go today," he replied. "Meanwhile do *everything* you do for Him who has loved you and given Himself for you."

I did not dare to stay any longer, and so came away quite puzzled. Dinner was ready, and as I sat down to the table, I said to myself:

"I eat this dinner for myself, not for God. What can Dr. Cabot mean?" Then I remembered the text about doing all for the glory of God, even in eating and drinking; but I do not understand it at all.

February 19

It has seemed to me for several days that it must be that I really do love God, though ever so little. But it shot through my mind today like a knife, that it is a miserable, selfish love at the best, not worth my giving, not worth God's accepting. All my old misery has come back with several other miseries more miserable than itself. I wish I had never been born! I wish I were thoughtless and careless, like so many other girls of my age, who seem to get along very well, and to enjoy themselves far more than I do.

February 21

Dr. Cabot came to see me today. I told him all about it. He could not help smiling as he said:

"When I see a little infant caressing its mother, would

you have me say to it, 'You selfish child, how dare you pretend to caress your mother in that way? You are quite unable to appreciate her character; you love her merely because she loves you, and treats you kindly?' "

It was my turn to smile now, at my own folly.

"You are as yet but a babe in Christ," Dr. Cabot continued. "You love your God and Saviour because He first loved you. The time will come when the character of your love will become changed into one which sees and feels the beauty and the perfection of its object, and if you could be assured that He no longer looked on you with favor, you would still cling to Him with devoted affection."

"There is one thing more that troubles me," I said. "Most persons know the exact moment when they begin real Christian lives. But I do not know of any such time in my history. This causes me many uneasy moments."

"You are wrong in thinking that most persons have this advantage over you. I believe that the children of Christian parents, who have been judiciously trained, rarely can point to any day or hour when they began to live this new life. The question is not, do you remember, my child, when you entered this world, and how! It is simply this, are you now alive and an inhabitant thereof? And now it is my turn to ask you a question. How does it happen that you, who have a mother of rich and varied experience, allow yourself to be tormented with these petty anxieties which she is as capable of dispelling as I am?"

"I do not know," I answered. "But we girls *can't* talk to our mothers about any of our sacred feelings, and we hate to have them talk to us."

Dr. Cabot shook his head.

"There is something wrong somewhere," he said. "A young girl's mother is her natural refuge in every perplexity. I hoped that you, who have rather more sense than most girls of your age, could give me some idea what the difficulty is."

After he had gone, I am ashamed to admit that I was in a perfect flutter of delight at what he had said about my having more sense than most girls. Meeting poor mother on the stairs while in this exalted state of mind, I gave her a very abrupt answer to a kind question, and made her unhappy, as I have made myself.

It is just a year ago today that I got frightened at my novel-reading propensities, and resolved not to look into one for twelve months. I was getting to dislike all other books, and night after night sat up late, devouring everything exciting I could get hold of. One Saturday night I sat up until the clock struck twelve to finish one, and the next morning I was so sleepy that I had to stay at home from church. Now I hope and believe that the back of this dangerous taste is broken, and that I shall never be a slave to it again. Indeed it does not seem to me now that I shall ever care for such books again.

February 24

Mother spoke to me this morning for the fiftieth time, I really believe, about my disorderly habits. I don't think I am careless because I like confusion, but the trouble is I am always in a hurry and a commotion about something. If

I want anything, I want it very much, and right away. So if I am looking for a book, or a piece of music, or a pattern, I tumble everything around, and can't stop to put them back in their rightful place. I wish I were not so eager and impatient. But I mean to try to keep my room and my drawers in order, to please mother.

She says, too, that I am growing careless about my hair and my dress. But that is because my mind is so full of graver, more important things. I thought I *ought* to be wholly occupied with my duty to God. But mother says duty to God includes duty to one's neighbor, and that untidy hair, put up in all sorts of rough bunches, rumpled cuffs and collars, and all that sort of thing, make one offensive to all one meets. I am sorry she thinks so, for I find it very convenient to twist up my hair almost anyhow, and it takes a good deal of time to look after collars and cuffs.

March 14

Today I feel discouraged and disappointed. I certainly thought that if God really loved me, and I really loved Him, I would find myself growing better day by day. But I am not improved in the least. Most of the time I spend on my knees I am either stupid, feeling nothing at all, or else my head is full of what I was doing before I began to pray, or what I am going to do as soon as I get through. I do not believe anybody else in the world is like me in this respect. Then when I feel differently, and can make a nice, glib prayer, with floods of tears running down my cheeks, I get all puffed up, and think how much pleased God must be to see me so fervent in spirit. I go down-stairs in this frame of mind, and begin to scold Susan for misplacing my music, till all of a sudden I catch myself doing it, and stop short, crestfallen and confounded. I have so many such experiences that I feel like a baby just learning to walk, who is so afraid of falling that it has half a mind to sit down once for all.

Then there is another thing. Seeing mother so fond of Thomas à Kempis, I have been reading it, now and then, and am not fond of it at all. From beginning to end it exhorts to self-denial in every form and shape. Must I then give up all hope of happiness in this world, and modify all my natural tastes and desires? Oh, I do love so to be happy! And I do so hate to suffer! The very thought of being sick, or of being forced to nurse sick people, with all their cross ways, and of losing my friends, or of having to live with disagreeable people, makes me shudder. I want to please God, and to be like Him. I certainly do. But I am so young, and it is so natural to want to have a good time! And now I am in for it I may as well tell the whole story. When I read the lives of good men and women who have died and gone to heaven, I find they all liked to sit and think about God and about Christ. Now I *don't*. I often try, but my mind flies off in a tangent. The truth of the matter is that I am perfectly discouraged.

March 17

I went to see Dr. Cabot again today, but he was out, so I thought I would ask for Mrs. Cabot, though I was determined not to tell her any of my troubles. But somehow she got the whole story out of me, and instead of being shocked, as I expected she would be, she actually burst out laughing! She recovered herself immediately however, and said, "Do excuse me for laughing at you, you dear child you! But I remember so well how I used to flounder through just such needless anxieties, and life looks so different, so very different, to me now from what it did then! What would you think of a man who, having just sowed his field, was astonished not to see it at once ripe for the harvest because his neighbor's, after long months of waiting, was just being gathered in?"

"Do you mean," I asked, "that by and by I shall naturally come to feel and think as other good people do?"

"Yes, I do. You must make the most of what little Christian life you have; be thankful God has given you so much, cherish it, pray over it, and guard it like the apple of your eye. Imperceptibly, but surely, it will grow, and keep on growing, for this is its nature."

"But I don't want to wait," I said, despondently. "I have just been reading a delightful book, full of stories of heroic deeds— not fables, but histories of real events and real people. It has quite stirred me up, and made me wish to possess such beautiful heroism, and that I were a man, that I might have a chance to perform some truly noble, self-sacrificing acts."

"I dare say your chance will come," she replied, "though you are not a man. I fancy we all get, more or less, what we want."

"Do you really think so? Let me see, then, what I want

most. But I am staying too long. Were you particularly busy?"

"No," she returned smilingly, "I am learning 'that the one who wants me is the one I want.'"

"You are very good to say so. Well, in the first place, I do really and truly want to be good. Not with common goodness, you know, but—"

"But *un*common goodness," she put in.

"I mean that I want to be very, very good. I would like next best to be learned and accomplished. Then I would want to be perfectly healthy and perfectly happy. And a pleasant home, of course, I must have, with friends to love me, and like me, too. And I can't get along without some pretty, tasteful things around me. But you are laughing at me! Have I said anything foolish?"

"If I laughed it was not at you, but at poor human nature that would yearn to grasp everything at once. Allowing that you would possess all you have just described, where is the heroism you so much admire to find room for exercise?"

"That's just what I was saying. That is just what troubles me."

"To be sure, while perfectly healthy and happy, in a pleasant home, with friends to love and admire you—"

"Oh, I did not say admire," I interrupted.

"That was just what you meant, my dear."

I am afraid it was, now that I come to think it over.

"Well, with plenty of friends, good in an uncommon way, accomplished, learned, and surrounded with pretty and tasteful objects, your life will certainly be in danger of not proving very sublime."

"It is a great pity," I said, musingly.

"Suppose then you content yourself for the present with doing in a faithful, quiet, persistent way all the little, homely tasks that return with each returning day, each one as unto God, and perhaps by and by you will thus have gained strength for a more heroic life."

"But I don't know how."

"You have some little home duties, I suppose?"

"Yes; I have the care of my own room, and mother wants me to have a general oversight of the parlor; you know we have but one parlor now."

"Is that all you have to do?"

"Why, my music and drawing take up a good deal of my time, and I read and study more or less, and go out some, and we have a good many visitors."

"I suppose, then, you keep your room in nice ladylike order, and that the parlor is dusted every morning, loose music put out of the way, books restored to their places—"

"Now I know mother has been telling you."

"Your mother has told me nothing at all."

"Well, then," I said, laughing, but a little ashamed, "I don't keep my room in nice order, and mother really sees to the parlor herself, though I pretend to do it."

"And is she never annoyed by this neglect?"

"Oh, yes, very much annoyed."

"Then, dear Katy, suppose your first act of heroism tomorrow would be the gratifying of your mother in these little things, little though they are. Surely your first duty, next to pleasing God, is to please your mother, and in every possible way to sweeten and beautify her life. You may depend upon it that a life of real heroism and self-sacrifice *must* begin and lay its foundation in this little world, wherein it learns its first lesson and takes its first steps."

"And do you really think that God notices such little things?"

"My dear child, what a question! If there is any one truth I would gladly impress on the mind of a young Christian, it is just this, that God notices the most trivial act, accepts the poorest, most threadbare little service, listens to the coldest, feeblest petition, and gathers up with parental fondness all our fragmentary desires and attempts at good works. Oh, if we could only begin to conceive how He loves us, what different creatures we would be!"

I felt inspired by her enthusiasm, though I don't think I quite understand what she means. I did not dare to stay any longer, for, with her great host of children, she must have her hands full.

March 25

Mother is very much astonished to see how nicely I am keeping things in order. I was flying about this morning, singing, and dusting the furniture, when she came in and began, "He that is faithful in that which is least—" but I ran at her with my brush, and would not let her finish. I really, really don't deserve to be praised. For I have been thinking that, if it is true that God notices every little thing we do to please Him, He must also notice every cross word we speak, every shrug of the shoulders, every ungracious look, and that they displease Him. And my list of such offenses is as long as my life!

March 29

Yesterday, for the first time since that dreadful blow, I felt some return of my natural gaiety and cheerfulness. It seemed to come hand in hand with my first real effort to go so far out of myself as to try to do exactly what would gratify dear mother.

But today I am all down again. I miss Amelia's friendship, for one thing. To be sure I wonder how I ever came to love such a superficial character so devotedly, but I *must* have somebody to love, and perhaps I invented a lovely creature, and called it by her name, and bowed down to it and worshiped it. I certainly did so in regard to him whose heartless cruelty has left me so sad, so desolate.

Evening

Mother has been very patient and forbearing with me all day. Tonight, after tea, she said, in her gentlest, most tender way,

"Dear Katy, I feel very sorry for you. But I see one path which you have not yet tried, which can lead you out of these sore straits. You have tried living for yourself a good many years, and the result is great weariness and heaviness of soul. Try now to live for others. Take a class in the Sunday-school. Go with me to visit my poor people. You will be astonished to find how much suffering and sickness there is in this world, and how delightful it is to sympathize with and try to relieve it."

This advice was very repugnant to me. My time is pretty fully occupied with my books, my music and my drawing. And of all places in the world I hate a sick-room. But, on the whole, I *will* take a class in the Sunday-school.

Chapter 5

I have taken it at last. I would not take one before, because I knew I could not teach little children how to love God, unless I loved Him myself. My class is perfectly delightful. There are twelve dear little things in it, of all ages between eight and nine. Eleven are girls, and the one boy makes me more trouble than all of them put together. When I get them all about me, and their sweet innocent faces look up into mine, I am so happy that I can hardly help stooping every now and then to kiss them. They ask the very strangest questions! I mean to spend a great deal of time in preparing the lesson, and in hunting up stories to illustrate it. Oh, I am so glad I was ever born into this beautiful world, where there will always be dear little children to love!

April 13

Sunday has come again, and with it my darling little class! Dr. Cabot has preached delightfully all day, and I feel that it must do me good. I long, I truly long to please God; I long to feel as the best Christians feel, and to live as they live.

April 20

Now that I have these twelve little ones to instruct, I am more than ever in earnest about setting them a good example throughout the week. It is true they do not, most of them, know how I spend my time, nor how I act. But *I* know, and whenever I am conscious of not practicing what I preach, I am bitterly ashamed and grieved. How much work, badly done, I am now having to undo! If I had begun in earnest to serve God when I was young, as these children are, how many wrong habits I could have avoided; habits that entangle me now, as in so many nets. I am trying to take each of these little gentle girls by the hand and to lead her to Christ. Poor Johnny Ross is not so manageable as they are, and tests my patience to the last degree.

April 27

This morning I had my little flock about me, and talked to them out of the very bottom of my heart about Jesus. They left their seats and got close to me in a circle, leaning on my lap and drinking in every word. All of a sudden I was aware, as by a magnetic influence, that a great lumbering man in the next seat was looking at me out of two of the blackest eyes I ever saw, and evidently listening to what I was saying. I was disconcerted at first, then angry. What impertinence. What rudeness! I am sure he must have seen the displeasure in my face, for he got up what I suppose he meant for a blush, that is he turned several shades darker than he was before, giving one the idea that he is full of black rather than red blood. I would not have remembered it, however— by it I mean his impertinence— if he had not shortly after made a really excellent address to the children. Perhaps it was a little above their comprehension, but it showed a good deal of thought and earnestness. I meant to ask who he was, but forgot it.

This has been a delightful Sunday. I have really feasted on Dr. Cabot's preaching. But I am convinced that there is something in religion I do not yet apprehend. I do wish I positively *knew* that God has forgiven and accepted me.

May 6

Last evening Clara Ray had a little party and I was there. She has a great knack at getting the right sort of people together, and of making them enjoy themselves.

I sang several songs, and so did Clara, but they all said my voice was finer and in better training than hers. It is delightful to be with such cultivated and agreeable people. I could have stayed all night, but mother sent for me before any one else had even thought of going, and so I had to leave.

May 7

I have been on a charming excursion today with Clara Ray and all her friends. I was rather tired, but had an invitation to a concert this evening, which I could not resist.

July 21

So much has been going on that I have not had time to write. There is no end to the picnics, drives, parties, etc., this summer. I am afraid that I am not getting on in my Christian life at all. My prayers are dull and short, and full of wandering thoughts. I am brimful of vitality and good humor in company, but then as soon as I get home am stupid and peevish. I suppose this will always be so, as it always has been; and I declare I would rather be so than such a vapid, flat creature as Mary Jones, or such a dull heavy one as big Lucy Merrill.

July 24

Clara Ray says the girls think me reckless and imprudent in speech. I've a good mind not to go with her gang any more. I am afraid I have been a good deal dazzled by the attentions I have received of late; and now comes this blow at my vanity.

On the whole, I feel greatly out of sorts this evening.

July 28

People talk about happiness to be found in a Christian life. I wonder why I do not find more! On Sundays I am pretty good, and always seem to start afresh; but on weekdays I am drawn along with those about me. All my pleasures are innocent ones; there is surely no harm in going to concerts, driving out, singing, and making little visits!

But these things distract me; They absorb me; they make religious duties irksome. I almost wish I could shut myself up in a cell, and so get out of the reach of temptation.

The truth is, the journey heavenward is all uphill. I have to *force* myself to keep on. The wonder is that anybody gets there with so much to oppose, and, apparently, so little to help one!

July 29

It is high time to stop and think. I have been like one running a race, and am stopping to take a breath. I do not like the way things have been going lately. I feel restless and ill at ease. I see that if I would be happy in God, I must give Him all. And there is a wicked reluctance to do that. I want Him— but I want to have my own way, too. I want to walk humbly and softly before Him, and I want to go where I shall be admired and applauded. To whom shall I yield? To God? Or to myself? This issue must be settled once and for all.

July 30

I met Dr. Cabot today, and could not help asking the question: "Is it right for me to sing and play in company when all I do it for is to be admired?"

"Are you sure it is all you do it for?" he returned.

"Oh," I said, "I suppose there may be a sprinkling of desire to entertain and please, mixed with the love of display."

"Do you suppose that your love of display, assuming you have it, would be forever slain by your merely refusing to sing in company?"

"I thought that might give it a pretty hard blow," I said, "if not its death-blow."

"Meanwhile, in punishing yourself you punish your poor innocent friends," he said laughing. "No, child, go on singing; God has given you this power of entertaining and gratifying your friends. But pray, without ceasing, that you may sing from pure benevolence and not from pure self-love."

"Why, do people pray about such things as that?" I cried.

"Of course they do. Why, I would pray about my little finger, if my little finger went astray."

I looked at his little finger, but saw no signs of its becoming schismatic.

August 3

This morning I took great delight in praying for my little students, and went to Sunday-school as on wings. But on reaching my seat, what was my horror to find Maria Perry there!

"Oh, your seat has been changed," said she. "I am to have half your class, and I like this seat better than those higher up. I suppose you don't care?"

"But I do care," I returned; "and you have taken my very best children— the very sweetest and the very prettiest. I shall speak to Mr. Williams about it immediately."

"At any rate, I would not fly into such a fury," she said. "It is just as pleasant to me to have sweet and pretty children to teach as it is to you. Mr. Williams said he had no doubt you would be glad to divide your class with me, as it is so large; and I doubt if you would gain anything by speaking to him."

There was no time for further discussion, as school was about to begin. I went to my new seat with great disgust, and found it very inconvenient. The children could not cluster around me as they did before, and I got on with the lesson very badly. I am sure Maria Perry has no gift at teaching little children, and I feel quite miffed and disappointed. This has not been a profitable Sunday, and I am going to bed, cheerless and uneasy.

August 9

Mr. Williams called this evening to say that I am to have my old seat and all the children again. All the mothers had been to see him, or had written him notes about it, and requested that I might continue to teach them. Mr. Williams said he hoped I would go on teaching for twenty years, and that as fast as his little girls grew old enough to come to Sunday-school he would want me to take charge of them. I should have been greatly elated by these compliments, but for the display I made of myself to Maria Perry on Sunday. Oh, that I could learn to bridle my miserable tongue!

January 15, 1835

Today I am twenty. That sounds very old, yet I feel pretty much as I did before. I have begun to visit some of mother's poor folks with her, and am astonished to see how they love her, and how plainly they let her talk to them. As a general rule, I do not think poor people are very interesting, and they are always ungrateful.

We went first to see old Jacob Stone. I have been there a good many times with the basket of nice things mother takes such comfort in sending him, but I never would bring myself to go in. I was shocked to see how worn away he was. He seemed in great distress of mind, and begged mother to pray with him. I do not see how she could. I am perfectly sure that no earthly power could ever induce me to go around praying on bare floors, with people sitting, rocking and staring all the time, as the two Stone girls stared at mother. How tenderly she prayed for him!

We then went to see Susan Green. She had made a carpet for her room by sewing together little bits of pieces given to her, I suppose, by persons for whom she works, for she goes about fitting and making carpets. It looked bright and cheerful. She had a nice bed in the corner, covered with a white quilt, and some little ornaments were arranged about the room. Mother complimented her on her neatness, and said a queen might sleep in such a bed as that, and hopes she found it as comfortable as it looked.

"Mercy on us!" she cried out, "it ain't to *sleep* in! I sleep in the loft, that I climb to by a ladder every night."

Mother looked a little amused, and then she sat and listened, patiently, to a long account of how the poor old thing had invested her money; how Mr. Jones did not pay the interest regularly, and how Mr. Stevens haggled about the percentage. After we came away, I asked mother how she could listen to such a rigmarole in patience, and what good she supposed she had done by her visit.

"Why the poor creature likes to show off her bright carpet and nice bed, her chairs, her vases and her knick-knacks, and she likes to talk about her beloved money, and her bank stock. I may not have done her any good; but I have given her some pleasure, and so have you."

"Why, I hardly spoke a word."

"Yes, but your mere presence gratified her. And if she ever gets into trouble, she will feel kindly towards us for the sake of our sympathy with her pleasures, and will let us sympathize with her sorrows."

I confess this did not seem a privilege to be coveted. She is not nice at all, and even takes snuff.

We went next to see Bridget Shannon. Mother had lost track of her for some years, and had just heard that she was sick and in great need. We found her in bed; there was no furniture in the room, and three little half-naked children sat with their bare feet in some ashes where there had been a little fire. Three such forlorn faces I never saw before. Mother sent me to the nearest baker's for bread; I ran nearly all the way, and I hardly know which I enjoyed most, mother's eagerness in distributing, or the children's in clutching at and devouring it. I am going to cut up one or more old dresses to make the poor things something to cover them. One of them has lovely hair that would curl beautifully if it were only brushed out. I told her to come see me tomorrow, she is so very pretty.

Those few visits used up the very time I usually spend in drawing. But on the whole I am glad I went with mother, because it has gratified her. Besides, one must either stop reading the Bible altogether, or else leave off spending one's whole time in just doing easy pleasant things one likes to do.

January 20

The little Shannon girl came, and I washed her face and hands, brushed out her hair and made it curl in lovely golden ringlets all around her sweet face, and carried her in great triumph to mother.

"Look at the dear little thing, mother!" I cried; "doesn't she look like a line of poetry?"

"You foolish, romantic child!" replied mother. "She looks, to me, like a very ordinary line of prose. A slice of bread and butter and a piece of gingerbread mean more to her than these elaborate ringlets possibly can. They get in her eyes, and make her neck cold; see, they are dripping with water, and the child is all in a shiver."

So saying, mother folded a towel around her neck, to catch the falling drops, and went for bread and butter, of which the child consumed a quantity that was absolutely appalling. To crown all, the ungrateful little thing would not so much as look at me from that moment on, but clung to mother, turning her back upon me in supreme contempt.

Moral— Mothers occasionally know more than their daughters do.

Chapter 6

January 24

A message came yesterday morning from Susan Green to the effect that she had had a dreadful fall, and was half killed. Mother wanted to set off at once to see her, but I would not let her go, as she has one of her worst colds. She then asked me to go in her place. I turned up my nose at the bare thought, though I dare say it turns up enough on its own account.

"Oh, mother!" I said, reproachfully, "that dirty old woman!"

Mother made no answer, and I sat down at the piano, and played a little. But I only played discords.

"Do you think it is my *duty* to run after such horrid old women?" I asked mother, at last.

"I think, dear, you must make your own duties," she said kindly. "I dare say that at your age I would have made a great deal out of my personal repugnance to such a woman as Susan, and very little out of her sufferings."

I believe I am the most fastidious creature in the world. Sick-rooms with their intolerable smells of camphor, and vinegar and mustard, their gloom and their whines and their groans, actually make me shudder. But was it not just such fastidiousness that made Cha— no, I won't utter his name— that made somebody weary of my possibilities? And has that terrible lesson really done me no good?

January 26

No sooner had I written the above than I scrambled into my cloak and bonnet, and flew, on the wings of holy indignation, to Susan Green. Such wings fly fast, and got me a little out of breath. I found her lying on that nice white bed of hers, in a frilled cap and night-gown. It seems she fell from her ladder in climbing to the dismal den where she sleeps, and lay all night in great distress with some serious internal injury. I found her groaning and complaining in a fearful way.

"Are you in such pain?" I asked, as kindly as I could.

"It isn't the pain," she said, "it isn't the pain. It's the way my nice bed is going to wreck and ruin, and the starch all getting out of my frills that I made with my own hands. And the doctor's bill, and the medicines, oh, dear, dear, dear!"

Just then the doctor came in. After examining her, he said to a woman who seemed to have charge of her:

"Are you the nurse?"

"Oh, no, I only stepped in to see what I could do for her."

"Who is to be with her tonight, then?"

Nobody knew.

"I will send a nurse, then," he said. "But some one else will be needed also," he added, looking at me.

"I will stay," I said. But my heart died within me.

The doctor took me aside.

"Her injuries are very serious," he said. "If she has any friends, they ought to be sent for."

"You don't mean that she is going to die?" I asked.

"I fear she is. But not immediately." He took leave, and I went back to the bedside. I saw there no longer a snuffy, repulsive old woman, but a human being about to make that mysterious journey to a far country whence there is no return. Oh, how I wished mother were there!

"Susan," I said, "have you any relatives?"

"No, I haven't," she answered sharply. "And if I had they needn't come prowling around me. I don't want no relations about my body."

"Would you like to see Dr. Cabot?"

"What would I want of Dr. Cabot? Don't tease, child."

Considering the deference with which she had heretofore treated me, this was quite a new order of things.

I sat down and tried to pray for her, silently, in my heart. Who was to go with her on that long journey, and where was it to end?

The woman who had been caring for her now went away, and it was growing dark. I sat still listening to my own heart, which beat till it half choked me.

"What were you and the doctor whispering about?" she suddenly burst out.

"He asked me, for one thing, if you had any friends that could be sent for."

"I've been my own best friend," she returned. "Who'd have raked and scraped and hoarded and counted for Susan Green if I hadn't ha' done it? I've got enough to make me comfortable as long as I live, and when I lie on my dying bed."

"But you can't carry it with you," I said. This highly original remark was all I had courage to utter.

"I wish I could," she cried. "I suppose you think I talk awful. They say you are getting most to be as much of a saint as your ma. It's born in some, and in some it ain't. Do get a light. It's lonesome here in the dark, and cold."

I was thankful enough to enliven the dark room with light and fire. But I saw now that the thin, yellow, hard face had changed sadly. She fixed her two little black eyes on me, evidently startled by the expression of my face.

"Look here, child, I ain't hurt to speak of, am I?"

"The doctor says you are hurt seriously."

My tone must have said more than my words did, for she caught me by the wrist and held me fast.

"He didn't say nothing about my— about its being

dangerous? I ain't dangerous, am I?"

I felt ready to sink.

"Oh, Susan!" I gasped out; "you haven't any time to lose. You're going, you're going!"

"Going!" she cried; "going where? You don't mean to say I'm a-dying? Why, it beats all my calculations. I was going to live ever so many years, and save up ever so much money, and then, when my time come, I was going to put on my best frilly night-gown and night-cap, and lay my head on my handsome pillow, and draw the clothes up over me, neat and tidy, and die decent. But here's my bed all in a toss, and my frills all in a crumple, and my room all upside down, and bottles of medicine setting around alongside of my vases, and nobody here but you, just a girl, and nothing else!"

All this came out by jerks, as it were, and at intervals.

"Don't talk so!" I fairly screamed. "Pray, pray to God to have mercy on you!"

She looked at me, bewildered, but yet as if the truth had reached her at last.

"Pray yourself!" she said, eagerly. "I don't know how. I can't think. Oh, my time's come! my time's come! And I ain't ready! I ain't ready! Get down on your knees and pray with all your might."

And I did; she holding my wrist tightly in her hard hand. All at once I felt her hold relax. After that the next thing I knew I was lying on the floor, and somebody was dashing water in my face.

It was the nurse. She had come at last, and found me by the side of the bed, where I had fallen, and had been trying to revive me ever since. I started up and looked about me. The nurse was closing Susan's eyes in a professional way, and performing other little services of the sort. The room wore an air of perfect desolation. The clothes Susan had on when she fell lay in a forlorn heap on a chair; her shoes and stockings were thrown hither and thither; the mahogany bureau, in which she had taken so much pride, was covered with vials, to make room for which some pretty trifles had been hastily thrust aside. I remembered what I had once said to Mrs. Cabot about having tasteful things about me, with a sort of shudder. What a mockery they are in the awful presence of death!

Mother met me with open arms when I reached home. She was much shocked at what I had to tell, and at my having encountered such a scene alone. I would have felt myself quite a heroine under her caresses if I had not been overcome with bitter regret that I had not, with firmness and dignity, turned poor Susan's last thoughts to her Saviour. Oh, how could I, through miserable cowardice, let those precious moments slip by!

February 27

I have learned one thing by yesterday's experience that is worth knowing. It is this: duty looks more repulsive at a distance than when fairly faced and met. Of course I

have read the lines,

> *Nor know we anything so fair*
> *As is the smile upon Thy face;*

but I seem to be one of the stupid sort, who never apprehend a thing till they experience it. Now however, I have seen the smile, and find it so "fair," that I shall gladly plod through many a hardship and trial to meet it again.

Poor Susan! Perhaps God heard my eager prayer for Susan's soul, and revealed Himself to her at the very last moment.

March 2

Such a strange thing has happened! Susan Green left a will, bequeathing her precious savings to whoever offered the last prayer in her hearing! I do not want, I never could touch a penny of that hardly-earned store; and if I did, no earthly motive would tempt me to tell a human being, that it was offered by me, an inexperienced trembling girl, driven to it by mere desperation! So it has gone to Dr. Cabot, who will be delighted to have it to give to poor people, who really besiege him. The last time he called to see her he talked and prayed with her, and says she seemed pleased and grateful, and promised to be more regular at church, which she had been, ever since.

March 28

I feel all out of sorts. Mother says it is due to the strain I went through at Susan's dying bed. She wants me to go to visit my aunt Mary, who is always urging me to come. But I do not like to leave my little Sunday School students, nor to give mother the occasion to deny herself in order to meet the expense of such a long journey. Besides, I would have to have some new dresses, a new bonnet, and lots of things.

Today Dr. Cabot has sent me some directions for which I have been begging him a long time. Lest I should wear out this precious letter by reading it over, I will copy it here. After alluding to my complaint that I still "saw men as trees walking," (Mark 8:24) he says:

> "Yet he who first uttered this complaint had had his eyes opened by the Son of God, and so have you. Now He never leaves His work incomplete, and He will gradually lead you into clear and open vision, if you will allow Him to do it. I say gradually because I believe this to be His usual method, while I do not deny that there are cases where light suddenly bursts in like a flood. To return to the blind man. When Jesus found that his cure was not complete, He put His hands again upon his eyes, and made him look up; and he was restored, and saw every man clearly. Now this must be done for you; and in order to have it done you must go to Christ Himself, not to one of His servants. Make your complaint, tell Him how obscure everything still looks to you, and beg Him to complete your cure. He may see fit to test your faith and patience by delaying this completion; but meanwhile you are safe in His presence, and while led by His hand, He will excuse the mistakes you make, and pity your falls. But you will imagine that it is best that He

should at once enable you to see clearly. If it is, you may be sure He will do it. He never makes mistakes. But He often deals far differently with His disciples. He lets them grope their way in the dark until they fully learn how blind they are, how helpless, how absolutely in need of Him.

"What His methods will be with you I cannot fore-tell. But you may be sure that He never works in an arbitrary way. He has a reason for everything He does. You may not understand why He leads you now in this way and now in that, but you may, nay, you must believe that perfection is stamped on His every act.

"I am afraid that you are in danger of falling into an error only too common among young Christians. You acknowledge that there has been enmity towards God in your secret soul, and that one of the first steps towards peace is to become reconciled to Him and to have your sins forgiven for Christ's sake. This done, you settle down with the feeling that the great work of life is done, and that your salvation is sure. Or, if not sure, that your whole business is to study your own case to see whether you get beyond this point. They spend their whole time in asking the question:

" 'Do I love the Lord or no?
Am I His or am I not?'

"I beg you, my dear child, if you are doing this aimless, useless work, to stop short at once. Life is too precious to spend in a tread-mill. Having been pardoned by your God and Saviour, the next thing you have to do is to show your gratitude for this infinite favor by consecrating yourself entirely to Him, body, soul, and spirit. This is the least you can do. He has bought you with a price,

and you are no longer your own. 'But,' you may reply, 'this is contrary to my nature. I love my own way. I desire ease and pleasure; I desire to go to heaven, but I want to be carried thither on a bed of flowers. Can I not give myself so far to God as to feel a sweet sense of peace with Him, and be sure of final salvation, and yet, to a certain extent, indulge and gratify myself? If I give myself entirely away to Him, and lose all ownership in myself, He may deny me many things I greatly desire. He may make my life hard and wearisome, depriving me of all that now makes it agreeable.' But, I reply, this is no matter of parley and discussion; it is not optional with God's children whether they will pay Him a part of the price they owe Him, and keep back the rest. He asks, and He has a right to ask, for all you have and all you are. And if you shrink from what is involved in such a surrender, you should fly to Him at once and never rest till He has conquered this secret disinclination to give to Him as freely and as fully as He has given to you. It is true that such an act of consecration on your part may involve no little future discipline and correction. As soon as you become the Lord's by your own deliberate and conscious act, He will begin that process of sanctification which is to make you holy as He is holy, perfect as He is perfect. He becomes at once your Physician as well as you dearest and best Friend, but He will use no painful remedy that can be avoided. Remember that it is His will that you should be sanctified, and that the work of making you holy is His, not yours. At the same time you are not to sit with folded hands, waiting for this blessing. You are to avoid laying hindrances in His way, and you are to exercise faith in Him as just as able and just as willing to give you sanctification as He was to give you redemption. And now if

*you ask how you may know that you have truly conse-
crated yourself to Him, I reply, observe every indication
of His will concerning you, no matter how trivial, and see
whether you at once close in with that will. Lay down
this principle as a law— God does nothing arbitrary. If
He takes away your health, for instance, it is because He
has some reason for doing so; and this is true of every
thing you value; and if you have real faith in Him you
will not insist on knowing this reason. If you find, in the
course of daily events, that your self-consecration was
not perfect— that is, that your will revolts at His will—
do not be discouraged, but fly to your Saviour and stay
in His presence till you obtain the spirit in which He cried
in His hour of anguish 'Father, if Thou be willing, remove
this cup from me: nevertheless, not my will but Thine be
done' (Luke 22:42). Every time you do this it will be easier
to do it; every such consent to suffer will bring you
nearer and nearer to Him; and in this nearness to Him
you will find such peace, such blessed, sweet peace, as will
make your life infinitely happy, no matter what may be
its mere outside conditions. Just think, my dear Katy, of
the honor and the joy of having your will one with the
Divine will, and so becoming changed into Christ's image from glory to glory!*

*"But I cannot say, in a letter, the tenth part of what
I want to say. Listen to my sermons from week to week,
and glean from them all the instruction you can, remembering that they are preached to you.*

*"In reading the Bible I advise you to choose de-
tached passages, or even one verse a day, rather than a
whole chapter. Study every word, ponder and pray over it
till you have gotten out of it all the truth it contains.*

"As to the other devotional reading, it is better to settle down on a few favorite authors, and read their works over and over and over until you have digested their thoughts and made them your own.

"It has been said 'that a fixed, inflexible will is a great assistance in a holy life.'

"You can will to choose for your associates those who are most devout and holy.

"You can will to read books that will stimulate you in your Christian life, rather than those that merely amuse.

"You can will to use every means of grace appointed by God.

"You can will to prefer a religion of principle to one of mere feeling; in other words, to obey the will of God when no comfortable glow of emotion accompanies your obedience.

"You cannot will to possess the spirit of Christ; that must come as His gift; but you can choose to study His life, and to imitate it. This will infallibly lead to such self-denying work as visiting the poor, nursing the sick, giving of your time and money to the needy, and the like.

"If the thought of such self-denial is repugnant to you, remember that it is enough for the disciple to be as his Lord. And let me assure you that as you penetrate the labyrinth of life in pursuit of Christian duty, you will often be surprised and charmed by meeting your Master Himself amidst its windings and turnings, and receive His soul-inspiring smile. Or, I should rather say, you will always meet Him wherever you go."

I have read this letter again and again. It has taken such hold of me that I can think of nothing else. The idea of seeking holiness had never so much as crossed my mind. And even now it seems like presumption for such a one as I to utter so sacred a word. And I shrink from committing myself to such a pursuit, lest after a time I should fall back into the old routine. And I have an undefined, wicked dread of being singular, as well as a certain terror of self-denial and loss of all liberty. But no choice seems left to me. Now that my duty has been clearly pointed out to me, I do not stand where I did before. And I feel, mingled with my indolence and love of ease and pleasure, some drawings towards a higher and better life. There is one thing I can do, and that is to pray that Jesus would do for me what He did for the blind man— put His hands yet again upon my eyes and make me to see clearly. And I will.

March 30

Yes, I have prayed, and He has heard me. I see that I have no right to live for myself, and that I *must* live for Him. I have given myself to Him as I never did before, and have entered, as it were, a new world. I was very happy when I first began to believe in His love for me, and that He had redeemed me. But this new happiness is deeper; it involves something higher than getting to heaven at last, which has hitherto, been my great aim.

March 31

The more I pray, and the more I read the Bible, the more I feel my ignorance. And the more earnestly I desire holiness, the more utterly unholy I see myself to be. But I have pledged myself to the Lord, and I must pay my vows, cost what it may.

I have begun to read Taylor's "Holy Living and Dying."[8] A month ago I would have found it a tedious, dry book. But I am now reading it with a sort of eagerness, like one seeking after hidden treasure. Mother, observing what I was doing, advised me not to read it straight through, but to mingle a passage now and then with some chapters from other books. She suggested my beginning with Baxter's "The Saints Everlasting Rest,"[9] and of that I have read every word. I shall read it over as Dr. Cabot advised till I have fully caugh its spirit. Even this one reading had taken away my lingering fear of death, and made heaven wonderfully attractive. I never mean to read worldly books again, and my music and my drawing I have given up forever.

Chapter 7

April 1

Mother asked me last evening to sing and play to her. I was embarrassed to know how to excuse myself without telling her my real reason for declining. But somehow she got it out of me.

"One need not be fanatical in order to be religious," she said.

"Is it fanatical to give up all for God?" I asked.

"What is it to give up all?" she asked, in reply.

"Why, to deny one's self every gratification and indulgence in order to mortify one's natural inclinations, and to live entirely for Him."

"God is then a hard Master, who allows His children no liberty," she replied. "Now let us see where this theory will lead you. In the first place you must shut your eyes to all the beautiful things He has made. You must shut your heart against all sweet human affections. You have a body, it is true, and it may revolt at such bondage—"

"We are told to keep under the body," I interrupted. "Oh, mother, don't hinder me! You know that my love for music is a *passion* and that it is my snare and temptation.

And how can I spend my whole time in reading the Bible and praying, if I go on with my drawing? It may do for other people to serve both God and Mammon, but not for me. I must belong wholly to the world or wholly to Christ."

Mother said no more, and I went on with my reading. But somehow my book seemed to have lost its flavor. Besides, it was time to retire for my evening devotions, which I never put off now till the last thing at night, as I used to do. When I came down, mother was lying on the sofa, by which I knew she was not well. I felt troubled that I had refused to sing to her. Think of the money she had spent on that part of my education! I went to her and kissed her with a pang of terror. What if she were going to be very sick, and die?

"It is nothing, darling," she said, "nothing at all. I am tired, and felt a little faint."

I looked at her anxiously, and the bare thought that she might die and leave me alone was so terrible that I could hardly help crying out. And I saw, as by a flash of lighting, that if God took her from me, I could not, would not say: "Thy will be done".

But she was better after taking a few drops of lavender[10], and what color she has came back to her dear, sweet face.

April 12

Dr. Cabot's letter has lost all its power over me. A stone has more feeling than I do. I don't love to pray. I am sick and tired of this dreadful struggle after holiness; good books are all alike, flat and meaningless. But I *must* have something to absorb and carry me away, and I have come back to my music and my drawing with new zest. Mother was right in warning me against giving them up. Maria Kelley is teaching me to paint in oil-colors, and says I have a natural gift for it.

April 13

Mother asked me to go to church with her last evening, and I said I did not want to go. She looked surprised and troubled.

"Are you not feeling well, dear?" she asked.

"I don't know. Yes. I suppose I am. But I could not be still at church five minutes. I am so nervous that I feel as if I could fly."

"I see how it is," she said; "you have forgotten that body of yours, of which I reminded you, and have been trying to live as if you were all soul and spirit. You have been straining every nerve to acquire perfection, whereas this is God's gift, and one that He is willing to give you, fully and freely."

"I have finished seeking for that or anything else that is good," I said, despondently. "And so I have gone back to my music and everything else."

"Here is just the rock upon which you split," she returned. "You speak of going away from God. Yet you rush from one extreme to another. The only true way to live in this world, constituted just as we are, is to make all our employments serve the one great end and aim of our existence, namely, to glorify God and to enjoy Him forever.

But in order to do this we must be wise task-masters, and not require of ourselves what we cannot possibly perform. Recreation we must have. Otherwise the strings of our soul, wound up to an unnatural tension, will break."

"Oh, I do wish," I cried, "that God had given us plain rules, about which we could make no mistake!"

"I think His rules *are* plain," she replied. "And some liberty of action He must leave us, or we would become mere machines. I think that those who love Him, and wait upon Him day by day, learn His will almost imperceptibly, and need not go astray."

"But, mother, music and drawing are sharp edged tools in such hands as mine. I cannot be moderate in my use of them. And the more I delight in them, the less I delight in God."

"Yes, this is human nature. But God's divine nature will supplant it, if we only consent to let Him work in us of His own good pleasure."

April 16, in New York

After all, mother has come off conqueror, and here I am at Aunty's. After our quiet, plain little home, in our quiet little town, this seems like a new world. The house is large, but it is full as it can hold. Aunty has six children of her own, and has adopted two. She says she always meant to imitate the old woman who lived in a shoe. She reminds me of mother, and yet she is very different; full of fun and energy; flying about the house as on wings, with a kind, bright word for everybody. All her household affairs go on like clock-work; the children are always nicely dressed; nobody ever seems out of humor; nobody is ever sick. Aunty is the central object around which everybody revolves; you can't forget her a moment, for she is always doing something for you, and then her unflagging good humor and cheerfulness keep you good-humored and cheerful. I don't wonder that Uncle Alfred loves her so.

I hope I shall have just such a home. I mean this is the sort of home I would like if I ever married, which I never intend to do. I would like to be just such a bright, loving wife as Aunty is; to have my husband lean on me as Uncle leans on her; to have just as many children, and to train them as wisely and kindly as she does hers. Then, indeed, I would feel that I had not been born, in vain, but had a high and sacred mission on earth. But as it is, I must just pick up what scraps of usefulness I can, and let the rest go.

April 18

Aunty says I sit writing and reading and thinking too much, and wants me to go out more. I tell her I don't feel strong enough to go out much. She says that is all nonsense, and drags me out. I get tired, and hungry, and sleep like a baby a month old. I see now mother's wisdom and kindness in making me leave home when I did. I had veered about from point to point till I was nearly ill. Now Aunty keeps me healthy by making me go out, and dear Dr. Cabot's precious letter can work a true and not a morbid work in my soul. I am very happy. I have delightful talks with Aunty, who sets me right at this point and at that; and it is beautiful to watch her home-life and to see with what sweet unconsciousness she carries her religion into every detail of life. I am sure it must do me good to be here; and yet, if I am growing better, how slowly, how slowly, it is! Somebody has said that "our course heavenward is like the plan of the zealous pilgrims of old, who for every three steps forward, took one backward."

April 30

Aunty's baby, my dear father's name-sake, and hitherto the merriest little fellow I ever saw, was taken sick last night, very suddenly. She sent for the doctor at once, who would not say positively what was the matter, but this morning pronounced it to be scarlet fever. The three youngest have all come down with it today. If they were my children, I would be in a perfect worry and flurry. Indeed, I am as it is. But Aunty is as bright and cheerful as ever. She flies from one sick child to another, and keeps up their spirits with her own gayety. I am mortified to find that at such a time as this I can think of myself, and that I find it irksome to be shut up in sick-rooms, instead of walking, driving, visiting and the like. But, as Dr. Cabot says, I can now *choose* to imitate my Master, who spent His whole life in doing good, and I do hope, too, to be of some little use to Aunty, after her kindness to me.

May 1

The doctor says the children are doing as well as could be expected. He made a short visit this morning, as it is Sunday. If I had ever seen him before I would say I had some unpleasant association with him. I wonder why Aunty employs such a great clumsy man. But she says he is very good, and very skillful. I wish I did not take such violent likes and dislikes to people. I want my religion to change me in every respect.

May 2

Oh, I know now! This is the very man who was so rude at Sunday-school, and afterwards made such a nice address to the children. Well he may know how to speak in public, but I am sure he doesn't in private. I never knew a man so shut-up within himself.

May 4

I have my hands as full as they can hold. The children have gotten so fond of me, and one or the other is in my lap nearly all the time. I sing to them, tell them stories, build block-houses, and relieve Aunty all I can. Dull and poky as the doctor is, I am not afraid of him, for he never notices anything I say or do, so while he is holding solemn consultations with Aunty in one corner, I can sing and talk all sorts of nonsense to my little pets in mine. What fearful black eyes he has, and what masses of black hair!

This busy life quite suits me, now I have gotten used to it. And it sweetens every bit of work to think that I am doing it in humble, far-off, yet real imitation of Jesus. I am indeed really and truly happy.

May 14

It is now two weeks since little Raymond was taken sick, and I have just lived in the nursery all the time, though Aunty has tried to make me go out. Little Emma was taken down today, though she has been kept on the third floor all the time. I feel dreadful myself. But this hard, cold doctor of Aunty's is so taken up with the children that he never so much as looks at me. I have been in a perfect shiver all day, but these merciless little folks call for stories as eagerly as ever. Well, let me be a comfort to them if I can! I hate selfishness more and more, and am shocked too see how selfish I have been.

May 15

I was in a burning fever all night, and my head ached, and my throat was and is very sore. If I knew I was going to die I would burn up this journal first. I would not have any one see it for the world.

May 24

Dr. Elliott asked me on Sunday morning a week ago if I still felt well. For an answer I behaved like a goose, and burst out crying. Aunty looked more anxious than I have seen her look yet, and reproached herself for having allowed me to be with the children. She took me by one elbow, and the doctor by the other, and they marched me off to my own room, where I was put through the usual routine on such occasions, and then ordered to bed. I fell asleep immediately and slept all day. The doctor came to see me in the evening, and made me a short, stiff little visit, gave me a powder, and said he thought I would soon be better.

I had two such visits from him the next day, when I began to feel quite like myself again, and in spite of his grave, stiff demeanor, could not help letting my good spirits run away with me in a style that evidently shocked him. He says persons nursing in the midst of scarlet fever often have such little attacks as mine; indeed every one of the servants have had a touch of sore throat and headache.

May 25

This morning, just as the doctor shuffled in on his big feet, it came over me how ridiculously I must have looked the day I was taken sick, being walked off between Aunty and himself, crying like a baby. I burst out laughing, and no consideration I could make to myself would stop me. I pinched myself, asked myself how I would feel if one of the children should die, and used other kindred devices all to no purpose. At last the doctor, gravity personified as he is, joined in, though not knowing in the least what he was laughing at. Then he said, "After this, I suppose, I shall have to pronounce you fully well."

"Oh, no!" I cried. "I am very sick indeed."

"This looks like it, to be sure!" said Aunty.

"I suppose this will be your last visit, Dr. Elliott," I went on, "and I am glad of it. After the way I behaved the day I was taken sick, I have been ashamed to look you in the face. But I really felt dreadfully ill at that time."

He made no answer whatever. I don't suppose he would speak a little flattering word by way of putting one in good humor with one's self for the whole world!

June 1

We are all as healthy as ever, but the doctor keeps some of the children still confined to the house for fear of bad consequences following the fever. He visits them twice a day for the same reason, or at least under that pretense, but I really believe he comes because he has gotten the habit of coming, and because he admires Aunty so much. She has a real affection for him, and is continually asking me if I don't like this and that quality in him which I can't see at all. We have begun to drive outside again. The weather is very warm, but I feel perfectly fine.

June 2

After the children's dinner today I took care of them while their nurse got hers and Aunty went to lie down, as she is all tired out. We were all full of life and fun, and some of the little ones wanted me to play a play of their own invention, which was to lie down on the floor, cover my face with a handkerchief, and make believe I was dead. They were to gather about me, and I was suddenly to come to life and jump up and try to catch them as they all ran scampering and screaming about. We had played in this interesting way for some time, and my hair, which I keep in nice order nowadays, was pulled down and flying every way, when in marched the doctor. I started up and came to life quickly enough when I heard his step, looking red and angry, no doubt.

"I should think you might have knocked, Dr. Elliott," I said, with much displeasure.

"I ask your pardon; I knocked several times," he returned. "I need hardly ask how my little patients are."

"No," I replied, still ruffled, and making desperate efforts to get my hair into some sort of order. "They are as healthy as possible."

"I came earlier than usual today," he went on, "because I am called to visit my uncle, Dr. Cabot, who is in a very critical state of health."

"Dr. Cabot!" I repeated, bursting into tears.

"Compose yourself," he entreated; "I hope that I may be able to relieve him. At all events—"

"At all events, if you let him die it will break my heart," I cried passionately. "Don't wait another moment; go this instant."

"I cannot go this instant," he replied. "The boat does not leave until four o'clock. And if I may be allowed, as a physician, to say one word, that my brief acquaintance hardly justifies, I do wish to warn you that unless you acquire more self-control—"

"Oh, I know that I have a quick temper, and that I spoke very rudely to you just now," I interrupted, not a little startled by the seriousness of his manner.

"I did not refer to your temper," he said. "I meant your whole passionate nature. Your vehement loves and hates, your ecstasies and your despondencies; your disposition to throw yourself headlong into whatever interests you."

I would rather have too little self-control," I retorted, resentfully, "than to be as cold as a stone, and as hard as a rock, and as silent as the grave, like some people I know."

His countenance fell; he looked disappointed, even pained.

"I shall probably see your mother." he said, turning to go; "your aunt wishes me to call on her; have you any message?"

"*No,*" I said

Another pained, disappointed look made me begin to compose myself. I was sorry, oh! so sorry, for my anger and rudeness. I ran after him, into the hall, my eyes full of tears, holding out both hands, which he took in both his.

"Don't go until you have forgiven me for being so angry!" I cried. "Indeed, Dr. Elliott, though you may not be able to believe it, I *am trying* to do right all the time!"

"I do believe it," he said earnestly.

"Then tell me that you forgive me!"

"If I once begin, I shall be tempted to tell something else," he said, looking me through and through with those great dusky eyes. "And I *will* tell it," he went on, his grasp on my hands growing firmer— "It is easy to forgive when one loves." I pulled my hands away, and burst out crying again.

"Oh, Dr. Elliot, this is *dreadful!,*" I said. "You do not, you cannot love me! You are so much older than I am! So grave and silent! You are not in earnest!"

"I am only too much so," he said, and went quietly out.

I went back to the nursery. The children rushed upon me, and insisted that I should "play die". I let them pull me about as they pleased. I only wished I could play it in earnest.

Chapter 8

June 28

Mother writes me that Dr. Cabot is out of danger, Dr.
Elliott having thrown new light on his case, and performed
some sort of an operation that relieved him at once. I am
going home. Nothing would tempt me to encounter those
black eyes again. Besides, the weather is growing warm, and
Aunty is getting ready to go out of town with the children.

June 29

Aunty insisted on knowing why I was hurrying home
so suddenly, and at last got it out of me inch by inch. On
the whole it was a relief to have some one to speak to.

"Well!" she said, and leaned back in her chair in a fit
of musing.

"Is that all you are going to say, Aunty?" I ventured to
ask at last.

"No, I have one more remark to add," she said, "and it
is this: I don't know which of you has behaved most ridiculously. It would relieve me to give you each a good shaking."

"I think *Dr. Elliott* has behaved ridiculously," I said, "and he has made me most unhappy."

"Unhappy!" she repeated. "I don't wonder you are unhappy. You have pained and wounded one of the noblest men that walks the earth."

"It is not my fault. I never tried to make him like me."

"Yes, you did. You were perfectly bewitching whenever he came here. No mortal man could help being fascinated."

I knew this was not true, and bitterly resented Aunty's injustice.

"If I wanted to 'fascinate' or 'bewitch' a man," I cried, "I would not choose one old enough to be my father, nor one who was as uninteresting, awkward and stiff as Dr. Elliott. Besides, how could I know he was not married? If I thought anything about it at all, I certainly thought of him as a middle-aged man, settled down with a wife, long ago."

"In the first place he is not old, or even middle-aged. He is not more than twenty-seven or eight. As to his being uninteresting, perhaps he is to you, who don't know him. And if he were a married man, what business had he to come here to see you, as he has done?"

"I did not know he came to see me; he never spoke to me. And I always said I would never marry a doctor."

"We all say scores of things we live to repent," she replied. "But I must admit that the doctor acted quite out of character when he expected you to take a fancy to him on such short notice, you romantic little thing. Of course knowing him as little as you do, and only seeing him in sick-rooms, you could not have done otherwise than as you did."

"Thank you, Aunty," I said, running and throwing my arms around her; "thank you with all my heart. And now won't you take back what you said about my trying to fascinate him?"

"I suppose I must, you dear child," she said. "I was not half in earnest. The truth is I am so fond of you both that the idea of your misunderstanding each other annoys me extremely. Why, you were made for each other. He would tone you down and keep you straight, and you would stimulate him and keep him awake."

"I don't want to be toned down or kept straight," I remonstrated. "I hate fuddy-duddys who keep their wives in leading-strings.[11] I do not intend to marry anyone, but if I should be left to such a piece of folly, it must be to one who will take me for better for worse, just as I am, and not as a wild plant for him to prune till he has got it into a shape to suit him. And now, Aunty, promise me one thing. Never mention Dr. Elliott's name to me again."

"I shall make no such promise," she replied, laughing. "I like him, and I like to talk about him, and the more you hate and despise him the more I shall love and admire him. I only wish my Lucy were old enough to be his wife, and that he could fancy her; but he never could!"

"On the contrary I would think that little model of propriety would just suit him," I exclaimed.

"Don't make fun of Lucy," Aunty said, shaking her head. "She is a dear, good child, after all."

"*After all*" means this (for what with my own observation, and what Aunty has told me, Lucy's portrait is easy to paint): The child is the daughter of a man who died from a lingering illness caused by an accident. She entered the family at a most inauspicious moment, two days after this accident. From the outset she comprehended the situation, and took the ground that a character of irreproachable dignity and propriety became an infant coming at such a time. She never cried, never put improper objects into her mouth, never bumped her head, or scratched herself. Once put to bed at night, you knew nothing more of her till such time next day as you found it convenient to attend her. If you forgot her existence, as was not seldom the case under the circumstances, she vegetated on, unmoved. It is possible that pangs of hunger sometimes assailed her, and it is a fact that she teethed, had the measles and the whooping-cough. But these minute ripples on her infant life only showed the more clearly what a wave-less, placid little sea it was. She got her teeth in the order laid down in "Dewees on Children";[12] her measles came out on the appointed day like well-behaved measles should. Her whooping-cough had a well-bred, methodical air, and left her conqueror of the field. As the child passed out of her babyhood, she remained still her mother's appendage and glory; a monument of pure white marble, displaying to the human race one instance at least of perfect parental training. Those smooth, round hands were always magically clean; the dress immaculate and uncrumpled; the hair dutifully shining and tidy. She was a model child, as she had been a model baby. No slamming of doors, no litter of carpets, no pattering of noisy feet on the stairs, no headless dolls, no soiled or torn books indicated her presence. Her dolls were subject to a methodical training, not unlike her own. They rose, they were dressed, they took the air, they retired for the night, with clock-like regularity. At the advanced age of eight, she ceased occupying herself with such trifles, and began a course of instructive reading. Her lessons were received in mute submission, like medicine; so many doses, so many times a day. An agreeable interlude of needlework was afforded, and Dorcas-like[13], many were the garments that resulted for the poor. Give her the very eyes out of your head, cut off your right hand for her if you choose, but don't expect a gush of enthusiasm that would crumple your collar; she would as soon strangle herself as run headlong to embrace you. If she has any passions or emotions, they are kept under complete control; but who asks for passion in blancmange[14], or seeks emotion in a comfortable apple-pudding?

When her father had been dead a year, her mother married a man with a large family of children and a very small purse. Lucy had a hard time of it, especially as her step-father, a quick, impulsive man, took a dislike to her. Aunty had no difficulty in persuading them to give the child to her. She took her from the purest motives, and it does seem as if she ought to have more reward than she gets. She declares, however, that she has all the reward she could ask in the conviction that God accepts this attempt to please Him.

Lucy is now nearly fourteen; very large for her age, with a dead white skin, pale blue eyes, and a little light hair. To hear her talk is most edifying. Her babies are all "babes"; she never begins anything but "commences" it; she never cries, she "weeps": never gets up in the morning, but "rises." But why am I writing all this? Why, to escape my own thoughts, which are anything but agreeable companions, and to put off answering the question which must be answered, "Have I really made a mistake in refusing Dr. Elliott? Could I not, in time, have come to love a man who has so honored me?"

July 5

Here I am again, safely at home, and very pleasant it seems to be with dear mother again. I have told her about Dr. E. She says very little about it one way or the other.

July 10

Mother sees that I am restless and out of sorts. "What is it, dear?" she asked, this morning. "Has Dr. Elliott anything to do with the unsettled state you are in?"

"Why, no, mother," I answered. "My going away has broken up all my habits; that's all. Still if I knew Dr. Elliott did not care much, and was beginning to forget it, I dare say I would feel better."

"If you were perfectly sure that you never could return his affection," she said, "you were quite right in telling him so at once. But if you had any misgivings on the subject, it would have been better to wait, and to ask God to direct you."

Yes, it would. But at the moment I had no misgivings. In my usual headlong style I settled one of the most weighty questions of my life, without reflection, without so much as one silent appeal to God, to tell me how to act. And now I have forever repelled, and thrown away a heart that truly loved me. He will go his way and I shall go mine. He never will know, what I am only just beginning to know myself, that I yearn after his love with unutterable yearning.

But I am not going to sit down in sentimental despondency to weep over this irreparable past. No human being could forgive such folly as mine; but God can. In my sorrowfulness and loneliness I fly to Him, and find, what is better than earthly felicity, the sweetest peace. He allowed me to bring upon myself, in one hasty moment, a shadow out of which I shall not soon pass, but He pities and He forgives me, and I have had many precious moments when I could say sincerely and joyfully, "whom have I in heaven but Thee, and there is none upon earth that I desire besides Thee" (Psalm 73:25).

With a character still so undisciplined as mine, I seriously doubt whether I could have made him happy who has honored me with his unmerited affection. Sometimes I think I am as impetuous and as quick-tempered as ever; I get angry with dear mother, and even with James, if they oppose me; how unfit, then, I am to become the mistress of a household and the wife of a good man! How he came to love me? I cannot, cannot imagine!

August 31

The last day of the very happiest summer I ever spent. If I had only been willing to believe the testimony of others I might have been just as happy long ago. But I wanted to have all there was in God and all there was in the world, at once, and there was a constant, painful struggle between the two. I hope that struggle is now over. I deliberately choose and prefer God. I have found a sweet peace in trying to please Him such as I never conceived of. I would not change it for all the best things this world can give.

But I have a great deal to learn. I am like a little child who cannot run to get what he wants, but approaches it step by step, slowly, timidly— and yet approaches it. I am amazed at the patience of my blessed Master and Teacher, but how I love His school!

September 29

This, too, has been a delightful month in a certain sense. Amelia's marriage, at which I had to be present, upset me a little, but it was but a little ruffle on a deep sea of peace.

I saw Dr. Cabot today. He is quite healthy again, and speaks of Dr. Elliott's skill with rapture. He asked about my Sunday School students and my poor folks, etc., and I could not help letting out a little of the new joy that has taken possession of me.

"This is as it should be," he said. "I would be sorry to see a person of your temperament enthusiastic in everything except religion. Do not be discouraged if you still have some ups and downs. "He that is down need fear no fall"; but you are away up on the heights, and may have one, now and then."

This made me a little uncomfortable. I don't want any falls. I want to go on to perfection!

October 1

Laura Cabot came to see me today, and seemed very affectionate.

"I hope we may see more of each other than we have done," she began. "My father wishes it, and so do I."

Katy [mentally]— "Ah! he sees how unworldly, how devoted I am, and so wants Laura under my influence."

Katy [aloud]— "I am sure that is very kind."

Laura— "Not at all. He knows it will be profitable to me to be with you. I get a good deal discouraged at times, and want a friend to strengthen and help me."

Katy [to herself]— "Yes, yes, he thinks me quite experienced and trustworthy."

Katy [aloud]— "I shall never dare to try to help you."

Laura— "Oh, yes, you must. I am so far behind you in Christian experience."

But I am ashamed to write down any more. After she had gone I felt delightfully puffed up for a while. But when I came up to my room this evening, and knelt down to pray, everything looked dark and chaotic. God seemed far away, and I took no pleasure in speaking to Him. I felt sure that I had done something or felt something wrong, and asked Him to show me what it was. There then flashed into my mind the remembrance of the vain, conceited thoughts I had had during Laura's visit and ever since.

How perfectly contemptible! I have had a fall indeed!

I think now my first mistake was in telling Dr. Cabot my secret, sacred joys, as if some merit of mine had earned them for me. That gave Satan a fine chance to triumph over me! After this I am determined to maintain the utmost reserve in respect to my religious experiences. Nothing is gained by running to tell them, and much is lost. I feel depressed and comfortless.

Chapter 9

October 10

We have very sad news from Aunty. She says my Uncle is quite broken down with some obscure disease that has been creeping imperceptibly along for months. All his physicians agree that he must give up his business and try the effect of a year's rest. Dr. Elliott proposes his going to Europe, which seems to me about as formidable as going to the next world. Aunty makes the best she can of it, but she says the thought of being separated from Uncle a whole year is dreadful. I pray for her day and night, that this wild project may be given up. Why, he would be on the ocean ever so many weeks, exposed to all the discomforts of narrow quarters and poor food, and that just as winter is drawing near!

October 12

Aunty writes that the voyage to Europe has been decided on, and that Dr. Elliott is to accompany Uncle, travel with him, amuse him, and bring him home a healthy man.

I hope Dr. E's power to amuse may exist somewhere, but must admit it was in a most latent form when I had the pleasure of knowing him. Poor, Aunty! How much better it would be for her to go with Uncle! There are all the children, to be sure. Well, I hope Uncle may be the better for this great undertaking, but I don't like the idea of it.

October 15

Another letter from Aunty, and new plans! The Dr. is to stay home, Aunty is to go with Uncle, and we— mother and myself— are to take possession of the house and children during their absence! In other words, all this is to be if we say amen. Could anything be more frightful? To refuse would be selfish and cruel. If we consent I thrust myself under Dr. Elliott's very nose.

October 16

Mother is surprised that I can hesitate one instant. She seems to have forgotten all about Dr. E. She says we can easily find a family to take this house for a year, and that she is delighted to do anything for Aunty that can be done.

November 4

Here we are, the whole thing settled. Uncle and Aunty started a week ago, and we are monarchs of all we survey, and this a great deal. I am determined that mother shall not be worn out with these children although, of course, I could not manage them without her advice and help. It is to be hoped they won't all have the measles in a body, or anything of that sort; I am sure it would be very annoying to Dr. E. to come here now.

November 25

Of course the baby must go on teething if only to have the doctor sent for to lance his gums. I told mother I was sure I could not be present when this was being done, so, though she looked surprised, and said people should accustom themselves to such things, she volunteered to hold the baby herself.

November 26

The baby was afraid of mother, not being used to her, so she sent for me. As I entered the room she gave him to me with an apology for doing so, since I shrank from witnessing the operation. What must Dr. E. think I am made of if I can't bear to see a child's gums lanced? However, its my own fault that he thinks me such a coward, for I made mother think me one. It was very embarrassing to hold the baby and have the doctor's face so close to mine. I really wonder mother could not see how awkwardly I am situated here.

November 27

We have a good many visitors, friends of Uncle and Aunty. How uninteresting most people are! They all say the same thing, namely, how strange that Aunty had courage to undertake such a voyage, and to leave her children, etc., etc., etc., and what *was* Dr. Elliott thinking of to *let* them go, etc., etc., etc.

Dr. Embury called today, with a pretty little fresh creature, his new wife, who hangs on his arm like a work-bag. He is Dr. Elliott's intimate friend, and spoke of him very warmly, and so did his wife, who says she has known him always, as they were born and brought up in the same village. I wonder he did not marry her himself, instead of leaving her for Dr. Embury!

She says he, Dr. Elliott, I mean, was the most devoted son she ever saw, and that he deserves his present success because he has made such sacrifices for his parents. I never met any on whom I liked so well on so short acquaintance— I mean Mrs. Embury, though you might fancy, you poor deluded journal you, that I meant somebody else.

November 30

I have so much to do that I have little time for writing. The way the children wear out their shoes and stockings, the speed with which their hair grows, the way they bump their heads and pinch their fingers, and the insatiable demand for stories, is something next to miraculous. Not a day passes that somebody doesn't need something bought; that somebody else doesn't choke itself, and that I don't have to tell stories till I feel my intellect reduced to the size of a pea. If ever I was alive and wide awake, however, it is just now, and in spite of some vague shadows of, I don't know what, I am very happy indeed. So is dear mother. She and the doctor have become bosom friends. He keeps her making beef-tea[15], scraping lint, and boiling calves feet for jelly, till the house smells like a hospital.

I suppose he thinks *me* a poor, selfish, frivolous girl, whom nothing would tempt to raise a finger for his invalids. But, of course, I do not care what he thinks.

December 4

Dr. Elliott came this morning to ask mother to go with him to see a child who had met with a horrible accident. She turned pale, and pressed her lips together, but went at once to get ready. Then my long-suppressed wrath burst out.

"How can you ask poor mother to go and see such sights?" I cried. "You must think her nothing but a stone, if you suppose that after the way in which my father died—"

"It was indeed most thoughtless of me," he interrupted; "but your mother is such a rare woman, so decided and self-controlled, yet so gentle, so full of tender sympathy, that I hardly know where to look for just the help I need today. If you could see this poor child, even you would justify me."

"Even you!" you monster of selfishness, heart of stone, floating bubble, *"even you* would justify it!"

How cruel, how unjust, how unforgiving he is!

I rushed out of the room, and cried until I was tired.

December 6

Mother says she feels really grateful to Dr. E. for taking her to see that child, and to help soothe and comfort it while he went through with a severe, painful operation which she would not describe, because she fancied I looked pale. I said I would think the child's mother the most proper person to soothe it on such an occasion.

"The poor thing has no mother," she said, reproachfully. "What *has* gotten into you, Kate? You do not seem at all like yourself."

"I would think you had enough to do with this great house to keep in order, so many mouths to fill, and so many servants to oversee, without wearing yourself out with nursing all Dr. Elliott's poor folks," I said, gloomily.

"The more I have to do the happier I am," she replied. "Dear Katy, the old wound isn't healed yet, and I like to be with those who have wounds and bruises of their own. And Dr. Elliott seems to have surmised this by instinct."

I ran and kissed her dear, pale face, which grows more beautiful every day. No wonder she misses father so! He loved and honored her beyond description, and never forgot one of those little courtesies which must have a great deal to do with a wife's happiness. People said of him that he was a gentleman of the old school, and that race is dying out. I feel a good deal out of sorts myself. Oh, I do so wish to get above myself and all my childish, petty ways, and to live in a region where there is no temptation and no sin!

December 22

I have been to see Mrs. Embury today. She did not receive me as cordially as usual, and I very soon resolved to come away. She detained me, however.

"Would you mind my speaking to you on a certain subject?" she asked, with some embarrassment.

I felt myself flush up.

"I do not want to meddle with affairs that don't concern me," she went on, "but Dr. Elliott and I have been intimate friends all our lives. And his disappointment has really distressed me."

One of my moods came on, and I couldn't speak a word.

"You are not at all the sort of a girl I supposed he would fancy," she continued. "He always has said he was waiting to find some one just like his mother, and she is one of the gentlest, meekest, sweetest, and fairest among women."

"You ought to rejoice then that he has escaped the snare," I said, in a husky voice, "and is free to marry his ideal, when he finds her."

"But that is just what troubles me. He is not free. He does not attach himself readily, and I am afraid that it will be a long, long time before he gets over this unfortunate passion for you."

"Passion!" I cried, contemptuously.

She looked at me with some surprise, and then went on.

"Most girls would jump at the chance of getting such a husband."

"I don't know that I particularly care to be classed with 'most girls,'" I replied, loftily.

"But if you only knew him as well as I do. He is so noble, so disinterested, and is so beloved by his patients. I could tell you scores of anecdotes about him that would show just what he is."

"Thank you," I said, "I think we have discussed Dr. Elliott quite enough already. I cannot say that he has elevated himself in my opinion by making you take up the cudgels[16] in his defence."

"You do him injustice, when you say that," she cried. "His sister, the only person to whom he confided the state of things, begged me to find out, if I could, whether you had any other attachment, and if her brother's case was quite hopeless. But I am sorry I undertook the task as it has annoyed you so much."

I came away a good deal ruffled. When I got home mother said she was glad I had been out at last for a little recreation, and that she wished I did not confine myself so to the children. I said that I did not confine myself more than Aunty did.

"But that is different," mother objected. "She is their own mother, and love helps her to bear her burden."

"So it does me," I returned. "I love the children exactly as if they were my own."

"That," she said, "is impossible."

"I certainly do," I persisted.

Mother would not dispute with me, though I wished she would.

"A mother," she went on, "receives her children one at a time, and gradually adjusts herself to gradually increasing burdens. But you take a whole houseful upon you at once, and I am sure it is too much for you. You do not look or act like yourself."

"It isn't the children," I said.

"What is it, then?"

"Why, it's nothing," I said, pettishly.

"I must say, dear," said mother, not noticing my manner, "that your wonderful devotion to the children, aside from its effect on your health and temper, has given me great delight."

"I don't see why," I said.

"Very few girls of your age would give up their whole time as you do to such work."

"That is because very few girls are as fond of children as I am. There is no virtue in doing exactly what one likes best to do."

"There, go away, you contrary child," said mother, laughing. "If you won't be praised, you won't."

So I came up here and moped a little. I don't see what ails me.

But there is an under-current of peace that is not entirely disturbed by any outside events. In spite of my follies and my shortcomings, I do believe that God loves and pities me, and will yet perfect that which concerns me. It is a great mystery. But so is everything.

Dr. Elliott to Mrs. Crofton:

. . . *"And now, my dear friend, having issued my usual bulletin of health, you may feel quite at ease about your dear children, and I come to a point in your letter which I would gladly pass over in silence. But this would be but a poor return for the interest you express in my affairs.*

"Both ladies are devoted to your little flock, and Miss Mortimer seems not to have a thought but for them. The high opinion I formed of her at the outset is more than justified by all I see of her daily, household life. I know what her faults are, for she seems to take delight in revealing them. But I also know her rare virtues, and what a wealth of affection she has to bestow on the man who is so happy as to win her heart. But I shall never be that man. Her growing aversion to me makes me dread a summons to your house, and I have hardly manliness enough to conceal the pain this gives me. I entreat you, therefore, never again to press this subject upon me. After all, I would not, if I could, dispense with the ministry of disappointment and unrest."

Mrs. Crofton, in reply—

. . . *"So she hates you, does she? I am charmed to hear it. Indifference would be an alarming symptom, but good, cordial hatred, or what looks like it, is a most hopeful sign. The next chance you get to see her alone, assure her that you never shall repeat your first offence. If nothing comes of it I am not a woman, and never was one; nor is she."*

March 25, 1836

The New Year and my birthday have come and gone, and this is the first moment I could find for writing down all that has happened.

The day after my last entry I was full of serious earnest thoughts, of new desires to live, without one reserve, for God. I was smarting under the remembrance of my folly at Mrs. Embury's, and with a sense of vague disappointment and discomfort, and had to fly closer than ever to Him. In the evening I thought I would go to the usual weekly service. It is true I don't like prayer-meetings, and that is a bad sign, I am afraid. But I am determined to go where good people go, and see if I can't learn to like what they like.

Mother went with me, of course.

What was my surprise to find that Dr. E. was to preside! I had no idea that he was that sort of a man.

The hymns they sang were beautiful, and did me good. So was his prayer. If all prayers were like that, I am sure I would like evening meetings as much as I now dislike them. He so evidently spoke to God in it, and as if he were used to such speaking.

He then made a little address on the ministry of disappointments, as he called it. He spoke so cheerfully and hopefully that I began to see almost for the first time God's reason for the petty trials and crosses that help to make up every day of one's life. He said there were few who were not constantly disappointed with themselves, with their childishness and weakness; disappointed with their friends who, strangely enough, were never quite perfect enough, and disappointed with the world, which was always promising so much and giving so little. Then he urged to a wise and patient consent to this discipline, which, if rightly used, would help to temper and strengthen the soul against the day of sorrow and bereavement. But I am not doing him justice in this meager report; there was something almost heavenly in his expression which words cannot describe.

Coming out I heard some one ask, "Who was that young clergyman?" and the answer, "Oh, that is only a doctor!"

Well! the next week I went again, with mother. We had hardly taken our seats when Dr. E. marched in with the sweetest looking little creature I ever saw. He was so taken up with her that he did not observe either mother or myself. As she sat by my side I could not see her full face, but her profile was nearly perfect. Her eyes were of that lovely blue one sees in violets and the skies, with long, soft eyelashes, and her complexion was as pure as a baby's. Yet she was not one of your doll beauties; her face expressed both feeling and character. They sang together from the same book, though I offered her a share of mine. Of course, when people do that it can mean but one thing.

So it seems he has forgotten me, and consoled himself with this pretty little thing. No doubt she is like his mother, that "gentlest, meekest, sweetest and fairest among women!"

Now if anybody should be sick, and he should come

here, I thought, what would become of me? I certainly could not help showing that a love that can so soon take up with a new object could not have been a sentiment of much depth.

It is not pleasant to lose even a portion of one's respect and esteem for another.

The next day mother went to visit an old friend of hers, who has a beautiful place outside of the city. The baby's nurse had ironing to do, so I promised to sit in the nursery till it was finished. Lucy came with her books, to sit with me. She always follows me like my shadow. After a while Mrs. Embury called. I hesitated a little about trusting the child to Lucy's care, for though her prim ways have given her the reputation of being wise beyond her years, I observe that she is apt to get into trouble which a quick-witted child would either avoid or jump out of in a twinkling. However, children are often left to much younger girls, so, with many cautions, I went down, resolving too stay only a few moments.

But I wanted so much to know all about that pretty little friend of Dr. E.'s that I let Mrs. Embury stay on and on, though not a ray of light did I get for my pains. At last I heard Lucy's step coming downstairs.

"Cousin Katy," she said, entering the room with her usual propriety, "I was seated by the window, engaged with my studies, and the children were playing about, as usual, when suddenly I heard a shriek, and one of them ran past me, all in a blaze and—"

I believe I pushed her out of my way as I rushed

upstairs, for I took it for granted I would meet the little figure all in a blaze, coming to meet me. But I found it
wrapped in a blanket, the flames extinguished. Meanwhile,
Mrs Embury had roused the whole house, and everybody
came running upstairs.

"Get the doctor, some of you," I cried, clasping the
poor little writhing form in my arms.

And then I looked to see which of them it was and
found it was Aunty's pet lamb, everybody's pet lamb, our
little loving, gentle Emma.

Dr. Elliott must have come on wings, for I had not
time to be impatient for his arrival. He was as tender as a
woman with Emma; we cut off and tore off her clothes
wherever the fire had touched her, and he dressed the
burns with his own hands. He did not speak a word to me,
or I to him. This time he did not find it necessary to advise
me to control myself. I was as cold and hard as a stone.

But when poor little Emma's piercing shrieks began to
subside, and she came a little under the influence of some
soothing drops he had given her at the outset, I began to
feel that sensation in the back of my neck that leads to conquest over the most stubborn and the most heroic. I had
just time to get Emma into the doctor's arms, and then
down I went. I got over it in a minute, and was up again
before any one had time to come to the rescue. But Dr. E.
gave Emma to Mrs. Embury, who had taken off her things
and been crying all the time, and said in a low voice,

"I beg you will now leave the room, and lie down.
And do not feel obliged to see me when I visit the child.

That annoyance, at least, you should spare yourself."

"No, consideration shall make me neglect little Emma," I replied, defiantly.

By this time Mrs. Embury had rocked her to sleep, and she lay, pale and with an air of complete exhaustion, in her arms.

"You *must* lie down now, Miss Mortimer," Dr. Elliott said, as he rose to go. "I will return in a few hours to see how you both do."

He stood looking at Emma, but did not go. Then Mrs. Embury asked the question I had not dared to ask.

"Is the poor child in danger?"

"I cannot say: I trust not. Miss Mortimer's presence of mind in extinguishing the flames at once, has, I hope, saved its life."

"It was not my presence of mind, it was Lucy's!" I cried, eagerly. Oh, how I envied her for being the heroine, and for the surprised, delighted smile with which he went and took her hand, saying, "I congratulate you, Lucy! How your mother will rejoice at this!"

I tried to think of nothing but poor little Emma, and of the reward Aunty had had for her kindness to Lucy. But I thought of myself, and how likely it was that under the same circumstances I would have been beside myself, and done nothing. This and many other emotions, made me burst out crying.

"Yes, cry, cry, with all your heart," said Mrs. Embury, laying Emma gently down, and coming to get me into her arms. "It will do you good, poor child!"

She cried with me, till at last I could lie down and try to sleep.

Well, the days and the weeks were very long after that.

Dear mother had a hard time, what with her anxiety about Emma, and my crossness and unreasonableness.

Dr. Elliott came and went, came and went. At last he said all danger was over, and that our patient little darling would get well. But his visits did not diminish; he came twice and three times every day. Sometimes I hoped he would tell us about his new flame, and sometimes I felt that I could not hear her mentioned. One day mother was so unhealthy that I had to help him dress Emma's burns, and I could not help saying:

"Even a mother's gentlest touch, full of love as it is, is almost rough when compared with that of one trained to such careful handling as you are."

He looked gratified, but said:

"I am glad you begin to find that even stones feel, sometimes."

Another time something was said about the fickleness of women. Mrs. Embury began it. I fired up, of course.

He seemed astonished at my attack.

"*I* said nothing," he declared.

"No, but you *looked* a good many things. Now the fact is, women are not fickle. When they lose what they value most, they find it impossible to replace it. But men console themselves with the first good thing that comes along."

I dare say I spoke bitterly, for I was thinking how soon

Ch—, I mean somebody, replaced me in his shallow heart, and how, with equal speed, Dr. Elliott had helped himself to a new love.

"I do not like these sweeping assertions," said Dr. Elliott, looking a good deal annoyed.

"I have to say what I think," I persisted.

"It is well to think rightly, then," he said gravely.

"By the bye, have you heard from Helen?" Mrs. Embury most irreverently asked.

"Yes, I heard yesterday."

"I suppose you will be writing her, then? Will you enclose a little note from me? Or rather let me have the least corner of your sheet?"

I was shocked at her lack of delicacy. Of course this Helen must be the new love, and how could a woman with two grains of sense imagine he would want to spare her a part of his sheet!

"I could hardly believe my ears," I said, "when I heard you ask leave to write on Dr. Elliott's sheet."

"No wonder," she said, laughing. "I suppose you never knew what it was to have to count every shilling, and to deny yourself the pleasure of writing to a friend because of what it would cost. I'm sure I never did till I was married."

"But to ask him to let you help write his love-letters," I objected.

"Ah! is that the way the wind blows?" she cried nodding her pretty little head. "Well, then, let me relieve your mind, my dear, by informing you that this "love-letter" is to his sister, my dearest friend, and the sweetest little thing you ever saw."

"Oh!" I said, and immediately felt quite rested, and like myself.

Like myself! And who is she, pray! Two souls dwell in my poor little body, and which of them is me, and which of them isn't, it would be hard to tell. This is the way they behave:

FIRST SCENE

Katy [to the other creature, whom I will call *Kate*]— Your mother looks tired, and you have been very cross. Run and put your arms around her, and tell her how you love her.

Kate— Oh, I can't; it would look odd. I don't like flattery. Besides, who would not be cross who felt as I do?

SECOND SCENE

Katy— Little Emma has nothing to do, and ought to be amused. Tell her a story, do.

Kate— I am tired, and need to be amused myself.

Katy— But the dear little thing is so patient and has suffered so much.

Kate— Well, I have suffered, too. If she had not climbed up on the fender[17] she would not have gotten burned.

THIRD SCENE

Kate— You are very irritable today. You had better go upstairs to your room and pray for patience.

Katy— One can't always be praying. I don't feel
like it.

FOURTH SCENE

Katy— You treat Dr. Elliott shamefully. I should think
he would really avoid you as you avoid him.

Kate— Don't let me hear his name. I don't avoid him.
Katy— You do not deserve his good opinion of you.
Kate— Yes, I do.

FIFTH SCENE

Just awake in the morning.

Katy— Oh, dear! how hateful I am! I am cross and
selfish, and domineering, and vain. I think of myself the
whole time; I behave like a heroine when Dr. Elliott is
present, and like a naughty, spoiled child when he is not.
Poor mother! how can she endure me? As to my piety, it is
worse than none.

Kate [a few hours later]— Well, nobody can deny that
I have a real gift in managing children! And I am very
lovable, or mother wouldn't be so fond of me. I am always
pleasant unless I am sick, or worried, and my temper is not
half so hasty as it used to be. I never think of myself, but
am all the time doing something for others. As to Dr. E., I
am thankful to say that I have never stooped to attract him
by putting on airs and graces. He sees me just as I am. And
I am very devout. I love to read good books and to be with
good people. I pray a great deal. The bare thought of doing

wrong makes me shudder. Mother is proud of me, and I don't wonder. Very few girls would have behaved as I did when Emma was burned. Perhaps I am not as sweet as some people. I am glad of it. I hate sweet people. I have great strength of character, which is much better, and am certainly very honorable.

But, my poor journal, you can't stand any more such stuff, can you? But tell me one thing, am I Katy or am I Kate?

Chapter 10

Yesterday I felt better than I have since the accident. I ran about the house quite cheerily, for me. I wanted to see mother for something, and flew singing into the parlor, where I had shortly left her before. But she was not there, and Dr. Elliott was. I started back, and was about to leave the room, but he detained me.

"Come in, I beg of you," he said, his voice growing hoarser and hoarser. "Let us put a stop to this."

"To what?" I asked, going nearer and nearer, and looking up into his face, which was quite pale.

"To your evident terror of being alone with me, of hearing me speak. Let me assure you, once for all, that nothing would tempt me to annoy you by urging myself upon you, as you seem to fear I may be tempted to do. I cannot force you to love me, nor would I if I could. If you ever want a friend you will find one in me. But do not think of me as your lover, or treat me as if I were always lying in wait for a chance to remind you of it. That I shall never do, never!"

"Oh, no, of course not!" I broke forth, my face all aglow, and tears of mortification raining down my cheeks. "I knew you did not care for me! I knew you had gotten over it!"

I don't know which of us began it, I don't think he did, and I am sure I did not, but the next moment I was folded all up in his great long arms, and a new life had begun!

Mother opened the door not long after, and seeing what was going on, trotted away on her dear old feet as fast as she could.

April 21

I am too happy to write. To think how much we love each other. And mother behaves beautifully.

April 25

One does not feel like saying much about it, when one is as happy as I am. I walk the streets as one treading on air. I fly about the house as on wings. I kiss everybody I see.

Now that I look at Ernest (for he makes me call him so) with unprejudiced eyes, I wonder that I ever thought him clumsy. And how ridiculous it was of me to confuse his dignity and manliness with age!

It is very odd, however, that such a cautious, well-balanced man should have fallen in love with me that day at Sunday school. And still stranger that with my headlong, impulsive nature, I deliberately walked into love with him!

I believe I shall never get through with what we have

to say to each other. I am afraid we are rather selfish to leave mother to herself every evening.

September 5

This has been a delightful summer. To be sure, we had to take the children to the country for a couple of months, but Ernest's letters are almost better than Ernest himself. I have written enough to him to fill a dozen books. We are going back to the city now. In his last letter Ernest says he has been home, and that his mother is delighted to hear of his engagement. He says, too, that he went to see an old lady, one of the friends of his boyhood, to tell the news to her.

"When I told her," he goes on, "that I had found the most beautiful, the noblest, the most loving of human beings, she only said, 'Of course, of course!' "

"Now you know, dear, that it is not at all of course, but the very strangest, most wonderful event in the history of the world."

And then he described a scene he had just witnessed at the deathbed of a young girl of my own age, who left this world and every possible earthly joy, with a delight in the going to be with Christ, that made him really eloquent. Oh, how glad I am that God has cast in my lot with a man whose whole business is to minister to others! I am sure this will, of itself, keep him unworldly and unselfish. How delicious it is to love such a character, and how happy I shall be to go with him to sick-rooms and to dying-beds! He has already taught me that lessons learned in such scenes far outweigh in value what books and sermons, even, can teach.

And now, my dear old journal, let me tell you a secret that has to do with life, and not with death.

I am going to be married!

To think that I am always to be with Ernest! To sit at the table with him every day, to pray with him, to go to church with him, to have him all mine! I am sure that there is not another man on earth whom I could love as I love him. The thought of *marrying* Ch——, I mean of having that silly, school-girl engagement end in marriage, was always repugnant to me. But I give myself to Ernest joyfully and with all my heart.

How good God has been to me! I do hope and pray that this new, this absorbing love, has not detached my soul from Him, will not detach it. If I knew it would, could I, would I have courage to cut it off and cast it from me?

January 16, 1837

Yesterday was my birthday, and today is my wedding-day. We meant to celebrate the one with the other, but Sunday would come this year on the fifteenth.

I am dressed, and have turned everybody out of this room, where I have suffered so much mortification, and experienced so much joy, that before I give myself to Ernest, and before I leave home forever, I may once more give myself away to God. I have been too much absorbed in my earthly love, and am shocked to find how it fills my thoughts. But I *will* belong to God I *will* begin my married life in His fear, depending on Him to make me an unselfish, devoted wife.

January 25

We had a delightful trip after the wedding was over. Ernest proposed to take me to his own home that I might see his mother and sister. He never has said that he wanted them to see me. But his mother is not well. I am heartily glad of it. I mean I was glad to escape going there to be examined and criticized. Every one of them would pick at me, I am sure, and I don't like to be picked at.

We have a home of our own, and I am trying to take kindly to housekeeping. Ernest is away a great deal more than I expected he would be. I am fearfully lonely. Aunty comes to see me as often as she can, and I go there almost every day, but that doesn't amount to much. As soon as I can venture to do it, I shall ask Ernest to let me invite mother to come and live with us. It is not right for her to be left all alone so. I hoped he would do that himself. But men are not like women. *We* think of everything.

February 16

Our honeymoon ends today. There hasn't been quite as much honey in it as I expected. I supposed that Ernest would be at home every evening, at least, and that he would read aloud, and have me play and sing, and that we would have delightful times together. But now that he has got me he seems satisfied, and goes about his business as if he had been married a hundred years. In the morning he goes off to see his list of patients; he is going in and out all day; after dinner we sit down to have a nice talk together, the door-bell invariably rings, and he is called away. Then in the evening he goes and sits in his office and studies; I don't mean every minute, but he certainly spends hours there. Today he brought me such a precious letter from dear mother! I could not help crying when I read it, it was so kind and so loving. Ernest looked amazed; he threw down his paper, came and took me in his arms and asked, "What *is* the matter, darling?" Then it all came out. I said I was lonely, and hadn't been used to spending my evenings all by myself.

"You must get some of your friends to come and see you, poor child," he said.

"I don't want friends," I sobbed out. "I want you."

"Yes, darling; why didn't you tell me so sooner? Of course I will stay with you if you wish it."

"If that is your only reason, I am sure I don't want you;" I pouted.

He looked puzzled.

"I really don't know what to do," he said, with a most comical look of perplexity. But he went to his office, and brought up a pile of musty old books.

"Now, dear," he said, "we understand each other, I think. I can read here just as well as downstairs. Get your book and we shall be as cozy as possible."

My heart felt sore and dissatisfied. Am I unreasonable and childish? What is married life? An occasional meeting, a kiss here and a caress there? or is it the sacred union of the twain who walk together side by side, knowing each other's joys and sorrows, and going Heavenward hand in hand?

February 17

Mrs. Embury has been here today. I longed to compare notes with her, and find out whether it really is my fault that I am not quite happy. But I could not bear to open my heart to her on so sacred a subject. We had some general conversation, however, which did me good for the time, at least.

She said she thought one of the first lessons a wife should learn is self-forgetfulness. I wondered if she had seen anything in me to call forth this remark. We meet pretty often; partly because our husbands are such good friends, partly because she is as fond of music as I am, and we like to sing and play together, and I never see her that she does not do or say something elevating; something that strengthens my own best purposes and desires. But she knows nothing of my conflict and dismay, and never will. Her gentle nature responds at once to holy influences. I feel truly grateful to her for loving me, for she really does love me, and yet she must see my faults.

I would like to know if there is *any* reason on earth why a woman should learn self-forgetfulness that does not apply to a man?

February 18

Uncle says he has no doubt he owes his life to Ernest, who, in the face of opposition to other physicians, insisted on his giving up his business and going off to Europe at just the right moment. For his partner, whose symptoms were very like his own, has been stricken down with paralysis, and will not recover.

It is very pleasant to hear Ernest praised, and it is a pleasure I have very often, for his friends come to see me, and speak of him with rapture. A lady told me that through the long illness of a sweet young daughter of hers, he prayed with her every day, ministering so skillfully to her soul, that all fear of death was taken away, and she just longed to go, and did go at last, with perfect delight. I think he spoke of her to me once, but he did not tell me that her preparations for death was *his* work. I could not conceive of him as doing that.

February 24

Ernest has been gone a week. His mother is worse and he had to go. I wanted to go too, but he said it was not worth while, as he would have to return directly. Dr. Embury takes charge of his patients during his absence, and Mrs. E. and Aunty and the children come to see me very often. I like Mrs. Embury more and more. She is not so sassy as I am, but I believe she agrees with me more than she will admit.

February 25

Ernest writes that his mother is dangerously ill, and seems in great distress. I am mean enough to want all his love myself, while I would hate him if he gave none to her. Poor Ernest! If she should die he would be sadly afflicted!

February 27

She died the very day he wrote. How I long to rush to him and to comfort him! I can think of nothing else. I pray day and night that God would make me a better wife.

A letter came from mother at the same time with Ernest's. She evidently misses me more than she will admit. Just as soon as Ernest returns home I will ask him to let her come and live with us. I am sure he will; he loves her already, and now that his mother has gone he will find her a real comfort. I am sure she will only make our home the happier.

February 28

Such a dreadful thing is going to happen! I have cried and called myself names repeatedly throughout the day. Ernest writes that it has been decided to give up the old homestead, and scatter the family about among the married sons and daughters. Our share is to be his father and his sister Martha, and he desires me to have two rooms prepared for them at once.

So all the glory and the beauty is snatched out of my married life at one swoop! And it is done by the hand I love best, and that I would not have believed could be so unkind.

I am torn in pieces by conflicting emotions and passions. One moment I am all tenderness and sympathy for poor Ernest, and ready to sacrifice everything for his pleasure. The next I am bitterly angry with him for disposing of all my happiness in this arbitrary way. If he had let me make common cause with him and share his interests with him, I know I am not so abominably selfish as to feel as I do now. But he forces two perfect strangers upon me, and forever shuts our doors against my darling mother. For, of course, she cannot live with us if they do.

And who knows what sort of people they are? It is not everybody I can get along with, nor is it everybody can get along with me. Now, if Helen were coming instead of Martha, that would be some relief. I could love her, I am sure, and she would put up with my ways. But your Marthas I am afraid of. Oh, dear, dear, what a nest of scorpions this affair has stirred up within me! Who would believe I could be thinking of my own misery while Ernest's mother, whom he loved so dearly, is barely in her grave! But I have no heart, I am stony and cold. It is good to have found out just what I am!

Since I wrote that I have been trying to tell God all about it. But I could not speak for crying. And I have been getting the rooms ready. How many little things I had planned to put in the best one, which I intended for mother! I have made myself arrange them just the same for Ernest's father. The stuffed chair I have had in my room, and enjoyed so much, has been rolled in, and the Bible with large print placed on the little table near which I had pictured mother with her sweet, pale face, as sitting year after year. The only thing I have taken away is the copy of father's portrait. *He* won't want *that*!

When I had finished this business I went and shook my fist at the creature I saw in the glass.

"You're beaten!" I cried. "*You* didn't want to give up the chair, nor your writing-table, nor the Bible in which you expect to record the names of your ten children! But you've had to do it, so there!"

March 3

They all got here at 7 o'clock last night, just in time for tea. I was so glad to get hold of Ernest once more that I was gracious to my guests, too. The very first thing, however, Ernest annoyed me by calling me Katherine, though he knows I hate that name, and want to be called Katy, as if I were a lovable person, as I certainly am (sometimes). Of course, his father and Martha called me Katherine.

His father is even taller, darker, blacker eyed, blacker haired than he is.

Martha is a spinster.

I had gotten up a nice little supper for them, thinking they would need something substantial after their journey. And perhaps there was some vanity in the display of dainties that needed the mortification I felt at seeing my guests both push away their plates in apparent disgust. Ernest, too, looked annoyed, and expressed some regret that they could find nothing to tempt their appetites.

Martha said something about not expecting much from young housekeepers, which I inwardly resented, for the light, delicious bread had been sent by Aunty, together with other luxuries from her own table, and I knew they were not the handiwork of a young housekeeper, but of old Chloe, who had lived in her own and her mother's family twenty years.

Ernest went out as soon as this unfortunate meal was over to hear Dr. Embury's report of his patients, and we passed a dreary evening, as my mind was preoccupied with longing for his return. The more I tried to think of something to say, the more I couldn't.

At last Martha asked at what time we ate breakfast.

"At half-past seven, precisely," I answered. "Ernest is very punctual about breakfast. The other meals are more irregular."

"That is very late," she returned. "Father rises early and needs his breakfast at once."

I said I would see that he had it as early as he liked, while I foresaw that this would cost me a battle with the divinity who reigned in the kitchen.

"You need not trouble yourself. I will speak to my brother about it," she said.

"Ernest has nothing to do with it," I said, quickly.

She looked at me in a speechless way, and then there was a long silence, during which she shook her head a number of times. At last she inquired: "Did you make the bread we had on the table tonight?"

"No, I do not know how to make bread," I said, smiling at her look of horror.

"Not know how to make bread?" she cried.

The very spirit of mischief got into me, and made me ask:

"Why, can you?"

Now I know there is but one other question I could

have asked her, less insulting than this, and that is:

"Do you know the Ten Commandments?"

A spinster fresh from a farm not know how to make bread, indeed!

But in a moment I was ashamed and sorry that I had yielded to myself so far as to forget the courtesy due to her as my guest, and one just come from a scene of sorrow, so I rushed across the room, seized her hand, and said eagerly:

"Do forgive me! It slipped out before I thought!"

She looked at me in blank amazement, unconscious that there was anything to forgive.

"How you startled me!" she said. "I thought you had suddenly gone crazy."

I went back to my seat crestfallen enough. All this time Ernest's father had sat grim and grave in his corner, without a word. But now he spoke.

"At what hour does my son have family worship? I would like to retire. I feel very weary."

Now family worship at night consists in our kneeling down together hand in hand, the last thing before going to bed, and in our own room. The awful thought of changing this sweet, informal habit into a formal one made me reply quickly:

"Oh, Ernest is very irregular about it. He is often out in the evening, and sometimes we are up quite late. I hope you never will feel obliged to wait for him."

"I trust I shall do my duty, whatever it costs," was the answer.

Oh, how I wished they would go to bed!

It was now ten o'clock, and I felt tired and restless. When Ernest is out late I usually lie on the sofa and wait for him, and so am bright and fresh when he comes in. But now I had to sit up, and there was no knowing for how long. I poked at the fire and knocked down the shovel and tongs, now I leaned back in my chair, and now I leaned forward; and then I listened for his step. At last he came.

"What, are you not all gone to bed?" he asked. As if I could go to bed when I had scarcely seen him a moment since his return!

I explained why we waited, and then we had prayers and escorted our guests to their rooms. When we got back to the parlor I was thankful to rest my tired soul in Ernest's arms, and to hear what little he had to tell about his mother's last hours.

"You must love me more than ever, now," he said, "for I have lost my best friend."

"Yes," I said, "I will." As if that were possible! All the time we were talking I heard the greatest racket overhead, but he did not seem to notice it. I found, this morning, that Martha, or her father, or both together, had changed the positions of every article of furniture in the room, making it look like a fright.

Chapter 11

March 10

Things are even worse than I expected. Ernest evidently looked at me with his father's eyes (and this father has got the jaundice, or something), and certainly is cooler towards me than he was before he went home. Martha still refuses to eat more than enough merely to keep body and soul together, and sits at the table with the air of a martyr. Her father lives on crackers and stewed prunes, and when he has eaten them, fixes his melancholy eyes on me, watching every mouthful with an air of lamentable regret that I would consume so much unwholesome food.

Then Ernest positively spends less time with me than ever, and sits in his office reading and writing nearly every evening.

Yesterday I came home from an exhilarating walk, and a charming call at Aunty's, and at the dinner-table gave a lively account of some of the children's exploits. Nobody laughed, and nobody made any response, and after dinner Ernest took me aside, and said, kindly enough, but still said it, "My little wife must be careful how she runs on in my father's presence. He has a great dread of everything that might be thought levity."

Then all the vials of my wrath exploded and went off.

"Yes, I see how it is," I cried, passionately. "You and your father and your sister have got a box about a foot square that you want to squeeze me into. I have seen it ever since they came. And I can tell you it will take more than three of you to do it. There was no harm in what I said—none, whatever. If you only married me for the sake of screwing me down and freezing me up, why didn't you tell me so before it was too late?"

Ernest stood looking at me like one staring at a problem he had gotten to solve, and didn't know where to begin.

"My very best is my real self," I cried. "To talk like a woman of forty is unnatural to a girl of my age. If your father doesn't like me I wish he would go away, and not come here putting notions into your head, and making you as cold and hard as a stone. *Mother* liked to have me 'run on,' as you call it, and I wish I had stayed with her all my life."

"Do you mean," he asked, very gravely, "that you really wish that?"

"No," I said, "I don't mean it," for his husky, troubled voice brought me to my senses. "All I mean is, that I love you so dearly, and you keep my heart feeling so hungry and restless; and then you went and brought your father and sister here and never asked me if I would like it; and you crowded mother out, and she lives all alone, and it isn't right! I always said that whoever married me had also to marry mother, and I never dreamed that you would disappoint me!"

"Will you stop crying, and listen to me?" he said.

But I could not stop. The floods of the great deep were broken up at last, and I had to cry. If I could have told my troubles to some one I could thus have found vent for them, but there was no one to whom I had a right to speak of my husband.

Ernest walked back and forth in silence. Oh, if I could have cried on his breast, and felt that he loved and pitied me!

At last, as I grew quieter, he came and sat by me.

"This has come upon me like a thunderclap," he said. "I did not know I kept your heart hungry. I did not know you wished your mother to live with us. And I took it for granted that my wife, with her high-toned, heroic character, would sustain me in every duty, and welcome my father and sister to our home. I do not know what I can do now. Shall I send them away?"

"No, no!" I cried. "Only be good to me, Ernest, only love me, only look at me with your own eyes, and not with other's. You knew I had faults when you married me; I never tried to conceal them."

"And did you fancy I had none myself?" he asked

"N—o," I replied. "I saw no faults in you. Everybody said you were such a noble, good man, and you spoke so beautifully one night at an evening meeting."

"Speaking beautifully is little to the purpose unless one lives beautifully," he said, sadly. "And now it is possible that you and I, a Christian man and a Christian woman, are going on and on with such scenes as this? Are you to wear your very life out because I have not your frantic way of loving, and am I to be made weary of mine because I cannot satisfy you?"

"But, Ernest," I said, "you used to satisfy me. Oh, how happy I was in those first days when we were always together, and you seemed so fond of me!" I was down on the floor by this time, and looking up into his pale, anxious face.

"Dear child," he said, "I do love you, and that more than you know. But you would not have me leave my work and spend my whole time telling you so?"

"You know I am not so silly," I cried. "It is not fair, it is not right to talk as if I were. I ask for nothing unreasonable. I only want those little daily assurances of your affection which I should suppose would be spontaneous if you felt at all towards me as I do to you."

"The fact is," he returned, "I am absorbed in my work. It brings many grave cares and anxieties. I spend most of my time amid scenes of suffering and at dying beds. This makes me seem abstracted and cold, but it does not make you less dear. On the contrary, the sense it gives me of the brevity and sorrowfulness of life makes you doubly precious, since it constantly reminds me that sick beds and dying beds must sooner or later come to our home as to those of others."

I clung to him as he uttered these terrible words in an agony of terror.

"Oh, Ernest, promise me, promise me that you will not die first," I pleaded.

"Foolish little thing!" he said, and was as silly, for a while, as the silliest heart could ask. Then he became serious again.

"Katy," he said, "if you can once make up your mind to the fact that I am an undemonstrative man, not all fire and fury and ecstasy as you are, yet loving you with all my heart, however it may seem, I think you will spare yourself much needless pain— and spare me, also."

"But I want you to be demonstrative," I persisted.

"Then you must teach me. And about my father and sister, perhaps, we may find some way of relieving you by and by. Meanwhile, try to bear with the trouble they make, for my sake."

"But I don't mind the trouble! Oh, Ernest, how you do misunderstand me! What I mind is their coming between you and me and making you love me less."

By this time there was a call for Ernest— it is a wonder there had not been forty— and he went.

I feel as heart-sore as ever. What has been gained by this tempest? Nothing at all! Poor Ernest! How can I worry him so when he is already full of care?

March 20

I have had such a truly beautiful letter today from dear mother! She gives up the hope of coming to spend her last years with us with a sweet patience that makes me cry whenever I think of it. What is the secret of this instant and cheerful consent to whatever God wills! Oh, that I had it, too! She begs me to be considerate and kind to Ernest's father and sister, and constantly to remind myself that my Heavenly Father has *chosen* to give me this care and trial on the very threshold of my married life. I am afraid I have quite lost sight of that in my indignation with Ernest for bringing them here.

April 3

Martha is shut up with Ernest in his office day and night. They never give me the least hint of what is going on in these secret meetings. Then this morning Sarah, my good, faithful cook, bounced into my room to give warning. She said she could not live where there were two mistresses giving contrary directions.

"But, really, there is but one mistress," I urged. Then it came out that Martha went down every morning to look after the soap-fat, and to scrimp in the house-keeping, and see that there was no food wasted. I remembered then that she had inquired whether I attended to these details, evidently ranking such duties with saying one's prayers and reading one's Bible.

I rushed to Ernest the moment he was at leisure and poured all my grievances into his ear.

"Well, dear," he said, "suppose you give up the house-keeping to Martha! She will be far happier and you will be freed from much annoying, petty care."

I bit my tongue lest it should say something, and went back to Sarah.

"Suppose Miss Elliott takes charge of the house-keeping, and I have nothing to do with it, will you stay?"

"Indeed, and I won't then. I can't bear her, and I won't put up with her nasty, scrimping, pinching ways!"

"Very well. Then you will have to go," I said, with great dignity, though just ready to cry. Ernest, on being approached for her wages, undertook to argue the question himself.

"My sister will take the whole charge," he began.

"And may and welcome for all me!" exclaimed Sarah. "I don't like her and never shall."

"Your liking or disliking her is of no consequence whatever," said Ernest. "You may dislike her as much as you please. But you must not leave us."

"Indeed, and I'm not going to stay and be put upon by her," persisted Sarah. So she has gone. We had to get dinner ourselves; that is to say, Martha did, for she said I got in her way, and put her out with my awkwardness. I have been running hither and thither to find some angel who will consent to live in this ill-assorted household. Oh, how different everything is from what I had planned! I wanted a cheerful home, where I would be the center of every joy; a home like Aunty's, without a cloud. But Ernest's father sits, the personification of silent gloom, like a nightmare on my spirits; Martha holds me in disfavor and contempt; Ernest is absorbed in his profession, and I hardly see him. If he wants advice he asks it of Martha, while I sit, humbled, degraded and ashamed, wondering why he ever married me at all. And then come interludes of wild joy when he appears just as he did in the happy days of our bridal trip, and I forget every grievance and hang on his words and looks like one intoxicated with bliss.

October 2

There has been another explosion. I held in as long as I could, and then flew into ten thousand pieces. Ernest had got into the habit of helping his father and sister at the table, and apparently forgetting me. It seems a little thing, but it chafed and fretted my already irritated soul till at last I was almost beside myself.

Yesterday they all three sat eating their breakfast and I, with empty plate, sat boiling over and looking on, when Ernest brought things to a crisis by saying to Martha,

"If you can find time today I wish you would go out with me for half an hour or so. I want to consult you about—"

"Oh!" I said, rising, with my face all in a flame, "do not trouble yourself to go out in order to escape me. I can leave the room and you can have your secrets to yourselves as you do your breakfast!"

I don't know which struck me most, Ernest's appalled, grieved look or the glance exchanged between Martha and her father.

He did not hinder my leaving the room, and I went upstairs, as pitiable an object as could be seen. I heard him go to his office, then take his hat and set forth on his rounds. What wretched hours I passed, thus left alone! One moment I reproached myself, the next I was indignant at the long series of offenses that had led to this disgraceful scene.

At last Ernest came.

He looked concerned, and a little pale.

"Oh, Ernest!" I cried, running to him, "I am so sorry I spoke to you as I did! But, indeed, I cannot stand the way things are going on; I am wearing all out. Everybody speaks of my growing thin. Feel of my hands. They burn like fire."

"I knew you would be sorry, dear," he said. "Yes, your hands are hot, poor child."

There was a long, dreadful silence. And yet I was speaking, and perhaps he was. I was begging and beseeching God not to let us drift apart, not to let us lose one jot or tittle of our love to each other, to enable me to understand my dear, dear husband and make him understand me.

Then Ernest began.

"What was it that vexed you, dear? What is it you can't stand? Tell me. I am your husband, I love you, I want to make you happy."

"Why, you are having so many secrets that you keep from me; and you treat me as if I were only a child, consulting Martha about everything. And of late you seem to have forgotten that I am at the table and never help me to anything!"

"Secrets!" he re-echoed. "What possible secrets can I have?"

"I don't know," I said, sinking wearily back on the sofa. "Indeed, Ernest, I don't want to be selfish or demanding, but I am very unhappy."

"Yes, I see it, poor child. And if I have neglected you at the table I do not wonder you are out of patience. I know how it has happened. While you were pouring out the coffee I busied myself in caring for my father and Martha, and so forgot you. I do not give this as an excuse, but as a reason. I have really no excuse, and am ashamed of myself."

"Don't say that, darling," I cried, "it is I who ought to be ashamed for making such an ado about a trifle."

"It is not a trifle," he said; "and now to the other points. I dare say I have been careless about consulting Martha. But she has always been a sort of oracle in our family, and we all look up to her, and she is so much older than you. Then as to the so-called secrets. Martha comes to my office to help me look over my books. I have been careless about my accounts, and she has kindly undertaken to attend to them for me."

"Could not I have done that?"

"No; why should your little head be troubled about money matters? But to go on. I see that it was thoughtless of me not to tell you what we were about. But I am greatly perplexed and harassed in many ways. Perhaps you would feel better to know all about it. I have only kept it from you to spare you all the anxiety I could."

"Oh, Ernest," I said, "ought not a wife to share in all her husband's cares?"

"No," he returned; "but I will tell you all that is annoying me now. My father was in business in our native town, and went on prosperously for many years. Then the tide turned— he met with loss after loss, till nothing remained but the old homestead, and on that there was a mortgage. We concealed the state of things from my mother; her health was delicate, and we never let her know a trouble we could spare her. Now she has gone, and we have found it necessary to sell our old home and to divide and scatter the family. My father's mental distress when he found others suffering from his own losses threw him into the state in which you see him now. I have therefore assumed his debts, and with God's help hope in time to pay them to the very last penny. It will be necessary for us to live prudently until this is done. There are two pressing cases that I am trying to meet at once. This has given me a preoccupied air, I have no doubt, and made you suspect and misunderstand me. But now you know the whole, my darling."

I felt my injustice and childish folly very keenly, and told him so.

"But I think, dear Ernest," I added, "if you will not be hurt at my saying so, that you have led me to it by not letting me share at once in your cares. If you had at the outset just told me the whole story, you would have enlisted my sympathies in your father's behalf, and in your own. I should have seen the reasonableness of your breaking up the old home and bringing him here, and it would have taken off the edge of my bitter, bitter disappointment about my mother."

"I feel very sorry about that," he said. "It would be a pleasure to have her here. But as things are now, she could not be happy with us."

"There is no room," I put in.

"No, I am truly sorry. And now my dear little wife must have patience with her stupid, blundering old husband, and we'll start together once more, fair and square. Don't wait, next time, till you are so full that you boil over; the moment I annoy you by my inconsiderate ways, come right out and tell me."

So then I called myself all the horrid names I could think of.

"May I ask one thing more, now that we are upon the subject?" I said, at last. "Why couldn't your sister Helen have come instead of Martha?"

He smiled a little.

"In the first place, Helen would be perfectly crushed if she had the care of father in his present state. She is too young to have such a burdensome responsibility. In the second place, my brother John, with whom she has gone to live, has a wife who would be quite overwhelmed by my father and Martha. She is one of those little tender, soft souls one could crush with one's fingers. Now, you are not of that sort; you have force of character enough to enable you to live with them, while maintaining your own dignity and remaining yourself in spite of circumstances."

"I thought you admired Martha above all things and wanted me to be exactly like her."

"I admire her, but I do not want you to be like anybody but yourself."

"But you nearly killed me by suggesting that I should take heed how I talked in your father's presence."

"Yes, dear; it was very stupid of me, but my father has a standard of excellence in his mind by which he tests every woman; this standard is my mother. She had none of your life and fun in her, and perhaps would not have appreciated your whimsical way of putting things any better than he and Martha do."

I could not help sighing a little when I thought what sort of people were watching my every word.

"There is nothing amiss to my mind," Ernest continued, "in your merry talk; but my father has his own views as to what constitutes a religious character and cannot understand that real earnestness and real, genuine mirthfulness are consistent with each other."

He had to go now, and we parted as if for a week's separation, this one talk had brought us so near to each other. I understand him now as I never have done, and feel that he has given me as real a proof of his affection by unlocking the door of his heart and letting me see its cares, as I give him in my wild pranks and caresses and foolish speeches. How truly noble it is in him to take up his father's burden in this way! I must contrive to help to lighten it.

Chapter 12

November 6

Aunty has put me in the way of doing that. I could not tell her the whole story, of course, but I made her understand that Ernest needed money for a generous purpose, and that I wanted to help him in it. She said the children needed both music and drawing lessons, and that she would be delighted if I would take them in hand. Aunty does not care a fig for accomplishments, but I think I am right in accepting her offer, as the children ought to learn to sing and to play and to draw. Of course I cannot have them come here, as Ernest's father could not bear the noise they would make; besides, I want to take him by surprise, and keep the whole thing a secret.

November 14

I have seen by the way Martha draws down the corners of her mouth of late, that I am unusually out of favor with her. This evening, Ernest, coming home quite late, found me lolling back in my chair, idling, after a hard day's work with my little cousins, and Martha sewing nervously away at the rate of ten knots an hour, which is the first pun I ever made.

"Why will you sit up and sew at such a rate, Martha?" he asked.

She twitched at her thread, broke it, and began with a new one before she replied.

"I suppose you find it convenient to have a whole shirt to your back."

I saw then that she was making his shirts! It made me both hot and cold at once. What must Ernest think of me?

It is plain enough what he thinks of her, for he said, quite warmly, for him—

"This is really too kind."

What right has she to prowl around among Ernest's things and pry into the condition of his wardrobe? If I had not had my time so broken up with giving lessons, I would have found out that he needed new shirts and set to work on them. Though I must admit I hate shirt-making. I could not help showing that I felt deeply grieved. Martha defended herself by saying that she knew young people would be young people, and would gad about, shirts or no shirts. Now it is not her fault that she thinks I waste my time gadding about, but I am just as angry with her as if she did. Oh, why couldn't I have had Helen, to be a pleasant companion and friend to me, instead of this old— well I won't say what.

And really, with so much to make me happy, what would become of me if I had no trials?

November 15

Today Martha has a house-cleaning mania, and has dragged me into it by representing the sin and misery of those deluded mortals who think servants know how to sweep and to scrub. In spite of my resolution not to get under her thumb, I have somehow let her rule and reign over me to such an extent that I can hardly sit up long enough to write this. Does the whole duty of woman consist in keeping her house distressingly clean and prim; in making and baking and preserving and pickling; in climbing to the top shelves of closets lest perhaps a little dust should lodge there, and getting down on her hands and knees to inspect the carpet? The truth is there is not one point of sympathy between Martha and myself, not one. One would think that our love to Ernest would furnish it. But her love aims at the abasement of his character and mine at its elevation. She thinks I should bow down to and worship him, jump up and offer him my chair when he comes in, feed him with every unwholesome dainty he fancies, and feel myself honored by his acceptance of these services. I think it is for him to rise and offer me a seat, because I am a woman and his wife; and that a silly subservience on my part is degrading to him and to myself. And I am afraid I make known these sentiments to her in a most unpalatable way.

November 18

Oh, I am so happy that I sing for joy! Dear Ernest has given me such a delightful surprise! He says he has persuaded James to come and spend his college days here, and finally study medicine with him. Dear, darling old James! He is to be here tomorrow. He is to have the little hall bedroom fitted up for him, and he will be here several years. Next to having mother, this is the nicest thing that could happen. We love each other so dearly, and get along so beautifully together. I wonder how he'll like Martha with her grim ways, and Ernest's father with his melancholy ones.

November 30

James has come, and the house already seems lighter and cheerier. He is not in the least annoyed by Martha or her father, and though he is as jovial as the day is long, they actually seem to like him. True to her theory on the subject, Martha invariably rises at his entrance, and offers him her seat! He pretends not to see it, and runs to get one for her! Then she takes comfort in seeing him consume her good things, since his gobbling them down is a sort of tacit tribute to their merits.

Mrs. Embury was here today. She says there is not much the matter with Ernest's father, that he has only got the *hypo*. I don't know exactly what this is, but I believe it is thinking something is the matter with you when there isn't. At any rate I put it to you, my dear old journal, whether it is pleasant to live with people who behave in this way?

In the first place all he talks about is his fancied disease. He gets book after book from the office and studies and ponders his case till he grows quite yellow. One day he says he has found out the seat of his disease to be the liver, and changes his diet to meet that view of the case. Martha has to do him up in mustard plaster, and he takes kindly to the little blue pills. In a day or two he finds his liver is all right, but that his brain is all wrong. The mustard goes now to the back of his neck, and he takes solemn leave of us all, with the assurance that his last hour has come. Finding that he survives the night, however, he transfers the seat of his disease to the heart, spends hours in counting his pulse, refuses to take exercise lest he should bring on palpitations, and warns us all to prepare to follow him. Everybody who comes in has to hear the whole story, every one prescribes something, and he tries each remedy in turn. These all failing to reach his case, he is plunged into ten-fold gloom. He complains that God has cast him off forever, and that his sins are like the sands of the sea for number. I am such a goose that I listen to all these varying moods and symptoms with the solemn conviction that he is going to die immediately; I bathe his head, and count his pulse, and fan him, and take down his dying depositions for Ernest's solace after he has gone. And I talk theology to him by the hour, while Martha bakes and brews in the kitchen, or makes mince pies, after eating which, one might give him the whole Bible at one dose, without the smallest effect.

Today I stood by his chair, holding his head and whispering such consoling passages as I thought might comfort him, when James burst in, singing and tossing his cap in the air.

"Come here, young man, and hear my last testimony. I am about to die. The end draws near," were the sepulchral words that made him bring his song to an abrupt close.

"I shall take it very ill of you, sir," said James, "if you go and die before giving me that cane you promised me."

Who could die decently under such circumstances? The poor old man revived immediately, but looked a good deal injured. After James had gone out, he said:

"It is very painful to one who stands on the very verge of the eternal world to see the young so thoughtless."

"But James is not thoughtless," I said. "It is only his merry way."

"Daughter Katherine," he went on, "you are very kind to the old man, and you will have your reward. But I wish I could feel sure of your state before God. I greatly fear you deceive yourself, and that the ground of your hope is delusive."

I felt the blood rush to my face. At first I was staggered a good deal. But is a mortal man who cannot judge of his own state to decide mine? It is true he sees my faults; anybody can, who looks. But he does not see my prayers, or my tears of shame and sorrow; he does not know how many hasty words I repress; how earnestly I am aiming, all the day long, to do right in all the little details of life. He does not know that it costs my meticulous nature an appeal to God every time I kiss his poor old face, and that what would be an act of worship in him is an act of self-denial in me. How could he know? The Christian life is a hidden life, known only by the eye that sees in secret. And I do believe this life is mine.

Up to this time I have contrived to get along without calling Ernest's father any name. I am now determined to make myself turn over a new leaf.

December 7

James is my perpetual joy and pride. We read and sing together, just as we used to do in our old school days. Martha sits by, with her work, grimly approving; for is he not a man? And, as if my cup of felicity were not full enough, I am to have my dear old pastor come here to settle over this church, and I shall once more hear his beloved voice in the pulpit. Ernest has managed the whole thing. He says the state of Dr. C.'s health makes the change quite necessary, and that he can avail himself of the best surgical advice this city affords, in case his old difficulties recur. I rejoice for myself and for this church, but mother will miss him sadly.

I am leading a very busy, happy life, only I am, perhaps, working a little too hard. What with my students, the extra amount of housework Martha contrives to get out of me, the practicing I must keep up if I am to teach, and the many steps I have to take, I have not only no idle moments, but none too many for recreation. Ernest is so busy himself that he fortunately does not see what a race I am running.

January 16, 1838

The first anniversary of our wedding-day, and like all days, has had its lights and its shades. I thought I would celebrate it in such a way as to give pleasure to everybody, and spent a good deal of time in getting up a little gift for each, from Ernest and myself. And I took special pains to have a good dinner, particularly for father. Yes, I had made up my mind to call him by that sacred name for the first time today, cost what it may. But he shut himself up in his room directly after breakfast, and when dinner was ready refused to come down. This cast a gloom over us all. Then Martha was nearly distracted because a valuable dish had been broken in the kitchen, and could not recover her equanimity at all. Worst of all Ernest, who is not in the least sentimental, never said a word about our wedding-day, and didn't give me a thing! I have kept hoping all day that he would make me some little present, no matter how small, but now it is too late; he has gone out to be gone all night, probably, and thus ends the day, an utter failure.

I feel a good deal disappointed. Besides, when I look back over this my first year of married life, I do not feel satisfied with myself at all. I can't help feeling that I have been selfish and unreasonable towards Ernest in a great many ways, and as unfavorable towards Martha as if I enjoyed a state of warfare between us. And I have felt a good deal of secret contempt for her father, with his moods and tenses, his pill-boxes and his plasters, his feastings and his fastings. I do not understand how a Christian *can* make such slow progress as I do, and how old faults can hang on so.

If I had made any real progress, would I not be sensible of it?

I have been reading over the early part of this journal, and when I came to the conversation I had with Mrs.

Cabot, in which I made a list of my wants, I was astonished that I could ever have had such contemptible ones. Let me think what I really and truly most want now.

First of all, then, if God should speak to me at this moment and offer to give just one thing, and that alone, I would say without hesitation, Love to Thee, O my Master![17]

Next to that, if I could have one thing more, I would choose to be a thoroughly unselfish, devoted wife. Down in my secret heart I know there lurks another wish, which I am ashamed of. It is that in some way or other, some *right* way, I could be delivered from Martha and her father. I shall never be any better while they are here to tempt me!

February 1

Ernest spoke today of one of his patients, a Mrs. Campbell, who is a great sufferer, but whom he describes as the happiest, most cheerful person he ever met. He rarely speaks of his patients. Indeed, he rarely speaks of anything. I felt strangely attracted by what he said of her, and asked so many questions that at last he proposed to take me to see her. I snatched at the idea very eagerly, and have just come home from the visit greatly moved and touched. She is confined to her bed, and is quite helpless, and at times her sufferings are terrible. She received me with a sweet smile, however, and led me on to talk more of myself than I ought to have done. I wish Ernest had not left me alone with her, so that I would have had the restraint of his presence.

February 14

I am so fascinated with Mrs. Campbell that I cannot help going to see her again and again. She seems to me like one whose conflict and dismay are all over, and who looks on other human beings with an almost divine love and pity. To look at life as she does, to feel as she does, to have such a personal love to Christ as she has, I would willingly go through every trial and sorrow. When I told her so, she smiled, a little sadly.

"Much as you envy me," she said, "my faith is not yet so strong that I do not shudder at the thought of a young enthusiastic girl like you, going through all I have done in order to learn a few simple lessons which God was willing to teach me sooner and without the use of a rod, if I had been ready for them."

"But you are so happy now," I said.

"Yes, I am happy," she replied, "and such happiness is worth all it costs. If my flesh shudders at the remembrance of what I have endured, my faith in God sustains me through the whole. But tell me a little more about yourself, my dear. I would so love to give you a helping hand, if I might."

"You know," I began, "dear Mrs. Campbell, that there are some trials that cannot do us any good. They only call out all there is in us that is unlovely and severe."

"I don't know of any such trials," she replied.

"Suppose you had to live with people who were perfectly uncongenial; who misunderstood you, and who were always getting into your way as stumbling-blocks?"

"If I were living with them and they made me unhappy, I would ask God to relieve me of this trial if He thought it best. If He did not think it best, I would then try to find out the reason. He might have two reasons. One would be the good they might do me. The other the good I might do them."

"But in the case I was supposing, neither party can be of the least use to the other."

"You forget perhaps the *indirect* good one may gain by living with uncongenial, tempting persons. First such people do good by the very self-denial and self-control their mere presence demands. Then, their making one's home less home-like and perfect than it would be in their absence, may help to render our real home in heaven more attractive."

"But suppose one cannot exercise self-control, and is always flying out and flaring up?" I objected.

"I should say that a *Christian* who was always doing that," she replied, gravely, "was in pressing need of just the trial God sent when He shut him up to such a life of hourly temptation. We only know ourselves and what we really are, when the force of circumstances bring us out into the open."

"It is very mortifying and painful to find how weak one is."

"That is true. But our mortifications are some of God's best physicians, and do much toward healing our pride and self-conceit."

"Do you really think, then, that God *deliberately*

appoints to some of His children a lot where their worst passions are excited, with a desire to bring good out of this seeming evil? Why I have always supposed the best thing that could happen to me, for instance, would be to have a home exactly to my mind; a home where all were forbearing, loving and good-tempered, a sort of little heaven below."

"If you have not such a home, my dear, are you sure it is not partly your own fault?"

"Of course it is my own fault. Because I am very quick-tempered I want to live with good-tempered people."

"That is very benevolent of you," she said, slyly.

I blushed, but went on.

"Oh, I know I am selfish. And therefore I want to live with those who are not so. I want to live with persons to whom I can look for an example, and who will constantly stimulate me to something higher."

"But if God chooses quite another lot for you, you may be sure that He sees that you need something totally different from what you want. You said just now that you would gladly go through any trial in order to attain a personal love to Christ that would become the ruling principle of your life. Now as soon as God sees this desire in you, is He not kind, is He not wise, in appointing such trials as He knows will lead to this very end?"

I meditated long before I answered. Was God really asking me not merely to let Martha and her father live with me on mere tolerance, but to rejoice that He had seen fit to let them harass and embitter my domestic life?"

"I thank you for the suggestion," I said, at last.

"I want to say one thing more," Mrs. Campbell resumed, after another pause. "We look at our fellow-men too much from the standpoint of our own prejudices. They may be wrong, they may have their faults and deficiencies, they may call out all that is meanest and most hateful in us. But they are not all wrong; they have their virtues, and when they excite our bad passions by their own, they may be as ashamed and sorry as we are irritated. And I think some of the best, most contrite, most useful of men and women, whose prayers prevail with God, and bring down blessings into the homes in which they dwell, often possess unlovely traits that furnish them with their best discipline. The very fact that they are ashamed of themselves drives them to God; they feel safe in His presence, and while they lie in the very dust of self-confusion at His feet they are dear to Him and have power with Him."

"That is a comforting word, and I thank you for it," I said. My heart was full, and I longed to stay and hear her talk on. But I had already exhausted her strength. On the way home I felt as I suppose people do when they have caught a basketful of fish. I always am delighted to catch a new idea; I thought I would get all the benefit out of Martha and her father, and as I went down to tea, after taking off my things, felt like a holy martyr who had as good as won a crown.

I found, however, that the butter was horrible. Martha had insisted that she alone was capable of selecting that article, and had ordered a quantity from her own village which I could not eat myself and was ashamed to have on my table. I pushed back my plate in utter disgust.

"I hope, Martha, that you have not ordered much of this odious stuff!" I cried.

Martha replied that it was of the very first quality, and appealed to her father and Ernest, who both agreed with her, which I thought very unkind and unjust. I rushed into a hot debate on the subject, during which Ernest maintained that ominous silence that indicates his not being pleased, and that irritated and led me on. I would far rather he would say, "Katy, you're acting like a child, and I wish you would stop talking."

"Martha," I said, "you will persist that the butter is good, because you ordered it. If you will only admit that, I won't say another word."

"I *can't* say it," she returned. "Mrs. Jones' butter is invariably good. I never heard it found fault with before. The trouble is you are so hard to please."

"No, I am not. And you can't convince me that if the buttermilk is not perfectly worked out, the butter could be fit to eat."

This speech I felt to be a masterpiece. It was time to let her know how learned I was on the subject of butter, though I wasn't brought up to make it or see it made.

But here Ernest put in a little oil.

"I think you are both right," he said. "Mrs. Jones makes good butter, but just this once she failed. I'm sure it won't happen again, and meanwhile this can be used to make seed-cakes, while we get a new supply."

This was *his* masterpiece! A whole firkin of butter made up into seed-cakes!

Martha turned to encounter him on that head, and I slipped off to my room to look, with a miserable sense of disappointment, at my folly and weakness in making so much ado about nothing. I find it hard to believe that it can do me good to have people live with me who like rancid butter, and who disagree with me in everything else.

Chapter 13

Aunty sent for us all to dine with her today to celebrate Lucy's fifteenth birthday. Ever since Lucy behaved so heroically in regard to little Emma, really saving her life, Ernest says Aunty seems to feel that she cannot do enough for her. The child has taken the most unaccountable fancy to me, strangely enough, and when we got there she came to meet me with something like cordiality.

"Mamma permits me to be the bearer of agreeable news," she said, "because this is my birthday. A friend, of whom you are very fond, has just arrived, and is impatient to embrace you."

"To *embrace* me?" I cried. "You foolish child!" And the next moment I found myself in my mother's arms!

The despised Lucy had been the means of giving me this pleasure. It seems that Aunty had told her she could choose her own birthday treat, and that, after solemn meditation, she had decided that to see dear mother again would be the most agreeable thing she could think of. I have never told you, dear journal, why I did not go home last summer, and never shall. If you choose to fancy that I couldn't afford it you can!

Well! wasn't it nice to see mother, and to read in her dear, loving face that she was satisfied with her poor, wayward Katy, and fond of her as ever! I only longed for Ernest's coming, that she might see us together, and see how he loved me.

He came; I rushed out to meet him and dragged him in. But it seemed as if he had grown stupid and awkward. All through the dinner I watched for one of those loving glances which would proclaim to mother the good understanding that exists between us, but watched in vain.

"It will come by and by," I thought. "When we get by ourselves mother will see how fond of me he is." But "by and by" it was just the same. I was preoccupied, and mother asked me if I were well. It was all very foolish I dare say, and yet I did want to have her know that with all my faults he still loves me. Then, besides this disappointment, I have to reproach myself for misunderstanding poor Lucy as I have done. Because she was not all fire and fury like myself, I need not have assumed that she had no heart. It is just like me; I hope I shall never be so severe in my judgment again.

April 30

Mother has just gone. Her visit has done me a world of good. She found out something to like in father at once, and then something good in Martha. She says father's sufferings are real, not fancied; that his error is not know-ing where to locate his disease, and is starving one week and over-eating the next. She charged me not to lay up future misery for myself by misjudging him now, and to treat him as a daughter ought without the smallest regard to his appreciation of it. Then as to Martha, she declares that I have no idea how much she does to reduce our expenses, to keep the house in order and to relieve us from care. "But, mother," I said, "did you notice what *horrid* butter we have? And it is all her doing."

"But the butter won't last forever," she replied. "Don't make yourself miserable about such a trifle. For my part, it is a great relief to me to know that with your delicate health you have this tower of strength to lean on."

"But my health is not delicate, mother."

"You certainly look pale and thin."

"Oh, well," I said, whereupon she fell to giving me all sorts of advice about getting up on step-ladders, and climbing on chairs, and sewing too much and all that.

June 15

The weather, or something, makes me rather languid and stupid. I begin to think that Martha is not an entire nuisance in the house. I have just been to see Mrs. Campbell. In answer to my routine of lamentations, she took up a book and read me what was called, as nearly as I can remember, "Four Steps that Lead to Peace."

"Be desirous of doing the will of another, rather than

thine own."

"Choose always to have less, rather than more."

"Seek always to the lowest place, and to be inferior to every one."

"Wish always, and pray, that the will of God may be wholly fulfilled in thee."

I was much struck with these directions; but I said, despondently:

"If peace can only be found at the end of such hard roads, I am sure I shall always be miserable."

"Are you miserable now?" she asked.

"Yes, just now I am. I do not mean that I have no happiness; I mean that I am in a disheartened mood, weary of going round and round in circles, committing the same sins, uttering the same confessions, and making no advance."

"My dear," she said, after a time, "have you a perfectly distinct, settled view of what Christ is to the human soul?"

"I do not know. I understand, of course, more or less perfectly, that my salvation depends on Him alone; it is His gift."

"But do you see, with equal clearness, that your sanctification must be as fully His gift, as your salvation is?"

"No," I said, after a little thought. "I have had a feeling that He has done His part, and now I must do mine."

"My dear," she said, with such tenderness and feeling, "then the first thing you have to do is to learn Christ."

"But how?"

"On your knees, my child, on your knees!" She was tired, and I came away; and I have indeed been on my knees.

July 1

I think that I do begin, dimly it is true, but really, to understand that this terrible work which I was trying to do myself, is Christ's work, and must be done and will be done by Him. I take some pleasure in the thought, and wonder why it has all this time been hidden from me, especially after what Dr. C. said in his letter. But I get hold of this idea in a misty, unsatisfactory way. If Christ is to do all, what am I to do? And have I not been told, over and over again, that the Christian life is one of conflict, and that I am to fight like a good soldier?

August 5

Dr. Cabot has come just as I need him most. I long for one of those good talks with him which always used to strengthen me so. I feel a perfect weight of depression that makes me a burden to myself and to poor Ernest, who, after visiting sick people all day, needs to come home to a cheerful wife. But he comforts me with the assurance that this is merely physical despondency, and that I shall get over it by and by. How kind, how even tender he is! My heart is getting all it wants from him, only I am too sluggish to enjoy him as I ought. Father, too, talks far less about his own bad feelings, and seems greatly concerned at mine. As to Martha I have finished trying to get sympathy or love from her. She cannot help it, I suppose, but she is very hard and dry towards me, and I feel such a longing to throw myself on her mercy, and to have one little smile to assure me that she has forgiven me for being Ernest's wife, and so different from what she would have chosen for him.

October 4, 1838

My Dear Katy's Mother—

You will rejoice with us when I tell you that we are the happy parents of a very fine little boy. My dearest wife sends "an ocean of love" to you, and says she will write herself to-morrow. That I shall not be very likely to allow, as you will imagine. She is doing extremely well, and we have every-thing to be grateful for.

Your affectionate Son,

J. E. Elliott

Mrs. Crofton to Mrs. Mortimer:

I am sure, my dear sister, that the doctor has not writ-ten you more than five lines about the great event which has made such a stir in our domestic circle. So I must supply the details you will want to hear. . . I need not add that our darling Katy behaved nobly. Her self-forgetfulness and con-sideration for others were really beautiful throughout the whole scene. The doctor may well be proud of her, and I took care to tell him so in presence of that dreadful sister of his. I never met so jagged, so uncompromising a person as she is in all my life. She does not understand Katy, and never can, and I find it hard to realize that living with such a person can furnish a wholesome discipline, which is even more desirable than the most delightful home. And yet I not only know that this is true in the abstract, but I see that it is so in the actual fact. Katy is acquiring both self-control and patience, and her Christian character is developing in a way that amazes me. I cannot but hope that God will, in time, deliver her from this trial; indeed, I feel sure that when it has done its beneficent work He will do so. Martha Elliott is a good woman, but her goodness is without grace or beauty. She takes excellent care of Katy, keeps her looking as if she had just come out of a band-box, as the saying is, and always has her room in perfect order. But one misses the loving word, the reassuring smile, the delicate, thoughtful little forbearance, that ought to adorn every sick-room, and light it up with genuine sunshine. There is one comfort about it, however, and that is, that I can spoil dear Katy to my heart's content.

As to the baby, he is a fine little fellow, and his mother is so happy in him that she can afford to do without some other pleasures. I shall write again in a few days. Meanwhile, you may rest assured that I love your Katy almost as well as you do, and shall be with her most of the time till she is quite herself again.

James to his mother:

Of course there never was such a baby before on the face of the earth. Katy is so nearly wild with joy, that you can't get her to eat or sleep or do any of the proper things that her charming sister-in-law thinks is fitting under the circumstances. You never saw anything so pretty in your life, as she is now. I hope the doctor is as much in love with her as I am. He is the best fellow in the world, and Katy is just the wife for him.

November 4

My darling baby is a month old today. I never saw such a splendid child. I love him so that I lie awake nights to watch him. Martha says, in her dry way, that I had better show my love by sleeping and eating for him, and Ernest says I shall, as soon as I get stronger. But I don't get strong, and that discourages me.

November 26

I begin to feel rather more like myself, and as if I could write with less labor. I have had in these few past weeks such a revelation of suffering, and such a revelation of joy, as mortal mind can hardly conceive of. The world I live in now is a new world; a world full of suffering that leads to unutterable felicity. Oh, this precious, precious baby! How can I thank God enough for giving him to me!

I see now why He has put some thorns into my domestic life; but for them I should be too happy to live. It does not seem just the moment to complain, and yet, as I can speak to no one, it is a relief, a great relief, to write about my trials. During my whole sickness, Martha has been so hard, so cold, so unsympathetic that sometimes it has seemed as if my cup of trial could not hold another drop. She routed me out of bed when I was so languid that everything seemed a burden, and when sitting up made me faint away. I heard her say to herself, that I had no constitution and had no business to get married. The worst of all is that during the dreadful night before the baby came, she kept asking Ernest to lie down and rest, and was sure he would kill himself, and all that, while she had not one word of pity for me. But, oh, why need I let this rankle in my heart! Why cannot I turn my thoughts entirely to my darling baby, my dear husband, and all the other sources of joy that make my home a happy one in spite of this one discomfort! I hope I am learning some useful lessons from my joys and from my trials, and that both will serve to make me in earnest, and to keep me so.

December 4

We have had a great time about poor baby's name. I expected to call him Raymond, for my own dear father, as a matter of course. It seemed a small gratification for mother in her loneliness. Dear mother! How little I have known all these years what I cost her! But it seems there has been a Jotham in the family ever since the memory of man, each eldest son handing down his father's name to the next in descent, and Ernest's real name is Jotham Ernest— of all the extraordinary combinations! His mother would add the latter name in spite of everything. Ernest behaved very well through the whole affair, and said he had no feeling about it all. But he was so gratified when I decided to keep up the family custom that I feel rewarded for the sacrifice.

Father is in one of his gloomiest moods. As I sat caressing baby today he said to me: "Daughter Katherine, I trust you make it a subject of prayer to God that you may be kept from idolatry."

"No, father," I returned, "I never do. An idol is something one puts in God's place, and I don't put baby there."

He shook his head and said the heart is deceitful above all things, and desperately wicked.

"I have heard mother say that we might love an earthly object as much as we pleased, if we only love God better." I might have added, but of course I didn't, that I prayed every day that I might love Ernest and baby better and better. Poor father seemed puzzled and troubled by what I did say, and after musing a while, went on thus:

"The Almighty is a great and terrible Being. He cannot bear a rival; He will have the whole heart or none of it. When I see a young woman so absorbed in a created being as you are in that infant, and in your other friends, I tremble for you, I tremble for you!"

"But, father," I persisted, "God gave me this child, and He gave me my heart, just as it is."

"Yes; and that heart needs renewing."

"I hope it *is* renewed," I replied. "But I know there is a great work still to be done in it. And the more effectually it is done the more loving I shall grow. Don't you see, father? Don't you see that the more Christ-like I become the more I shall be filled with love for every living thing?"

He shook his head, but pondered long, as he always

does, on whatever he considers audacious. As for me, I am vexed with my presumption in disputing with him, and am sure, too, that I was trying to show off what little wisdom I have picked up. Besides, my mountain does not stand so strong as it did. Perhaps I *am* making idols out of Ernest and the baby.

January 16, 1839

This is our second wedding anniversary. I did not expect much from it, after last year's failure. Father was very gloomy at breakfast, and retired to his room immediately after it. No one could get in to make his bed, and he would not come down to dinner. I wonder why Ernest lets him go on so. But his rule seems to be to let everybody have their own way. He certainly lets me have mine. After dinner he gave me a book I have been wanting for some time, and had asked him for— "The Imitation of Christ." Ever since that day at Mrs. Campbell's I have felt that I should like it, though I did think, in old times, that it preached too hard a doctrine. I read aloud to him the "Four Steps to Peace"; he said they were admirable, and then took it from me and began reading to himself, here and there. I felt the precious moments when I had gotten him all to myself were passing away, and was becoming quite out of patience with him when the words "Constantly seek to have less, rather than more," flashed into my mind. I suppose this direction had reference to worldly good, but I despise money, and despise people who love it. The riches I crave are not silver and gold, but my husband's love and esteem. And of these must I desire to have less rather than more? I puzzled myself over this question in vain, but when I silently prayed to be satisfied with just what God chose to give me of the wealth I crave, yes, hunger and thirst for, I certainly felt a sweet content, for the time, at least, that was quite resting and quieting. And just as I had reached that acquiescent mood Ernest threw down his book, and came and caught me in his arms.

"I thank God," he said, "my precious wife, that I married you this day. The wisest thing I ever did was when I fell in love with you and made a fool of myself!"

What a speech for my silent old darling to make! Whenever he says and does a thing out of character, and takes me all by surprise, how delightful he is! *Now* the world is a beautiful world, and so is everybody in it. I met Martha on the stairs after Ernest had gone, and caught her and kissed her. She looked perfectly astonished.

"What spirits the child has!" I heard her whisper to herself; "no sooner down than up again."

And she sighed. Can it be that under that stern and hard crust, there lie hidden affections and perhaps hidden sorrows?

I ran back and asked, as kindly as I could, "What makes you sigh, Martha? Is anything troubling you? Have I done anything to annoy you?"

"You do the best you can," she said, and pushed past me to her own room.

Chapter 14

Who would have thought I would have anything more to do with poor old Susan Green? Dr. Cabot came to see me today, and told me the strangest thing. It seems that the nurse who performed the last offices for her was taken sick about six months ago, and that Dr. Cabot visited her from time to time. Her physician said she needed nothing but rest and good, nourishing food to restore her strength, yet she did not improve at all, and at last it came out that she was not taking the food the doctor ordered, because she could not afford to do so, having lost what little money she had designed to save. Dr. Cabot, on learning this, gave her enough out of Susan's inheritance to meet her case, and in doing so told her about this extraordinary will. The nurse then assured him that when she reached Susan's room and saw the state that she was in, and that I was praying with her, she had remained waiting in silence, fearing to interrupt me. She saw me faint, and sprang forward just in time to catch me and keep me from falling.

"I take great pleasure, therefore," Dr. Cabot continued, "in making over Susan's little property to you, to whom it belongs; and I cannot help congratulating you that you have had the honor and the privilege of perhaps leading that poor, benighted soul to Christ, even at the eleventh hour."

"Oh, Dr. Cabot!" I cried, "what a relief it is to hear you say that! For I have always reproached myself for the cowardice that made me afraid to speak to her of her Saviour. It takes less courage to speak to God than to man."

"It is my belief," replied Dr. Cabot, "that every prayer offered in the name of Jesus is sure to have its answer. Every such prayer is dictated by the Holy Spirit, and therefore finds acceptance with God; and if your cry for mercy on poor Susan's soul did not prevail with Him in her behalf, as we may hope it did, then He has answered it in some other way."

These words impressed me very much. To think that every one of my poor prayers is answered! Every one!

Dr. Cabot then returned to the subject of Susan's will, and in spite of all I could say to the contrary, insisted that he had no legal right to this money, and that I had. He said he hoped that it would help to relieve us from some of the petty financial concerns now rendered necessary by Ernest's struggle to meet his father's liabilities. Instantly my idol was rudely thrown down from his pedestal. How *could* he reveal to Dr. Cabot a secret he had pretended it cost him so much to confide to me, his wife? I could hardly restrain tears of shame and vexation, but did control myself so far as to say that I would sooner die than appropriate Susan's hard earnings to such a purpose, and that I would use it for the poor, as I was sure he would have done. He then advised me to invest the principal, and use the interest from year to year, as occasions presented themselves. So I shall have more than a hundred dollars to give away each year, as long as I live! How perfectly delightful. I can hardly conceive of anything that could give me so much pleasure! Poor old Susan! How many hearts she shall cause to sing for joy!

February 25

Things have not gone on well of late. Dearly as I love Ernest, he has lowered himself in my eye by telling that to Dr. Cabot. It would have been far nobler to be silent concerning his sacrifices; and he certainly grows harder, graver, sterner every day. He is all shut up within himself, and I am growing afraid of him. It must be that he is bitterly disappointed in me, and takes refuge in this awful silence. Oh, if I could only please him, and could know that I pleased him, how different my life would be!

Baby does not seem healthy. I have often prided myself on the thought that having a doctor as his father would be such an advantage to him, as he would be ready to attack the first symptoms of disease. But Ernest hardly listens to me when I express anxiety about this or that, and if I ask a question he replies, "Oh, you know better than I do. Mothers know by instinct how to manage babies." But I do not know by instinct, or in any other way, and I often wish that the time I spent over my music had been spent in learning how to meet all the little emergencies that are constantly arising since our baby came. How I used to laugh in my sleeve at those anxious mothers who lived near us and always seemed to be in hot water. Martha will take baby when I have other things to attend to, and she keeps him every Sunday afternoon that I may go to church, but she knows no more about his physical training than I do. If my dear mother were only here! I feel a good deal worn out. What with the care of baby, who is restless at night, and with whom I walk about lest he should keep Ernest awake, the depressing influence of father's presence, Martha's disdain, and Ernest keeping so aloof from me, life seems to me little better than a burden that I have not strength to carry and would gladly lay down.

March 3

If it were not for James I believe I would sink. He is so kind and affectionate, so ready to fill up the gaps Ernest leaves empty, and is so sunshiny and merry that I cannot be entirely sad. Baby, too, is a precious treasure; it would be wicked to cloud his little life with my depression. I try to look at him always with a smiling face, for he already distinguishes between a cheerful and a sad countenance.

I am sure that there is something in Christ's gospel that would soothe and sustain me amid these varied trials, if I only knew what it is, and how to put forth my hand and take it. But as it is I feel very desolate. Ernest often congratulates me on having had such a good night's rest, when

I have been up and down every hour with baby, half asleep and frozen and exhausted. But *he* shall sleep at any rate.

April 5

The first rays of spring make me more languid than ever. Martha cannot be made to understand that nursing such a large, insatiable baby, losing sleep, and confinement within doors, are enough to account for this. She is constantly speaking in terms of praise of those who keep up even when they do feel a little out of sorts, and says she always does. In the evening, after baby gets to sleep, I feel fit for nothing but to lie on the sofa, dozing; but she sees in this only a lazy habit, which ought not to be tolerated, and is constantly devising ways to rouse and set me at work. If I had more leisure for reading, meditation and prayer, I might still be happy. But all the morning I must have baby till he takes his nap, and as soon as he gets to sleep I must put my room in order, and by that time all the best part of the day is gone. And at night I am so tired that I can hardly feel anything but my weariness. That, too, is my only chance of seeing Ernest, and if I lock my door and fall upon my knees, I keep listening for his step, ready to spring to welcome him should he come. This is wrong, I know, but how can I live without one loving word from him, and every day I am hoping it will come.

May 2

Aunty was here today. I had not seen her for some weeks. She exclaimed at my looks in a tone that seemed to upbraid Ernest and Martha, though of course she did not mean to do that.

"You are not fit to have the whole care of that great boy at night," said she, "and you ought to begin to feed him, for his sake and yours."

"I am willing to take the child at night," Martha said, a little stiffly. "But I supposed his mother preferred to keep him herself."

"And so I do," I cried. "I would be perfectly miserable if I had to give him up just as he is getting teeth, and so wakeful."

"What are you taking to keep up your strength?" asked Aunty.

"Nothing in particular," I said.

"Very well, it is time the doctor looked after that," she cried. "It really never will do to let you get run down in this way. Let me look at baby. Why, my child, his gums need lancing."

"So I have told Ernest half a dozen times," I declared. "But he is always in a hurry, and says another time will do."

"I hope baby won't have convulsions while he is waiting for that other time," said Aunty, looking almost savagely at Martha. I never saw Aunty so nearly out of humor.

At dinner Martha began.

"I think, brother, the baby needs attention. Mrs. Crofton has been here and says so. And she seems to find Katherine run down. I am sure if I had known it I would have taken her in hand and built her up. But she did not complain."

"She never complains," father here put in, calling all

the blood I had into my face, my heart so leaped for joy at his kind word.

Ernest looked at me and caught the illumination of my face.

"You look well, dear," he said. "But if you do not feel so you ought to tell us. As to baby, I will attend to him directly."

So Martha's one word prevailed where my twenty fell to the ground.

Baby is much relieved, and has fallen into a sweet sleep. And I have had time to carry my tired, oppressed heart to my compassionate Saviour, and to tell Him what I cannot utter to any human ear. How strange it is that when, through many years of leisure and strength, prayer was only a task, it is now my chief solace if I can only snatch time for it.

Mrs. Embury has a little daughter. How glad I am for her! She is going to give it my name! That is a real pleasure.

July 4

Baby is ten months old today, and in spite of everything is bright and healthy. I have come home to mother. Ernest woke up at last to see that something must be done, and when he is awake he is very wide awake. So he brought me home. Dear mother is perfectly delighted, only she will make a tumult about my health. But I feel a good deal better, and think I shall get nicely rested here. How pleasant it is to feel myself observed by friendly eyes, my faults excused and forgiven, and what is best in me called out. I have been writing to Ernest, and have told him honestly how annoyed and pained I was at learning that he had told his secret to Dr. Cabot.

July 12

Ernest writes that he has had no communication with Dr. Cabot or any one else on a subject that, touching his father's honor as it does, he regards as a sacred one.

"You say, dear," he said, "you often say, that I do not understand you. Are you sure that you understand me?"

Of course I don't. How can I? How can I reconcile his marrying me and professing to do it with delight, with his indifference to my company, his reserve, his carelessness about my health?

But his letters are very kind, and really warmer than he is. I can hardly wait for them, and then, though my pride bids me to be reticent as he is, my heart runs away with me, and I pour out upon him such floods of affection that I am sure he is half drowned.

Mother says baby is *splendid!*

August 1

When I took leave of Ernest I was glad to get away. I thought he would perhaps find after I was gone that he missed something out of his life and would welcome me home with a little of the old love. But I did not dream that he would not find it easy to do without me till summer was over, and when, this morning, he came suddenly upon us, suitcase in hand, I could do nothing but cry in his arms like a tired child.

And now I finally had the silly triumph of having mother see that he loved me!

"How could you get away?" I asked at last. "And what made you come? And how long can you stay?"

"I *could* get away because I *would*," he replied. "And I came because I wanted to come. And I can stay three days."

Three days of Ernest all to myself!

August 5

He has gone, but he has left behind him a happy wife and the memory of three happy days.

After the first joy of our meeting was over, we had time for just such nice long talks as I delight in. Ernest began by upbraiding me a little for my injustice in fancying he had betrayed his father to Dr. Cabot.

"That is not all," I interrupted, "I even thought you had made a boast of the sacrifices you were making."

"That explains your coldness," he returned.

"My coldness! Of all the ridiculous things in the world!" I cried.

"You were cold, for you and I felt it. Don't you know that we undemonstrative men prefer loving winsome little women like you, just because you are our own opposites? And when the pet kitten turns into a cat with claws—"

"Now, Ernest, that is really too bad! To compare me to a cat!"

"You certainly did say some sharp things to me about that time."

"Did I, really? Oh, Ernest, how could I?"

"And it was at a moment when I particularly needed your help. But do not let us dwell upon it. We love each other; we are both trying to do right in all the details of life. I do not think we shall ever get very far apart.

"But, Ernest— tell me— are you very much disappointed in me?"

"Disappointed? Why, Katy!"

"Then what did make you seem so indifferent? What made you so slow to observe how miserably I was, as to health?"

"Did I seem indifferent? I am sure I never loved you better. As to your health, I am ashamed of myself. I ought to have seen how feeble you were. But the truth is, I was deceived by your bright ways with baby. For him you were all smiles and felicity."

"That was from principle," I said, and felt a good deal elated as I made the announcement.

He fell into a fit of musing, and none of my usual devices for arousing him had any effect. I pulled his hair and his ears, and shook him, but he remained unmoved. At last he began again.

"Perhaps I owe it to you, dear, to tell you that when I brought my father and sister home to live with us, I did not dream how trying a thing it would be to you. I did not know that he was a confirmed invalid, or that she would prove to possess a nature so entirely antagonistic to yours. I thought my father would interest himself in reading, visiting, etc., as he used to do. And I thought Martha's judgment would be of service to you, while her household skill would relieve you of some care. But the whole thing has proved a failure. I am harassed by the sight of my father, sitting there in his corner so penetrated with gloom; I reproach myself for it, but I almost dread coming home. When a man has been all day encompassed with sounds and sights of suffering, he naturally longs for cheerful faces and cheerful voices in his own house. Then Martha's pertinacious— I won't say hostility to my little wife— what shall I call it?"

"It is only a lack of sympathy. She is too really good to be hostile to any one."

"Thank you, my darling," he said, "I believe you do her justice."

"I am afraid I have not been as forbearing with her as I ought," I said. "But, oh, Ernest, it is because I have been jealous of her all along!"

"That is really too absurd."

"You certainly have treated her with more deference than you have me. You looked up to her and looked down upon me. At least it seemed so."

"My dear child, you have misunderstood the whole thing. I gave Martha just what she wanted most; she likes to be looked up to. And I gave you what I thought you wanted most— my most tender love. And I expected that I would have your sympathy amidst the trials with which I am burdened, and that with your strong nature I might look to you to help me bear them. I know you have the worst of it, dear child, but then you have twice my strength. I believe women almost always have more than men."

"I have, indeed, misunderstood you. I thought you liked to have them here, and that Martha's not fancying me influenced you against me. But now I know just what you want of me, and I can give it, darling."

After this all our cloud melted away. I only long to go home and show Ernest that he shall have one cheerful face about him, and have one cheerful voice.

August 12

I have had a long letter from Ernest today. He says he hopes he has not been selfish and unkind in speaking of his father and sister as he has done, because he truly loves and honors them both, and wants me to do so, if I can. His father had called them up twice to see him die and to receive his last messages. This always happens when poor Ernest has been up all the previous night; there seems a fatality about it.

Chapter 15

Home again, and with my dear Ernest delighted to see me. Baby is a year old today, and, as usual, father, who seems to abhor anything like a merry-making, took himself off to his room. Tomorrow he will be all the worse for it, and will be sure to have a theological battle with somebody.

October 5

The somebody was his daughter Katherine, as usual. Baby was asleep in my lap and I reached out for a book which proved to be a volume of Shakespeare which had done long service as an ornament to the table, but which nobody ever read on account of the small print. The battle then began thus:

Father— "I regret to see that worldly author in your hands, my daughter."

Daughter— a little mischievously— "Why, were you wanting to talk, father?"

"No, I am too feeble to talk today. My pulse is very weak."

"Let me read aloud to you, then."

"Not from that profane book."

"It would do you good. You never take any recreation. Do let me read a little."

Father gets nervous.

"Recreation is a snare. I must keep my soul ever fixed on divine things."

"But can you?"

"No, alas, no. It is my grief and shame that I do not."

"But if you would indulge yourself in a little harmless mirth now and then, your mind would get rested and you would return to divine things with fresh zeal. Why should not the mind have its seasons of rest as well as the body?"

"We shall have time to rest in heaven. Our business here on earth is to be sober and vigilant because of our adversary; not to be reading plays."

"I don't make reading plays my business, dear father. I make it my rest and amusement."

"Christians do not need amusement; they find rest, refreshment, all they want, in God."

"Do you, father?"

"Alas, no. He seems a great way off."

"To me He seems very near. So near that He can see every thought of my heart. Dear father, it is your disease that makes everything so unreal to you. God is really so near, really loves us so; is so sorry for us! And it seems hard, when you are so good, and so intent on pleasing Him, that you get no comfort out of Him."

"I am not good, my daughter. I am a vile worm of the dust."

"Well, God is good, at any rate, and He would never have sent His Son to die for you if He did not love you." So then I began to sing. Father likes to hear me sing, and the sweet sense I had that all I had been saying was true and more than true, made me sing with joyful heart.

I hope it is not a mere miserable presumption that makes me dare to talk so to poor father. Of course, he is ten times better than I am, and knows ten times as much, but his disease, whatever it is, keeps his mind befogged. I mean to begin now to pray that light may shine into his soul. It would be delightful to see the peace of God shining in that pale, stern face!

March 28

It is almost six months since I wrote that. About the middle of October father had one of his ill turns one night, and we were all called up. He asked for me particularly, and Ernest came for me at last. I was a good deal agitated, and would not stop to half dress myself, and as I had a slight cold already, I suppose I added to it then. At any rate I was taken very sick, and the worst cough I ever had has racked my poor frame almost to pieces. Nearly six months confinement to my room; six months of uselessness during which I have been a mere cumberer of the ground.[19] Poor Ernest! What a hard time he has had! Instead of the cheerful welcome home I was to give him whenever he entered the house, here I have lain exhausted, woe-begone and good for nothing. It is the bitterest disappointment I ever had. My ambition is to be the sweetest, brightest, best of wives;

and what with my childish follies, and my sickness, what a weary life my dear husband has had! But how often I have prayed that God would do His will in defiance, if need be, of mine! I have tried to remind myself of that every day. But I am too tired to write any more.

March 30

This experience of suffering has filled my mind with new thoughts. At one time I was so sick that Ernest sent for mother. Poor mother, she had to sleep with Martha. It was a great comfort to have her here, but I knew by her coming how sick I was, and then I began to ponder the question whether I was ready to die. Death looked to me as a most solemn, momentous event— but there was something very pleasant in the thought of being no longer a sinner, but a redeemed saint, and of dwelling forever in Christ's presence. Father came to see me when I had just reached this point.

"My dear daughter," he asked, "are you prepared to face the Judge of all the earth?"

"No, dear father," I said, "Christ will do that for me."

"Have you no misgivings?"

I could only smile; I had no strength to talk.

Then I heard Ernest— my dear, calm, self-controlled Ernest— burst out crying and rush out of the room. I looked after him, and how I loved him! But I felt that I loved my Saviour infinitely more, and that if He now let me come home to be with Him I could trust Him to be a thousand-fold more to Ernest than I could ever be, and to take care of my darling baby and my precious mother far better than I could. The very gates of heaven seemed open to let me in. And then they were suddenly shut in my face, and I found myself a poor, weak, tempted creature here upon earth. I, who fancied myself an heir of glory, was nothing but a peevish, human creature— very human indeed, overcome if Martha shook the bed, as she always did, irritated if my food did not come at the right moment, or was not of the right sort, hurt and offended if Ernest behaved less anxious and tender than he had been when I was very ill, and in short, my own poor faulty self once more. Oh, what fearful battles I fought for patience, forbearance and unselfishness! What sorrowful tears of shame I shed over hasty, impatient words and fretful tones! No wonder I longed to be gone where weakness would be swallowed up in strength, and sin give place to eternal perfection!

But here I am, and suffering and work lie before me, for which I feel little physical or mental courage. But "blessed be the will of God."

April 5

I was alone with father last evening, Ernest and Martha both being out, and soon saw by the way he fidgeted in his chair that he had something on his mind. So I laid down the book I was reading, and asked him what it was.

"My daughter," he began, "can you bear a plain, honest word from an old man?"

I felt frightened, for I knew I had been impatient to

Martha of late, in spite of all my efforts to the contrary. I am still so miserably unhealthy.

"I have seen many death-beds," he went on; "but I never saw one where there was not some dread of the King of Terrors[20] exhibited; nor one where there was such absolute *certainty* of having found favor with God as to make the hour of departure entirely free from such doubts and such humility as is fitting for a guilty sinner about to face his Judge."

"I never saw such a one, either," I replied; "but there have been many such deaths, and I hardly know of any scene that so honors and magnifies the Lord."

"Yes," he said, slowly; "but they were old, mature, ripened Christians."

"Not always old, dear father. Let me describe to you a scene Ernest described to me only yesterday."

He waved his hand in token that this would delay his coming to the point he was aiming at.

"To speak plainly," he said, "I feel uneasy about you, my daughter. You are young and in the bloom of life, but when death seemed staring you in the face, you expressed no anxiety, asked for no counsel, showed no alarm. It must be pleasant to possess so comfortable a persuasion of our acceptance with God; but is it safe to rest on such an assurance while we know that the human heart is deceitful above all things and desperately wicked?"

"I thank you for the suggestion," I said; "and, dear father, do not be afraid to speak still more plainly. You live in

Your FREE Catalog is ready and waiting for you!*

Just complete and mail us back this card.
Or for faster service—
Call us, toll-free, at:
800.789.8175
or Fax us back at:
516.789.3690

Name _____

Street _____

City _____ State _____

Zip/Postal Code _____ Phone _____

＊ Send our free catalog of great Christian books to all your friends!

Name _____

Street _____

City _____ State _____

Zip/Postal Code _____ Phone _____

Name _____

Street _____

City _____ State _____

Zip/Postal Code _____ Phone _____

Calvary Press Publishing
Catalog Request Processing
P.O. Box 805
Amityville, NY 11701-0805

the house with me, see all my shortcomings and my faults, and I cannot wonder that you think me a poor, weak Christian. But do you really fear that I am deceived in believing that notwithstanding this I do really love my God and Saviour and am His Child?"

"No," he said, hesitating a little, "I can't say that, exactly— I can't say that."

This hesitation distressed me. At first it seemed to me that my life must have uttered a very uncertain sound if those who saw it could misunderstand its language. But then I reflected that it was, at best, a very faulty life, and that its springs of action were not necessarily seen by those looking on.

Father saw my distress and perplexity, and seemed to be touched by them.

Just then Ernest came in with Martha, but seeing that something was wrong, the latter took herself off to her room, which I thought really kind of her.

"What is it, father? What is it, Katy?" asked Ernest, looking from one troubled face to the other.

I tried to explain.

"I think, father, you may safely trust my wife's spiritual interest to me," Ernest said, with some warmth. "You do not understand her. I do. Because there is nothing morbid about her, because she has a sweet, cheerful confidence in Christ, you doubt and misjudge her. You may depend upon it that people are as individual in their piety as in other things, and cannot all be run in one mold. Katy has a playful way of speaking, I know, and often expresses her strongest feelings with what seems like levity, and is, perhaps, a little reckless about being misunderstood in consequence."

He smiled on me, as he thus sought to stand up in my defence, and I never felt so grateful to him in my life. The truth is, I hate sentimentalism so cordially, and have besides such an instinct to conceal my deepest, most sacred emotions, that I do not wonder people misunderstand and misjudge me.

"I did not refer to her playfulness," father returned. "Old people must make allowances for the young; they must make allowances. What pains me is that this child, full of life and felicity as she is, sees death approach without that appropriate awe and terror which is fitting for mortal man."

Ernest was going to reply, but I broke in eagerly upon his answer:

"It is true that I expressed no anxiety when I believed death to be at hand. I felt none. I had given myself away to Christ, and He had received me, and why should I be afraid to take His hand and go where He led me? And it is true that I asked for no counsel. I was too weak to ask questions or to like to have questions asked; but my mind was bright and wide awake while my body was so feeble, and I took counsel of God. Oh, let me read to you two passages from the life of Caroline Fry[21] which will make you understand how a poor sinner looks upon death. The first is an extract from a letter written after learning that her days on earth were numbered.

" 'As many will hear and will not understand, why I want no time of preparation, often desired by far holier ones than I, I tell you why, and shall tell others, and so shall you. It is not because I am so holy, but because I am so sinful. The peculiar character of my religious experience has always been a deep, and agonizing sense of sin; the sin of yesterday, of today, confessed with anguish hard to be endured, and cried for pardon that could not be unheard; each day cleansed anew in Jesus' blood, and each day more and more hateful in my own sight; what can I do in death I have not done in life? What do in this week, when I am told I cannot live, other than I did last week, when I knew it not? Alas, there is but one thing undone, to serve Him better; and the death-bed is no place for *that*. Therefore I say, if I am not ready now, I shall not be by delay, so far as I have to do with it. If *He* has more to do in *me* that is His part. I need not ask Him not to spoil His work by too much haste.' "

"And these are her dying words, a few days later:

" 'This is my bridal-day, the beginning of my life. I wish there could be no mistake about the reason for my desire to depart and to be with Christ. I confess myself the vilest, chiefest of sinners, and I desire to go to Him that I may be rid of the burden of sin— the sin of my nature— not the past, repented of every day, but the present, hourly, momentary sin, which I do commit, or may commit— *the sense of which at times drives me half mad with grief !* "

I shall never forget the expression on father's face, as I

finished reading these remarkable words. He rose slowly from his seat, and came and kissed me on the forehead. Then he left the room, but returned with a large volume, and pointing to a blank page, requested me to copy them there. He complains that I do not write legibly, so I printed them as plainly as I could, with my pen.

June 20

On the first of May, there came to us, with other spring flowers, our little fair-haired, blue-eyed daughter. How rich I felt when I heard Ernest's voice, as he replied to a question asked at the door, proclaim, "Mother and children all well." To think that we, who thought ourselves rich before, are made so much richer now!

But she is not large and vigorous, as little Ernest was, and we cannot rejoice in her without some misgiving. Yet her very frailty makes her precious to us. Little Ernest hangs over her with an almost lover-like pride and devotion, and should she live I can imagine what a protector he will be for her. I have had to give up the care of him to Martha. During my illness I do not know what would have become of him but for her. One of the pleasant events of every day at that time, was her bringing him to me in such exquisite order, his face shining with health and happiness, his hair and clothing so beautifully neat and clean. Now that she has the care of him, she has become very fond of him, and he certainly forms one bond of union between us, for we both heartily agree that he is the handsomest, best, most remarkable child that ever lived, or ever will live.

July 6

I have come home to dear mother with both my children. Ernest says our only hope for baby is to keep her out of the city during the summer months.

What a *petite* wee maiden she is! Where *does* all the love come from? If I had had her always I do not see how I could be more fond of her. And do people call it *living* who never had any children?

July 10

If this darling baby lives, I shall always believe it is owing to my mother's prayers.

I find little Ernest has a passionate temper, and a good deal of self-will. But he has fine qualities. I wish he had a better mother. I am so impatient with him when he is wayward and perverse! What he needs is a firm, gentle hand, moved by no caprice, and controlled by the constant fear of God. He never ought to hear an irritable word, or a sharp tone; but he does hear them, I must admit with grief and shame. The truth is, it is so long since I really felt strong and healthy that I am not myself, and cannot do him justice, poor child. Next to being a perfect wife I want to be a perfect mother. How mortifying, how dreadful in all things to come short of even one's own standard! What approach, then, does one make to God's standard?

Mother seems very happy to have us here, though we make so much trouble. She encourages me in all my attempts to control myself and to control my dear little boy, and the chapters she gives me out of her own experience are as interesting as a novel, and a good deal more instructive.

August 18

Dear Ernest has come to spend a week with us. He is all tired out, as there has been a great deal of sickness in the city, and father has had quite a serious attack. He brought with him a nurse for baby, as one more desperate effort to strengthen her constitution.

I reproached him for doing it without consulting me, but he said mother had written to tell him that I was all worn out and not in a state to have the care of the children. It has been a terrible blow to me. One by one I am giving up the sweetest maternal duties. God means that I shall *be* nothing and do nothing; a mere useless sufferer. But when I tell Ernest so, he says I am everything to him, and that God's children please him just as well when they sit patiently with folded hands, if that is His will, as when they are hard at work. But to be at work, to be useful, to be *necessary* to my husband and children, is just what I want, and I do find it hard to be set against the wall, as it were, like an old piece of furniture no longer of any service. I see now that my first desire has not been to please God, but to please myself, for I am restless under His restraining hand, and find my prison a very narrow one. I would be willing to bear any other trial, if I could only have health and strength for my beloved ones. I pray for patience with bitter tears.

Chapter 16

October 4

We are all at home together once more. The parting with mother was very painful. Every year that she lives now increases her loneliness, and makes me long to give her the shelter of my home. But in the midst of these anxieties, how much I have to make me happy! Little Ernest is the life and soul of the house; the sound of his feet pattering about, and all his prattle, are the sweetest music to my ear; and his heart is brimful of love and joy, so that he shines on us all like a sunbeam. Baby is improving every day, and is one of those tender clinging little things that appeal to everybody's love and sympathy. I never saw a more angelic face than hers. Father sits by the hour looking at her. Today he said:

"Daughter Katherine, this lovely little one is not meant for this sinful world."

"This world needs to be adorned with lovely little ones," I said. "And baby was never so healthy as she is now."

"Do not set your heart too fondly upon her," he returned. "I feel that she is far too dear to me."

"But, father, we could give her to God if He should ask

for her. Surely, we love Him better than we love her."

But as I spoke a sharp pang shot through and through my soul, and I held my little fair daughter closely in my arms, as if I could always keep her there. It may be my conceit, but it really does seem as if poor father was getting a little fond of me. Ever since my own sickness I have felt great sympathy for him, and he feels, no doubt, that I give him something that neither Ernest nor Martha can do, since they were never sick one day in their lives. I do wish he could look more at Christ and at what He has done and is doing for us. The way of salvation is to me a wide path, absolutely radiant with the glory of Him who shines upon it; I see my shortcomings; I see my sins, but I feel myself bathed, as it were, in the resplendent glow that proceeds directly from the throne of God and the Lamb. It seems as if I ought to have some misgivings about my salvation, but I can hardly say that I have one. How strange, how mysterious that is! And here is father, so much older, so much better than I am, creeping along in the dark! I spoke to Ernest about it. He says I owe it to my training, in a great measure, and that my mother is fifty years in advance of her age. But it can't be all that. It was only after *years* of struggle and prayer that God gave me this joy.

November 24

Ernest asked me yesterday if I knew that Amelia and her husband had come here to live, and that she was very ill.

"I wish you would go to see her, dear," he added. "She is a stranger here, and in great need of a friend." I felt extremely disturbed. I have lost my old affection for her, and the idea of meeting her husband was unpleasant.

"Is she very sick?" I asked.

"Yes. She is completely broken down. I promised her that you would go to see her."

"Are you attending her?"

"Yes; her husband came for me himself."

"I don't want to go," I said. "It will be very disagreeable."

"Yes, dear, I know it. But she needs a friend, as I said before."

I put on my things very reluctantly, and went. I found Amelia in a richly-furnished house, but looking untidy and ill-cared-for. She was lying on a couch in her bedroom; three delicate-looking children were playing about, and their nurse sat sewing at the window.

A terrible fit of coughing made it impossible for her to speak for some moments. At last she recovered herself sufficiently to welcome me, by throwing her arms around me and bursting into tears.

"Oh, Katy!" she cried, "would you have known me if we had met in the street? Don't you find me sadly altered?"

"You are changed," I said, "but so am I."

"Yes, you do not look strong. But then you never did. And you are as pretty as ever, while I— oh, Kate! do you remember what round, white arms I used to have? Look at them now!"

And she drew up her sleeve, poor child. Just then I heard a step in the entrance, and her husband sauntered into the room, smoking.

"Do go away, Charles," she said impatiently. "You know how your cigar sets me coughing."

He held out his hand to me with the easy, nonchalant air of one who is accustomed to success and popularity.

I looked at him with an aversion I could not conceal. The few years since we met has changed him so completely that I almost shuddered at the sight of his already bloated face, and at the air that told of a life worse than wasted.

"Do go away, Charles," Amelia repeated.

He threw himself into a chair without paying the least attention to her, and still addressing himself to me again, said:

"Upon my word, you are prettier than ever, and—"

"I will come to see you at another time, Amelia," I said, putting on all the dignity I could condense in my small frame, and rising to take leave.

"Don't go, Katy!" he cried, starting up, "don't go. I want to have a good talk about old times."

Katy, indeed! How dared he? I came away burning with anger and mortification. Is it possible that I ever *loved* such a man? That to gratify that love I defied and grieved my dear mother through a whole year! Oh, from what hopeless misery God saved me, when He snatched me out of the depth of my folly!

December 1

Ernest says I can go to see Amelia with safety now, as her husband has sprained his ankle, and keeps to his own room. So I am going. But, I am sure I shall say something imprudent or unwise, and wish I could think it right to stay away. I hope God will go with me and teach me what words to speak.

December 2

I found Amelia more unhealthy than on my first visit, and she received me again with tears.

"How good you are to come so soon," she began. "I did not blame you for running off the other day; Charley's impertinence was shameful. He said, after you left, that he perceived you had not yet lost your quickness to take offence, but I know he felt that you showed a just displeasure, and nothing more."

"No, I was really angry," I replied. "I find the road to perfection lies up-hill, and I slip back so often that sometimes I despair of ever reaching the top."

"What does the doctor say about me?" she asked. "Does he think me very sick?"

"I dare say he will tell you exactly what he thinks," I returned, "if you ask him. This is his rule with all his patients."

"If I could get rid of this cough I would soon be myself again," she said. "Some days I feel quite bright and well. But if it were not for my poor little children, I would not care much how the thing ended. With the life Charley leads me, I haven't much to look forward to."

"You forget that the children's nurse is in the room," I whispered.

"Oh, I don't mind Charlotte. Charlotte knows how he neglects me, don't you, Charlotte?"

Charlotte was discreet enough to pretend not to hear

this question, and Amelia went on: "It began very soon after we were married. He would go around with other girls exactly as he did before; then when I spoke about it he would just laugh in his easy, good-natured way, but pay no attention to my wishes. Then when I grew more in earnest he would say, that as long as he let me alone I ought to let him alone. I thought that when our first baby came that would sober him a little, but he wanted a boy and it turned out to be a girl. And my being unhappy and crying so much, made the poor thing fretful; it kept him awake at night, so he took another room. After that I saw him less than ever, though now and then he would have a little love-fit, when he would promise to be at home more and treat me with more consideration. We had two more little girls— twins; and then a boy. Charley seemed quite fond of him, and did certainly seem improved, though he was still out a great deal with a set of idle young men, smoking, drinking wine, and I don't know what else. His uncle gave him too much money, and he had nothing to do but to spend it."

"You must not tell me any more now," I said. "Wait until you are stronger."

The nurse rose and gave her something which seemed to refresh her. I went to look at the little girls, who were all pretty, pale-faced creatures, very quiet and mature in their ways.

"I am rested now," said Amelia, "and it does me good to talk to you, because I can see that you are sorry for me."

"I am, indeed!" I cried.

"When our little boy was three months old I took this terrible cold and began to cough. Charley at first reprimanded me for coughing so much; he said it was a habit I had got, and that I ought to cure myself of it. Then the baby began to pine and pine, and the more it wasted away the more I wasted away. And at last it died."

Here the poor child burst out again, and I wiped away her tears as fast as they fell, thankful that she *could* cry.

"After that," she went on, after awhile, "Charley seemed to lose his last particle of affection for me; he kept away more than ever, and once when I besought him not to neglect me and my children so, he said he was well paid for not keeping up his engagement with you, that you had some strength of character, and—"

"Amelia," I interrupted, "do not repeat such things. They only pain and mortify me."

"Well," she sighed, wearily, "this is what he has at last brought me to. I am sick and broken-hearted, and care very little what becomes of me."

There was a long silence. I wanted to ask her if, when earthly refuge failed her, she could not find shelter in the love of Christ. But I have what is, I fear, a morbid terror of seeking the confidence of others. I knelt down at last, and kissed the poor faded face.

"Yes, I knew you would feel for me," she said. "The only pleasant thought I had when Charley insisted on coming here to live was, that I would see you."

"Does your uncle live here, too?" I asked.

"Yes, he came first, and it was that which put it into Charley's head to come. He is very kind to me."

"Yes," I said, "and God is kind, too, isn't He?"

"Kind to let me get sick and disgust Charley? Now, Katy, how can you talk so?" I replied by repeating two lines from a hymn of which I am very fond:

" 'O Saviour, whose mercy severe in its kindness,
  Hath chastened my wanderings, and guided my way.' "

"I don't much care for hymns," she said. "When one is healthy, and everything goes quite to one's mind, it is nice to go to church and sing with the rest of them. But, sick as I am, it isn't so easy to be religious."

"But isn't this the very time to look to Christ for comfort?"

"What's the use of looking anywhere for comfort?" she said, peevishly. "Wait till you are sick and heart-broken yourself, and you'll see that you won't feel much like doing anything but just groan and cry your life out."

"I have been sick, and I know what sorrow means," I said. "And I am glad that I do. For I have learned Christ in that school, and I know that He can comfort when no one else can."

"You always were an odd creature," she replied. "I never pretended to understand half of what you said."

I saw that she was tired, very tired, and so came away. Oh, how I wish that I had been able to make Christ appear to her as He did to me all the way home.

December 24

Father says he does not like Dr. Cabot's preaching. He thinks that it is not doctrinal enough, and that he does not preach enough to sinners. But I can see that it has influenced him already, and that he is beginning to think of God, as manifested in Christ, far more than he used to do. With me he has endless discussions on his and my favorite subjects, and though I can never tell along what path I walked to reach a certain conclusion, the earnestness of my convictions does impress him strangely. I am sure there is a great deal of conceit mixed up with all I say, and then when I compare my life with my own standard of duty, I wonder I ever dare to open my mouth and undertake to help others.

Baby is not at all well. To see a little frail, tender thing really suffering, tears my soul to pieces. I think it would distress me less to give her to God just as she is now, a vital part of my very heart, than to see her live a mere invalid life. But I try to feel, as I know I say, Thy will be done! Little Ernest is the very picture of health and beauty. He has vitality enough for two children. He and his little sister will make very interesting contrasts as they grow older. His ardor and vivacity will rouse her, and her gentleness will soften him.

January 1, 1841

Every day brings its own duty and its own discipline. How is it that I make such slow progress while this is the case? It is a marvel to me why God allows characters like mine to defile His church. I can only account for it with the thought that if I ever am perfected, I shall be a great honor to His name, for surely worse material for building up a temple of the Holy Ghost was never gathered together before. The time may come when those who know me now, crude, childish, incomplete, will look upon me with amazement, saying, "What hath God wrought!" If I knew such a time would never come, I would want to flee into the holes and caves of the earth.

I have everything to inspire me to devotion. My dear mother's influence is always upon me. To her I owe the habit of flying to God in every emergency, and of *believing in prayer*. Then I am in close fellowship with a true man and a true Christian. Ernest has none of my fluctuations; he is always calm and self-possessed. This is partly his natural character; but he has studied the Bible more than any other book, his convictions of duty are fixed because they are drawn from there, and his constant contact with the sick and the suffering has revealed life to him just as it is. How he has helped me on! God bless him for it!

Then I have James. To be with him one half hour is an inspiration. He lives in such blessed communion with Christ that he is in perpetual sunshine, and his happiness fertilizes even this disordered household; there is not a soul in it that does not catch somewhat of his joyousness.

And there are my children! My darling, precious children! For their sakes I am continually constrained to seek after an amended, sanctified life; what I want them to become I must become myself.

So I enter on a new year, not knowing what it will

bring forth, but surely with a thousand reasons for thanksgiving, for joy and for hope.

January 16

One more desperate effort to make harmony out of the discords of my house, and one more failure. Ernest forgot that it was our wedding anniversary, which mortified and pained me, especially as he had made an engagement to dine out. I am always expecting something from life that I never get. Is it so with everybody? I am very uneasy, too, about James. He seems to be growing fond of Lucy's society. I am perfectly sure that she could not make him happy. Is it possible that he does not know what a brilliant young man he is, and that he can have whomever he pleases? It is easy, in theory, to let God plan our own destiny, and that of our friends. But when it comes to a specific case, we imagine we can help His judgments with our poor reason. Well, I must go to Him with this new anxiety, and trust my darling brother's future to Him, if I can.

I shall try to win James' confidence. If it is not Lucy, who or what is it that is making him so thoughtful and serious, yet so wondrously happy?

January 17

I have been trying to find out whether this is a mere notion of mine about Lucy. James laughs, and evades my questions. But he admits that a very serious matter is occupying his thoughts, of which he does not wish to speak presently. May God bless him in whatever it is.

May 1

My delicate little Una's first birthday. Thank God for sparing her to us a year. If He should take her away I would still rejoice that this life was mingled with ours, and has influenced them. Yes, even an unconscious infant is an ever-felt influence in the household; what an amazing thought!

I have given this precious little one away to her Saviour and to mine; living or dying, she is His.

December 13

Writing journals does not seem to be my mission on earth of late. My busy hands find so much else to do! And sometimes when I have been particularly exasperated and tested by the jarring elements that form my home, I have not dared to indulge myself with recording things that ought to be forgotten.

How I long to live in peace with all men, and how I resent interference in the management of my children! If the time ever comes that I live, a spinster of a certain age, in the family of an elder brother, what a model of forbearance, charity, and sisterly lovingkindness I shall be!

Chapter 17

January 1, 1842

I intend to resume my journal, and be more faithful to it this year. How many precious things, said by dear Mrs. Campbell and others, are lost forever, because I did not record them at the time!

I have seen her today. At Ernest's suggestion I have let Susan Green provide her with a comfortable chair, which enables her to sit up during a part of each day. I found her in it, full of gratitude, her sweet, tranquil face shining, as it always is, with a light reflected from heaven itself. She looks like one who has had her struggle with life and conquered it. During last year I visited her often, and gradually learned much of her past history, though she does not love to talk of herself. She has outlived her husband, a houseful of girls and boys, and her ill-health is chiefly the result of years of watching by their sick-beds, and grief at their loss.

For she does not pretend not to grieve, but always says, "It is *complaining* that dishonors God, not grief."

I said to her today: "Doesn't it seem hard when you think of the many happy homes there are in the world, that you should be singled out for such bereavement and loneliness?"

She replied, with a smile: "I am not singled out, dear. There are thousands of God's own dear children, scattered over the world, suffering far more than I do, and I do not think there are many persons in it who are happier than I am. I was bound to my God and Saviour before I knew a sorrow, it is true. But it was by a chain of many links; and every link that dropped away, brought me to Him, till at last, having nothing left, I was shut up to Him, and learned fully, what I had only learned partially, how soul-satisfying He is in Himself."

"You think, then," I said, while my heart died within me, "that husband and children are obstacles in our way, and hinder our getting near to Christ."

"Oh, no!" she cried. "God never gives us hindrances. On the contrary, He means, in making us wives and mothers, to put us into the very conditions of holy living. But if we abuse His gifts by letting them take His place in our hearts, it is an act of love on His part to take them away, or to destroy our pleasure in them. It is delightful," she added, after a pause, "to know that there are some generous souls on earth, who love their dear ones with all their hearts, yet give those hearts unreservedly to Christ. Mine was not one of them."

I had some little service to render her which interrupted our conversation. The offices I have had to have rendered me in my own long days of sickness have taught me to be less meticulous about waiting upon others. I am thankful that God has at last made me willing to do anything in a sick-room that must be done. She thanked me, as she always does, and then I said:

"I have a great many little trials, but they don't do me a bit of good. Or, at least, I don't see that they do."

"No, we never see plants growing," she said.

"And do you really think then, that perhaps I am growing, though unconsciously?"

"I *know* you are, dear child. There can't be life without growth."

This comforted me. I came home, praying all the way, and striving to commit myself entirely to Him in whose school I sit as a learner. Oh, that I were a better scholar! But I do not half learn my lessons, I am heedless and inattentive, and I forget what is taught. Perhaps this is the reason that weighty truths float before my mind's eye at times, but do not fix themselves there.

March 20

I have been much impressed by Dr. Cabot's sermons today. While I am listening to his voice and hear him speak of the beauty and desirableness of the Christian life, I feel as he feels, that I am willing to count all things but dross that I may win Christ. But when I come home to my worldly cares, I get completely absorbed in them, and it is only by a painful wrench that I force my soul back to God. Sometimes I almost envy Lucy her calm nature, which gives her so little trouble. Why do I need to throw my whole soul into whatever I do? Why can't I make so much as an apron for little Ernest without the ardor and eagerness of a soldier marching to battle? I wonder if people of my temperament ever get toned down, and finally learn to take life more coolly?

June 10

My dear little Una has had a long and very severe illness. It seems wonderful that she could survive such sufferings. And it is almost as wonderful that I could look upon them, week after week, without losing my senses.

At first Ernest paid little attention to my repeated entreaties that he would prescribe medicine for her, and some precious time was thus lost. But the moment he was fully aroused to see her danger, there was something beautiful in his devotion. He often walked the room with her by the hour together, and it was touching to see her lying like a pale, crushed lily in his strong arms. One morning she seemed almost gone, and we knelt around her with bursting hearts, to commend her parting soul to Him in whose arms we were about to place her. But it seemed as if all He asked of us was to come to that point, for then He gave her back to us, and she is still ours, only seven-fold dearer. I was so thankful to see dear Ernest's faith triumphing over his heart, and making him so ready to give up even this little lamb without a word. Yes, we will give our children to Him if He asks for them. He shall never have to *snatch* them from us by force.

October 4

We have had a quiet summer in the country, that is, I have with my darling little ones. This is the fourth birthday of our son and heir, and he has been full of health and vitality, enjoying everything with all his heart. How he lights up our somber household! Father has been fasting today, and is so worn out and so nervous in consequence, that he could not bear the sound of the children's voices. I wish, if he must fast, he would do it moderately, and do it all the time. Now he goes without food until he is ready to sink, and then he eats quantities of improper food. If Martha could only see how mischievous all this is for him. After the children had been hustled out of the way, and I had got them both off to bed, he said in his most doleful manner, "I hope, my daughter, that you are faithful to your son. He has now reached the age of four years, and is a remarkably intelligent child. I hope you teach him that he is a sinner, and that he is in a state of condemnation."

"Now, father, don't" I said. "You are all tired out, and do not know what you are saying. I would not have little Ernest hear you for the world."

Poor father! He fairly groaned.

"You are responsible for that child's soul," he said; "you have more influence over him than all the world beside."

"I know it," I said, "and sometimes I feel ready to sink when I think of the great work God has entrusted to me. But my poor child will learn that he is a sinner only too soon, and before that dreadful day arrives I want to fortify his soul with the only antidote against the misery that knowledge will give him. I want him to see his Redeemer in all His love, and all His beauty, and to love Him with all his heart and soul, and mind and strength. Dear father, pray for him, and pray for me, too."

"I do, I will," he said, solemnly. And then followed the inevitable long fit of silent musing, when I often wonder what is passing in that suffering soul. For a sufferer he certainly is who sees a great and good and terrible God who cannot look upon iniquity, and does not see His risen Son, who has paid the debt we owe, and lives to intercede for us before the throne of the Father.

January 1, 1843

James came to me yesterday with a letter he had been writing to mother. "I want you to read this before it goes," he said, "for you ought to know my plans as soon as mother does."

I did not get time to read it until after tea. Then I came up here to my room, and sat down curious to know what was coming.

Well, I thought I loved him as much as one human being could love another, already, but now my heart embraced him with a fervor and delight that made me so happy that I could not speak a word when I knelt down to tell my Saviour all about it.

He said that he had been led, within a few months, to make a new consecration of himself to Christ and to Christ's cause on earth, and that this had resulted in his choosing the life of a missionary, instead of settling down, as he had intended to do, as a city physician. Such expressions of personal love to Christ, and delight in the thought of serving Him, I never read. I could only marvel at what God had wrought in his soul.

For me to live to Christ seems natural enough, for I have been driven to Him not only by sorrow but by sin. Every outbreak of my hasty temper sends me weeping and penitent to the foot of the cross, and I love much because I have been forgiven much. But James, as far as I know, has never had a sorrow, except my father's death, and I that had no apparent religious effect. And his natural character is perfectly beautiful. He is as warm-hearted and loving and simple and guileless as a child, and has nothing of my intemperance, hastiness and quick temper. I have often thought that she would be a rare woman who could win and wear such a heart as his. Life has done little but smile upon him; he is handsome and talented and attractive; everybody is fascinated by him, everybody caresses him; and yet he has turned his back on the world that has dealt so kindly with him, and given himself, as Edwards[22] says, "clean away to Christ!" Oh, how thankful I am! And yet to let him go! My only brother— mother's only son! But I know what *she* will say; she will bid him God-speed!

Ernest came upstairs, looking tired and worn-out. I read the letter to him. It impressed him strangely; but he only said:

"This is what we might expect, who knew James, dear fellow!"

But when we knelt down to pray together, I saw how

he was touched, and how his soul kindled within him in harmony with that consecrated, devoted spirit. Dear James! it must be mother's prayers that have done for him this wondrous work that is usually the slow growth of years; and this is the mother who prays for you, Katy! So take courage!

January 2

James means to study theology as well as medicine, it seems. That will keep him with us for some years. Oh, is it selfish to take his view of it? Alas, the spirit is willing to have him go, but the flesh is weak, and cries out.

October 22

Amelia came to see me today. She has been traveling, for her health, and certainly looks much improved.

"Charley and I are quite good friends again," she began. "We have traveled about everywhere, and have a delightful time. What a snug little box of a house you have!"

"It is inconveniently small," I said, "for our family is large, and the doctor needs more office room."

"Does he receive patients here? How horrid! Don't you hate to have people with all sorts of ills and aches in the house? It must depress your spirits."

"I dare say it would if I saw them; but I never do."

"I would like to see your children. Your husband says you are perfectly devoted to them."

"As I suppose all mothers are," I replied, laughing.

"As to that," she returned, "people differ."

The children were brought down. She admired little Ernest, as everybody does, but only glanced at the baby.

"What a sickly-looking little thing!" she said. "But this boy is a splendid fellow! Ah, if mine had lived he would have been just such a child! But some people have all the trouble and others all the comfort. I am sure I don't know what I have done that I should have to lose my only boy, and have nothing left but girls. To be sure, I can afford to dress them elegantly, and as soon as they get old enough I mean to have them taught all sorts of accomplishments. You can't imagine what a relief it is to have plenty of money!"

"Indeed I can't!" I replied; "it is quite beyond the reach of my imagination."

"My uncle— that is to say Charley's uncle— has just given me a carriage and horses for my own use. In fact, he heaps everything upon me. Where do you go to church?"

I told her, reminding her that Dr. Cabot was its pastor.

"Oh, I forgot! Poor Dr. Cabot! Is he as old-fashioned as ever?"

"I don't know what you mean," I cried. "He is as good as ever, if not better. His health is very delicate, and that one thing seems to be a blessing to him."

"A blessing! Why, Kate Mortimer! Kate Elliott, I mean. It is a blessing I, for one, am very willing to dispense with. But you always did say peculiar things. Well, I dare say Dr. Cabot is very good and all that, but his church is not a fashionable one, and Charley and I go to Dr. Bellamy's.

That is, I go once a day, pretty regularly, and Charley goes when he feels like it. Good-bye. I must go now; I have all my fall shopping to do. Have you done yours? Suppose you jump into the carriage and go with me? You can't imagine how it passes away the morning to drive from shop to shop looking over the new goods."

"There seem to be a number of things I can't imagine," I replied, dryly. "You must excuse me this morning."

She took her leave. I looked at her rich dress as she gathered it about her and swept away, and recalled all her empty, frivolous talk with contempt.

She and Ch—, her husband, I mean, are well matched. They need their money, and their palaces and their fine clothes and handsome furnishings, for they have nothing else. How thankful I am that I am as unlike them as ex—

October 30

I'm sure I don't know what I was going to say when I was interrupted just then. Something in the way of self-glorification, most likely. I remember the contempt with which I looked after Amelia as she left our house, and the pinnacle on which I sat perched for some days, when I compared my life with hers. Alas, it was my view of life of which I was lost in admiration, for I am sure that if I ever come under the complete dominion of Christ's gospel I shall not know the sentiment of contempt. I feel truly ashamed and sorry that I am still so far from being penetrated with that spirit.

My pride has had a terrible fall. As I sat on my throne, looking down on all the Amelias in the world, I felt a profound pity at their delight in petty trifles, their love of position, of mere worldly show and passing vanities.

"They are all alike," I said to myself. "They are incapable of understanding a character like mine, or the exalted, ennobling principles that govern me. They crave the applause of this world, they are satisfied with fine clothes, fine houses, fine furnishings. They think and talk of nothing else; I have not one idea in common with them. I see the emptiness and hollowness of these things. I am absolutely unworldly; my ambition is to attain whatever they, in their blind folly and ignorance, absolutely despise."

Thus communing with myself, I was not a little pleased to hear Dr. Cabot and his wife announced. I hastened to meet them and to display to them the virtues I so admired in myself. They had hardly a chance to utter a word. I spoke eloquently of my contempt for worldly vanities, and of my enthusiastic longings for a higher life. I even went into particulars about the shortcomings of some of my acquaintances, though faint misgivings as to the propriety of such remarks on those absent made me half repent of the words I still kept uttering. When they finally left I rushed to my room with my heart beating, my cheeks all in a glow, and caught up and caressed the children in a way that seemed to astonish them. Then I took my work and sat down to sew. What a horrible reaction now took place! I saw my refined, subtle, disgusting pride, just as I suppose Dr.

and Mrs. Cabot saw it! I sat covered with confusion, shocked at myself, shocked at the weakness of human nature. Oh, to get back the good opinion of my friends! To recover my own self-respect! But this was impossible. I threw down my work and walked about my room. There was a terrible struggle in my soul. I saw that instead of brooding over the display I had made of myself to Dr. Cabot I ought to be thinking solely of my appearance in the sight of God, who could see far more plainly than any earthly eye could all my miserable pride and self-conceit. But I could not do that, and fretted about till I was worn out, body and soul. At last I sent the children away, and knelt down and told the whole story to Him who *knew what I was* when He had compassion on me, called me by my name, and made me His own child. And here I found a certain peace. Christian, on his way to the celestial city, met and fought his Apollyons and his giants, too; but he got there at last!

Chapter 18

November 12

This morning Ernest received an early summons to visit Amelia. I got out of all manner of patience with him because he would take his bath and eat his breakfast before he went, and would have driven any one else distracted by my hurry and flurry.

"She has had a hemorrhage!" I cried. "Do, Ernest, make haste."

"Of course," he returned, "that would come, sooner or later."

"You don't mean," I said, "that she has been in danger of this all along?"

"I certainly do."

"Then it was very unkind of you not to tell me so."

"I told you at the outset that her lungs were diseased."

"No, you told me no such thing. Oh, Ernest, is she going to die?"

"I did not know you were so fond of her," he said, apologetically.

"It is not that," I cried. "I am distressed at the thought

of the worldly life she has been living— at my never try-ing to influence her for her good. If she is in danger, you will tell her so? Promise me that."

"I must see her before I make such a promise," he said, and left.

I flew up to my room and threw myself on my knees, sorrowful, self-condemned. I had thrown away my last opportunity of speaking a word to her in season, though I had seen how much she needed one, and now she was go-ing to die! Oh, I hope God will forgive me, and hear the prayers I have offered for her!

Evening

Ernest says he had a most distressing scene at Amelia's this morning. She insisted on knowing what he thought of her, and then burst out into bitter complaints and lamenta-tions, charging it to her husband that she had this disease, declaring that she could not, and would not die, and insist-ing that he *must* prevent it. Her uncle urged for a consulta-tion of physicians, to which Ernest consented, of course, though he says no mortal power can save her now. I asked him how her husband appeared, to which he made the evasive answer that he appeared just as one would expect him to do.

December 6

Amelia was so determined to see me that Ernest thought it best for me to go. I found her looking very feeble.

"Oh, Katy," she began at once, "do make the doctor say

that I shall get well!"

"I wish he could say so with truth," I answered. "Dear Amelia, try to think how happy God's own children are when they are with Him."

"I can't think," she replied. "I do not want to think. I want to forget all about it. If it were not for this terrible cough I could forget it, for I am really a great deal better than I was a month ago."

I did not know what to say or what to do.

"May I read a hymn or a few verses from the Bible?" I finally asked.

"Just as you like," she said, indifferently.

I read a verse now and then, but she looked tired, and I prepared to go.

"Don't go," she cried. "I do not dare to be alone. Oh, what a terrible, terrible thing it is to die! To leave this bright, beautiful world, and be nailed up in a coffin and buried up in a cold, dark grave!"

"Nay," I said, "to leave this poor sick body there, and to fly to a world ten thousand times brighter, more beautiful than this."

"I had just got to feeling nearly well," she said, "and I had everything I wanted, and Charley was quite good to me, and I kept my little girls looking like fairies, just from fairy-land. Everybody said they wore the most picturesque costumes when they were dressed according to my taste. And I have got to go and leave them, and Charley will be marrying somebody else, and saying to her all the nice things he has said to me."

"I really must go now," I said. "You are wearing

yourself all out."

"I declare you are crying." she exclaimed. "You do pity me after all."

"Indeed I do," I said, and came away, heartsick.

Ernest says there is nothing I can do for her now but to pray for her, since she does not really believe herself in danger, and has a vague feeling that if she can once convince him how much she wants to live, he will use some vigorous measures to restore her. Martha is to watch with her tonight. Ernest will not let me.

January 18, 1843

Our wedding anniversary passed unobserved. Amelia's suffering condition absorbs us all. Martha spends much time with her, and prepares almost all the food she eats.

January 20

I have seen poor Amelia once more, and perhaps for the last time. She has failed rapidly of late, and Ernest says may drop away at almost any time.

When I went in she took me by the hand, and with great difficulty, and at intervals said something like this:

"I have made up my mind to it, and I know it must come. I want to see Dr. Cabot. Do you think he would be willing to visit me after my neglecting him so?"

"I am sure he would," I cried.

"I want to ask him if he thinks I was a Christian at that time— you know when. If I was, then I need not be so afraid to die."

"But, dear Amelia, what he thinks is very little to the purpose. The question is not whether you ever gave yourself to God, but whether you are His now. But I ought not to talk to you. Dr. Cabot will know just what to say."

"No, but I want to know what *you* thought about it."

I felt distressed, as I looked at her wasted dying figure, to be called on to help decide such a question. But I knew what I ought to say, and said it: "Don't look back to the past; it is useless. Give yourself to Christ right now."

She shook her head.

"I don't know how," she said. "Oh, Katy, pray to God to let me live long enough to get ready to die. I have led a worldly life. I shudder at the bare thought of dying; I *must* have time."

"Don't wait for time," I said, with tears, "get ready now, this minute. A thousand years would not make you more fit to die."

So I came away, weary and heavy-laden, and on the way home stopped to tell Dr. Cabot all about it, and by this time he is with her.

March 1

Poor Amelia's short race on earth is over. Dr. Cabot saw her every few days and says he hopes she did depart in Christian faith, though without Christian joy. I have not seen her since that last interview. That moved me so much that Ernest would not let me go back again.

Martha has been there nearly the whole time for three or four weeks, and I really think it has done her good. She seems less absorbed in mere outside things, and more lenient toward me and my failings.

I do not know what is to become of those motherless little girls. I wish I could take them into my own home, but, of course, that is not even to be thought of at this juncture. Ernest says their father seemed nearly distracted when Amelia died, and that his uncle is going to send him off to Europe immediately.

I have been talking with Ernest about Amelia. "What do you think," I asked, "about her last days on earth? Was there really any preparation for death?"

"These scenes are very painful," he returned. "Of course there is but one real preparation for Christian dying, and that is Christian living."

"But the sick-room often does what a prosperous life never did!"

"Not often. Sick persons delude themselves, or are deluded by their friends; they do not believe they are really about to die. Besides, they are bewildered and exhausted by disease, and what mental strength they have is occupied with studying symptoms, watching for the doctor, and the like. I do not now recall a single instance where a worldly Christian died a happy, joyful death, in all my practice."

"Well, in one sense it makes no difference whether they die happily or not. The question is do they die in the Lord?"

"It may make no vital difference to them, but we must not forget that God is honored or dishonored by the way a Christian dies, as well as by the way in which he lives.

There is great significance in the description given in the Bible of the death by which Peter would *'Glorify God'* (John 21:19); to my mind it implies that to die well is to live well."

"But how many thousands die suddenly, or of such exhausting disease that they cannot honor God by even one feeble word."

"Of course, I do not refer to such cases. All I ask is that those whose minds are clear, who are able to attend to all other final details, should let it be seen what the gospel of Christ can do for poor sinners in the great demands of life, giving Him the glory. I can tell you, my darling, that standing, as I so often do, by dying beds, this whole subject has become one of great magnitude to my mind. And it gives me positive personal pain to see heirs of the eternal kingdom, made such by the ignominious death of their Lord, go shrinking and weeping to the full possession of their inheritance."

Ernest is right, I am sure, but how shall the world, even the Christian world, be convinced that it may have blessed foretastes of heaven while yet plodding upon earth, and faith to go there joyfully, for the simple asking?

Poor Amelia! But she understands it all now. It is a blessed thing to have this great faith, and it is a blessed thing to have a Saviour who accepts it when it is but a mere grain of mustard-seed!

May 24

I celebrated my little Una's third birthday by presenting her with a new brother. Both the children welcomed him with delight that was of itself compensation enough for all it cost me to get up such a celebration. Martha takes a most prosaic view of this proceeding, in which she detects *malice prepense* on my part. She says I shall now have one mouth the more to fill, and two feet the more to shoe; more disturbed nights, more laborious days, and less leisure for visiting, reading, music, and drawing.

Well! this is one side of the story, to be sure, but I look at the other. Here is a sweet, fragrant mouth to kiss; here are two more feet to make music with their pattering about my nursery. Here is a soul to train for God, and the body in which it dwells is worthy all it will cost, since it is the abode of a kingly tenant. I may see less of friends, but I have gained one dearer than them all, to whom, while I minister in Christ's name, I make a willing sacrifice of what little leisure for my own recreation my other darlings had left me. Yes, my precious baby, you are welcome to your mother's heart, welcome to her time, her strength, her health, her most tender cares, to her life-long prayers! Oh, how rich I am, how truly, how wondrously blest!

June 5

We begin to be woefully crowded. We need a larger house, or a smaller household. I am afraid I secretly, down at the bottom of my heart, wish Martha and her father could give place to my little ones. May God forgive me if this is so! It is a poor time for such emotions when He has just given me another darling child, for whom I have as rich and ample a love as if I had spent no affection on the other two. I have made myself especially kind to poor father and to Martha, lest they should perceive how inconvenient it is to have them here, and be pained by it. I would not for the world rob them of what little satisfaction they may derive from living with us. But, oh! I am so selfish, and it is so hard to practice the very law of love I preach to my children! Yet I want this law to rule and reign in my home, that it may be a little heaven below, and I will not, no, I *will* not, cease praying that it may be such, no matter what it costs me. Poor father! poor old man! I will try to make your home so sweet and home-like to you that when you change it for heaven it shall be but a transition from one bliss to a higher!

Evening

Soon after writing that I went down to see father, whom I have had to neglect of late, baby has so used up both time and strength. I found him and Martha engaged in what seemed to be an exciting debate, as Martha had a fiery little red spot on each cheek, and was knitting furiously. I was about to retreat, when she got up in a flurried way and went off, saying, as she went:

"You tell her, father; I can't."

I went up to him tenderly and took his hand. Ah, how gentle and loving we are when we have just been speaking to God!

"What is it, dear father?" I asked; "is anything troubling you?"

"She is going to be married," he replied.

"Oh, father!" I cried, "how n—" nice, I was going to

say, but stopped just in time.

All my abominable selfishness that I thought I had left at my Master's feet ten minutes before now came trooping back in full force.

"She's going to be married; she'll go away, and will take her father to live with her! I can have room for my children, and room for mother! Every element of discord will now leave my home, and Ernest will see what I really am!"

These were the thoughts that rushed through my mind, and that illuminated my face.

"Does Ernest know?" I asked.

"Yes, Ernest has known it for some weeks."

Then I felt injured and inwardly accused Ernest of unkindness in keeping so important a fact a secret. But when I went back to my children, vexation with him took flight at once. The coming of each new child strengthens and deepens my desire to be what I would have it become; makes my faults more loathsome in my eyes, and elevates my whole character. What a blessed discipline of joy and of pain my married life has been; how thankful I am to reap its fruits even while pricked by its thorns!

June 21

It seems that the happy man who has wooed Martha and won her is no less a personage than old Mr. Underhill. His ideal of a woman is one who has no nerves, no sentiment, no backaches, no headaches, who will see that the wheels of his household machinery are kept well oiled, so that he need never hear them creak, and who, in addition to her other accomplishments, believes in him and will be kind enough to live for ever for his private accommodation. This *exposé* of his sentiments he has made to me in a loud, cheerful, pompous way, and he has also favored me with a description of his first wife, who lacked all these qualifications, and was obliging enough to depart in peace at an early stage of their married life, meekly preferring thus to make way for a worthier successor. Mr Underhill, with all his foibles, however, is on the whole a good man. He intends to take Amelia's little girls into his own home, and be a father, as Martha will be a mother, to them. For this reason he hurries on the marriage, after which they will all go at once to his home in the country, which is of easy access, and which he says he is sure father will enjoy. Poor old father! I hope he will, but when the subject is alluded to he maintains a somber silence, and it seems to me he never spent so many days alone in his room, brooding over his misery, as he has of late. Oh, that I could comfort him.

July 12

The marriage was scheduled for the first of the month, as old Mr. Underhill wanted to get out of town before the Fourth. As the time drew near, Martha began to pack father's trunk as well as her own, and brush in and out of his room till he had no rest for the sole of his foot, and seemed as forlorn as a pelican in the wilderness.[23]

I know no more striking picture of desolation than

that presented by one of these quaint birds, standing upon a single leg, feeling as the story has it, "den Jammer und das Elend der Welt."[24]

On the last evening in June we all sat together on the porch, enjoying, each in our own way, a refreshing breeze that had sprung up after a sultry day. Father was quieter than usual, and seemed very languid. Ernest who, out of regard to Martha's last evening at home, had joined our little circle, observed this, and said, cheerfully:

"You will feel much better as soon as you are once more out of the city, father."

Father made no reply for some minutes, and when he did speak we were all startled to find that his voice trembled as if he were shedding tears. We could not understand what he said. I went to him and made him lean his head upon me as he often did when it ached. He took my hand in both his.

"You do love the old man a little?" he asked in the same tremulous and faltering voice.

"Indeed, I do!" I cried, greatly touched by his helpless appeal, "I love you dearly father. And I shall miss you sadly."

"Must I go away then?" he whispered. "Cannot I stay here until the Lord summons me? It will not be long, it will not be long, my child."

With the cry of a hurt animal, Martha sprang up and rushed past us into the house. Ernest followed her, and we heard them talking together a long time. At last Ernest joined us.

"Father," he said, "Martha is a good deal wounded and disappointed at your reluctance to go with her. She threatens to break off her engagement rather than to be separated from you. I really think you would be better off with her than with us. You would enjoy country life, because it is what you have been accustomed to; you could spend hours of every day in driving around; just what your health requires."

Father did not reply. He took Ernest's arm and tottered into the house. Then we had a most painful scene. Martha reminded him with bitter tears that her mother had committed him to her with her last breath and set before him all the advantages he would have in her house over ours. Father sat pale and inflexible, tear after tear rolling down his cheeks. Ernest looked distressed and ready to sink. As for me I cried with Martha, and with her father by turns, and clung to Ernest with a feeling that all the foundations of the earth were giving way. It came time for evening prayers, and Ernest prayed as he rarely does, for he is rarely so moved. He quieted us all by a few simple words of appeal to Him who loved us, and father then consented to spend the summer with Martha if he might call our home his home, and be with us through the winter. But this was not till long after the rest of us went to bed, and a hard battle with Ernest. He says Ernest is his favorite child, and that I am his favorite daughter, and our children inexpressibly dear to him. I am ashamed to write down what he said of me. Besides, I am sure there is a wicked, wicked triumph over Martha in my secret heart. I am too elated with his extraordinary preference for us, to sympathize with her mortification and grief as I ought. Something whispered that she who has never pitied me deserves no pity now. But I do not like this mean and narrow spirit in myself, nay more, I hate and abhor it.

The marriage took place and they all went off together, father's rigid, white face, whiter, more rigid than ever. I am to go to mother's with the children at once. I feel that a great stone has been rolled away from before the door of my heart; the one human being who refused me a kindly smile, a sympathizing word, has gone, never to return. May God go with her and give her a happy home, and make her true and loving to those motherless little ones!

Chapter 19

October 1

I have had a charming summer with dear mother; and now I have the great joy, so long deferred, of having her in my own home. Ernest has been very cordial about it, and James has settled up all her worldly affairs, so that she has nothing to do now but to love us and let us love her. It is a pleasant picture to see her with my little darlings about her, telling the old sweet story she told me so often, and making God and Heaven and Christ such blissful realities. As I listen, I realize that it is to her I owe that early, deep-seated longing to please the Lord Jesus, which I never remember as having a beginning, or an ending, though it did have its fluctuations. And it is another pleasant picture to see her sit in her own old chair, which Ernest was thoughtful enough to have brought for her, pondering cheerfully over her Bible and her Thomas à Kempis just as I have seen her do ever since I can remember. And there is still a third pleasant picture, only that it is a new one; it is as she sits at my right hand at the table, the living personification of the blessed gospel of good tidings, with father, opposite, the fading image of the law given by Moses. For father has come back; father and all his ailments, his pill-boxes, his fits of despair and his fits of dying. But he is quiet and gentle, and even loving, and as he sits in his corner, his Bible on his knees, I see how much more he reads the New Testament than he used to do, and that the fourteenth chapter of St. John almost opens to him of itself.

I must do Martha the justice to say that her absence, while it increases my domestic peace and happiness, increases my cares also. What with the children, the housekeeping, the thought for mother's little comforts and the concern for father's, I am like a bit of chaff driven before the wind, and always in a hurry. There are so many stitches to be taken, so many things to pass through one's brain! Mother says no mortal woman ought to undertake so much, but what can I do? While Ernest is straining every nerve to pay off those debts, I must do all the needlework, and we must get along with servants whose lack of skill makes them willing to put up with low wages. Of course I cannot tell mother this, and I really believe she thinks I scrimp and pinch and overdo out of mere stinginess.

December 30

Ernest came to me today with our accounts for the last three months. He looked quite worried, for him, and asked me if there were any expenses we could cut down.

My heart jumped up into my mouth, and I said in an irritated way:

"I am killing myself with over-work now. Mother

says so. I sew every night till twelve o'clock, and I feel all worn out."

"I did not mean that I wanted you to do any more than you are doing now, dear," he said, kindly. "I know you are all worn out, and I look on this state of feverish activity with great anxiety. Are all these stitches absolutely necessary?"

"You men know nothing about such things," I said, while my conscience pricked me as I went on hurrying to finish the fifth tuck in one of Una's little dresses. "Of course I want my children to look decent."

Ernest sighed.

"I really don't know what to do," he said, in a hopeless way. "Father's persisting in living with us is throwing a burden on you, that with all your other cares is quite too much for you. I see and feel it every day. Don't you think I had better explain this to him and let him go to Martha's?"

"No, indeed!" I said. "He'll stay here if it kills me, poor old man!"

Ernest began once more to look over the bills. "I don't know how it is," he said, "but since Martha left us our expenses have increased a good deal."

Now the truth is that when Aunty paid me most generously for teaching her children, I did not dare to offer my earnings to Ernest, lest he should be annoyed. So I had quietly used it for household expenses, and it had held out until about the time of Martha's marriage. Ernest's injustice was just as painful, just as insufferable as if he had known this, and I now burst out with whatever my grated, overtaxed nerves impelled me to say, like one possessed.

Ernest was annoyed and surprised.

"I thought we had finished with these things," he said, and gathering up the papers he went off.

I rose and locked my door and threw myself down upon the floor in an agony of shame, anger, and physical exhaustion. I did not know how large a part of what seemed mere childish ill-temper was really the cry of exasperated nerves, that had been on too strained a tension, and silent too long, and Ernest did not know it either. How could he? His profession kept him for hours every day in the open air; there were times when his work was done and he could take entire rest; and his health is absolutely perfect. But I did not make any excuse for myself at the moment. I was overwhelmed with the sense of my utter unfitness to be a wife and a mother.

Then I heard Ernest try to open the door, and finding it locked, he knocked, calling pleasantly: "It is I, darling; let me in."

I opened it reluctantly enough.

"Come," he said, "put on your things and drive about with me on my rounds. I have no long visits to make, and while I am seeing my patients you will be getting the air, which you need."

"I do not want to go," I said. "I do not feel well enough. Besides, there's my work."

"You can't see to sew with these red eyes," he declared. "Come! I prescribe a drive, as your physician."

"Oh, Ernest, how kind, how forgiving you are!" I cried, running into the arms he held out to me. "If you knew how ashamed, how sorry, I am!"

"And if you only knew how ashamed and sorry I am!" he returned. "I ought to have seen how you were taxing and over-taxing yourself, doing your own work and Martha's too. It must not continue."

By this time, with a veil over my face, he had gotten me downstairs and out into the air, which fanned my fiery cheeks and cooled my heated brain. It seemed to me that I have had all this tempest about nothing at all, and that with a character still so undisciplined, I was utterly unworthy to be either a wife or a mother. But when I tried to say so in broken words, Ernest comforted me with the gentleness and tenderness of a woman.

"Your character is not undisciplined, my darling," he said. "Your nervous organization is very peculiar, and you have had unusual cares and trials from the beginning of our married life. I ought not to have confronted you with my father's debts at a moment when you had every reason to look forward to freedom from most petty financial concerns and other cares."

"Don't say so," I interrupted. "If you had not told me you had this draft on your resources I would have always suspected you of meanness. For you know, dear, you have kept me— that is to say— well you could not help it, but I suppose men can't understand how many demands are made upon a mother for money almost every day. I got along very well until the children came, but since then it has been very hard indeed."

"Yes," he said, "I am sure it has. But let me finish what

I was going to say. I want you to make a distinction for yourself, which I made for you, between mere ill-temper, and the irritability that is the result of a goaded state of the nerves. Until you do that, nothing can be done to relieve you from what I am sure distresses and grieves you exceedingly. Now, I suppose that whenever you speak to me or the children in this irritated way you lose your own self-respect, for the time, at least, and feel degraded in the sight of God also."

"Oh, Ernest! there are no words in any language that mean enough to express the anguish I feel when I speak quick, impatient words to you, the one human being in the universe whom I love with all my heart and soul, and to my darling little children who are almost as dear! I pray and mourn over it day and night. God only knows how I hate myself on account of this one horrible sin!"

"It is a sin only as you deliberately and willfully fulfill the conditions that lead to such results. Now I am sure if you could once make up your mind in the fear of God, *never* to undertake more work of any sort than you can carry on calmly, quietly, without hurry or flurry, and the *instant* you find yourself growing nervous and like one out of breath, would stop and take breath, you would find this simple, common-sense rule doing for you what no prayers or tears could ever accomplish. Will you try it for one month, my darling?"

"But we can't afford it," I cried, with almost a groan. "Why, you have told me this very day that our expenses must be cut down, and now you want me to add to them by doing less work. But the work must be done. The children must be clothed, and there is not end to the stitches to be taken for them, and your stockings must be mended—you make enormous holes in them! and you don't like it if you ever find a button lacking to a shirt or your supply of shirts getting low."

"All you say may be very true," he returned, "but I am determined that you shall not be driven to desperation as you have been of late."

By this time we had reached the house where his visit was to be made, and I had nothing to do but lean back and consider all he had been saying, over and over again, and to see its reasonableness while I could not see what was to be done for my relief. Ah, I have often felt in moments of bitter grief at my impatience with my children, that perhaps God pitied more than He blamed me for it! And now my dear husband was doing the same!

When Ernest had finished his visit we drove on again in silence.

At last I asked: "Do tell me, Ernest, if you worked out this problem all by your self?"

He smiled a little.

"No, I did not. But I have had a patient for two or three years whose case has interested me a good deal, and for whom I finally prescribed just as I have done for you. The thing worked like a charm, and she is now physically and morally quite well."

"I dare say her husband is a rich man," I said.

"He is not as poor as your husband, at any rate,"

Ernest replied. "But rich or poor I am determined not to sit looking on while you exert yourself so far beyond your strength. Just think, dear, suppose for fifty or a hundred or two hundred dollars a year you could buy a sweet, cheerful, quiet tone of mind, would you hesitate one moment to do so? And you can do it if you will. You are not *ill*-tempered but *quick*-tempered; the irritability which annoys you so is a physical infirmity which will disappear the moment you cease to be goaded into it by that exacting mistress you have hitherto been to yourself."

All this sounded very plausible while Ernest was talking, but the moment I got home I snatched up my work from mere force of habit.

"I may as well finish this as it is begun," I said to myself, and the stitches flew from my needle like sparks of fire. Little Ernest came and begged for a story, but I put him off. Then Una wanted to sit in my lap, but I told her I was too busy. In the course of an hour the influence of the fresh air and of Ernest's talk had nearly lost their power over me; my thread kept breaking, the children leaned on and tired me, the baby woke up and cried, and I got all out of patience.

"Do go away, Ernest," I said, "and let mamma have a little peace. Don't you see how busy I am? Go and play with Una like a good boy." But he would not go, and kept teasing Una till she, too, began to cry, and she and baby made a regular concert of it.

"Oh, dear!" I sighed, "this work will never be done!" and threw it down impatiently, and took the baby impatiently, and began to walk up and down with him impatiently. I was not willing that this little darling, whom I love so dearly, should get through with his nap and interrupt my work; yet I was displeased with myself, and tried by kissing him to make some amends for the hasty, unpleasant tones with which I had grieved him and frightened the other children. This evening Ernest came to me with a larger sum of money than he had ever given me at one time.

"Now every cent of this is to be spent," he said, "in having work done. I know any number of poor women who will be thankful to have all you can give them."

Dear me! it is easy to talk, and I do feel grateful to Ernest for his thoughtfulness and kindness. But I am almost in rags, and *need* every cent of this money to make myself decent. I am positively ashamed to go anywhere, my clothes are so shabby. Besides, supposing I leave off sewing and all sorts of over-doing of a similar nature, I must still nurse my baby, I suppose, and be up with him nights and the others will have their cross days and their sick days, and father will have his. Alas, there can be for me no royal road to a "sweet, cheerful, quiet tone of mind!"

January 1, 1844

Mother says Ernest is entirely right in forbidding my working so hard. I must admit that I already feel better. I have all the time I need to read my Bible and to pray now, and the children do not irritate and annoy me as they did. Who knows but I shall yet become quite amiable?

Ernest made his father very happy today by telling him that the last of those wretched debts is paid. I think that he might have told me that this deliverance was near at hand. I did not know but that we had years of these struggles with poverty before us. What with the relief from this anxiety, my improved state of health, and father's pleasure, I am in splendid spirits today. Ernest, too, seems wonderfully cheerful, and we both feel that we may now look forward to a quiet happiness we have never known. With such a husband and such children as mine, I ought to be the most grateful creature on earth. And I have dear mother and James besides. I don't quite know what to think about James' relation to Lucy. He is so brimful and running over with happiness that he is also full of fun and of love, and after all he may only like her as a cousin.

February 14

Father has not been so well of late. It seems as if he kept up until he was relieved about those debts, and then sunk down. I read to him a good deal, and so does mother, but his mind is still dark, and he looks forward to the hour of death with painful misgivings. He is getting a little childish about my leaving him, and clings to me exactly as if I were his own child. Martha spends a good deal of time with him, and fusses over him in a way that I wonder she does not see is annoying to him. He wants to be read to, to hear a hymn sung or a verse repeated, and to be left otherwise in perfect quiet. But she is continually pulling out and shaking up his pillows, bathing his head in hot vinegar and soaking his feet. It looks so odd to see her in one of the elegant silk dresses old Mr. Underhill makes her wear, with her sleeves rolled up, the skirt hid away under a large apron, continually rubbing away at poor father until it seems as if his tired soul would fly out of him.

February 20

Father grows weaker every day. Ernest has sent for his other children, John and Helen. Martha is no longer able to come; her husband is very sick with a fever, and cannot be left alone. No doubt he enjoys her bustling way of nursing, and likes to have his pillows pushed from under him every five minutes. I am afraid I feel glad that she is kept away, and that I have father all to myself. Ernest never was so fond of me as he is now. I don't know what to make of it.

February 22

John and his wife and Helen have come. They stay at Martha's, where there is plenty of room. John's wife is a little soft dumpling of a thing, and looks up to him as a mouse would look up at a steeple. He strikes me as a very selfish man. He steers straight for the best seat, leaving her standing, if need be, accepts her humble attentions with the air of one collecting his just debts, and is continually snubbing and setting her right. Yet in some things he is very like Ernest, and perhaps a wife destitute of self-assertion and without much individuality would have spoiled him as Helen has spoiled John. For I think it must be partly her fault that he dares to be so egotistical.

Helen is the dearest, prettiest creature I ever saw. Oh, why would James take a fancy to Lucy! I feel the new delight of having a sister to love and to admire. And she will love me in time; I feel sure of it.

March 1

Father is very feeble and in great mental distress. He gropes about in the dark, and shudders at the approach of death. We can do nothing but pray for him. And the cloud will be lifted when he leaves this world, if not before. For I know he is a good, yes, a saintly man, dear to God and dear to Christ.

March 4

Dear father has gone. We were all kneeling and praying and weeping around him, when suddenly he called me to come to him. I went and let him lean his head on my breast, as he loved to do. Sometimes I have stood so by the hour together ready to sink with fatigue, and only kept up with the thought that if this were my own precious father's bruised head I could stand and hold it forever.

"Daughter Katherine," he said, in his faint, quivering way, "you have come with me to the very brink of the river. I thank God for all your cheering words and ways. I thank God for giving you to be a helpmeet to my son. Farewell, now," he added, in a low, firm voice, "I feel the bottom, and it is good!"[25]

He lay back on his pillow looking upward with an expression of angelic peace and joy on his worn, withered face, and so his life passed gently away.

Oh, the abundance of God's payments! What a recompense for the poor love I had given my husband's father, and the poor little services I had rendered him! Oh, that I had never been impatient with him, never smiled at his peculiarities, never in my secret heart felt him unwelcome to my home! And how wholly I overlooked, in my blind selfishness, what he must have suffered in feeling himself homeless, dwelling with us on sufferance,[26] but master and head nowhere on earth! May God carry these lessons home to my heart of hearts, and make this cloud of mingled remorse and shame which now envelops me to descend in showers of love and benediction on every human soul that mine can bless!

Chapter 20

April 9

I have had a new lesson which has almost broken my heart. In looking over his father's papers, Ernest found a little journal, brief in its records indeed, but we learn from it that on those anniversaries and birthdays, when I assumed his austere religion made him aloof from our merrymaking, he was spending the time in fasting and praying for us and for our children! Oh, shall I ever learn the sweet charity that thinks no evil, and believes all things? What rich blessings may have descended upon us and our children through those prayers! What evils may they have been instrumental in warding off! Dear old father! Oh, that I could once more put my loving arms about him and bid him welcome to our home! And how gladly would I now confess to him all my unjust judgments concerning him and entreat his forgiveness! Must life always go on thus? Must I always be erring, ignorant and blind? How I hate this arrogant sweeping past my brother man; this utter ignoring of his hidden life?

I see now that it is good for mother that she did not come to live with me at the beginning of my married life. I would not have borne with her little peculiarities, nor have made her half so happy as I can now. I thank God that my varied disappointments and discomforts, my feeble health, my poverty, my mortifications have done me some little good, and driven me to Him a thousand times because I could not get along without His help. But I am not satisfied with my condition in His sight. I am sure something is lacking, though I know not what it is.

May 2

Helen is going to stay here and live with Martha. How glad, how enchanted I am! Old Mr. Underhill is getting well; I saw him today. He can talk of nothing but his illness, of Martha's wonderful skill in nursing him, declaring that he owes his life to her. I felt a little peeved at this speech, because Ernest was very attentive to him, and no doubt did his share towards the cure. We have fitted up father's room for a nursery. Hitherto all the children have had to sleep in our room, which has been bad for them and bad for us. I have been so afraid they would keep Ernest awake if they were unhealthy and restless. I have secured an excellent nurse, who is as fresh and blooming as the flower whose name she bears. The children are already attached to her, and I feel that the worst of my life is now over.

June 3

Little Ernest was taken sick on the very day I wrote that. The attack was fearfully sudden and violent. He is still very, very ill. I have not forgotten that I said once that I would give my children to God should He ask for them. And I will. But, oh, this agony of suspense! It eats into my soul and eats it away. Oh, my little Ernest! My first-born son! My pride, my joy, my hope! And I thought the worst of my life was all over!

August 8

We have come into the country with what God has left us, our two youngest children. Yes, I have tasted the bitter cup of bereavement, and drunk it down to the dregs. I *gave* my darling to God, I gave him, I gave him! But, oh, with what anguish I saw those round, dimpled limbs wither and waste away, the glad smile fade forever from that beautiful face! What a fearful thing it is to be a mother! But I have given my child to God. I would not recall him if I could. I am thankful He has counted me worthy to present Him so costly a gift.

I cannot shed a tear, and I must find relief in writing, or I shall lose my senses. My noble, beautiful boy! My first-born son! And to think that my delicate little Una still lives, and that death has claimed that bright, glad creature who was the sunshine of our home!

But let me not forget my mercies. Let me not forget that I have a precious husband and two darling children, and my kind, sympathetic mother still left to me. Let me not forget how many kind friends gathered about us in our sorrow. Above all let me remember God's lovingkindness and tender mercy. He has not left us to the bitterness of a grief that refuses and spurns to be comforted. We believe in

Him, we love Him, we worship Him as we never did before.

My dear Ernest has felt this sorrow to his heart's core. But he has not for one moment questioned the goodness or the love of our Father in thus taking from us the child who promised to be our greatest earthly joy. Our consent to God's will has drawn us together very closely; together we bear the yoke in our youth, together we pray and sing praises in the very midst of our tears. "I was dumb with silence because Thou didst it" (Psalm 39:9).

September 1

The old pain and cough have come back with the first cool nights of this month. Perhaps I am going to my darling— I do not know. I am certainly very feeble. *Consenting* to suffer does not annul the suffering. Such a child could not go hence without rending and tearing its way out of the heart that loved it. This world is wholly changed to me and I walk in it like one in a dream. And dear Ernest is changed, too. He says little, and is all kindness and goodness to me, but I can see that here is a wound that will never be healed.

I am confined to my room now with nothing to do but to think, think, think. I do not believe that God has taken our child in mere displeasure, but I cannot but feel that this affliction might not have been necessary if I had not so chafed and writhed, and secretly murmured at the way in which my home was invaded, and at our galling poverty. God has exchanged the one discipline for the other; and oh, how far more bitter is this cup!

October 4

My darling boy would have been six years old today. Ernest still keeps me shut up in doors, but he rather urges my seeing a friend now and then. People say very strange things in the way of consolation. I begin to think that a tender clasp of the hand is about all one can give to the afflicted. One says I must not grieve, because my child is better off in heaven. Yes, he *is* better off; I know it, I feel it; but I miss him none the less. Others say he might have grown up to be a bad man and broken my heart. Perhaps he might, but I cannot make myself believe that likely. One lady asked me if this affliction was not a rebuke of my idolatry of my darling; and another, if I had not been in a cold, worldly condition, needing this severe blow on that account.

But I find no consolation or support in these remarks. My comfort is in my perfect confidence in the goodness and love of my Father, my certainty that He had a reason in thus afflicting me that I would admire and adore if I knew what it was. And in the midst of my sorrow I have had and do have a delight in Him before unknown, so that sometimes this room in which I am a prisoner seems like the very gate of heaven.

May 12

A long winter in my room and all sorts of painful remedies and applications and deprivations. And now I am getting well, and drive outside every day. Martha sends her carriage, and mother goes with me. Dear mother! How nearly perfect she is! I never saw a sweeter face, nor ever heard sweeter expressions of faith in God, and love to all about her than hers. She has been my tower of strength all through these weary months, and yet she has shared my sorrow and made it her own.

I can see that dear Ernest's affliction and this prolonged anxiety about me have been a heavenly benediction to him. I am sure that every mother whose sick child he visits will have a sympathy he could not have given while all our own little ones were alive and well. I thank God that He has thus increased my dear husband's usefulness, as I think that He has mine also. How tenderly I already feel towards all suffering children, and how easy it will now be to bear patiently with them!

July 12, Keene, N. H.

It is a year ago this day that the brightest sunshine faded out of our lives, and our beautiful boy was taken from us. I have been tempted to spend this anniversary in bitter tears and lamentations. For oh, this sorrow is not healed by time! I feel it more and more. But I begged God when I first awoke this morning not to let me so dishonor and grieve Him. I may suffer, I must suffer, He means it, He wills it; but let it be without murmuring, without gloomy despondency. The world is full of sorrow; it is not I alone who taste its bitter draughts, nor have I the only right to a sad countenance. Oh, for patience to bear on, cost what it may!

"Cheerfully and gratefully I lay myself and all I am or own at the feet of Him who redeemed me with His precious blood, determining to follow Him, bearing the cross He lays upon me." This is the least I can do, and I do it while my heart still lies broken and bleeding at His feet.

My dear little Una has improved somewhat in health, but I am never free from anxiety about her. She is my milk-white lamb, my dove, my fragrant flower. One cannot look in her pure face without a sense of peace and rest. She is the sentinel who voluntarily guards my door when I am engaged at my devotions; she is my little comforter when I am sad, my companion and friend at all times. I talk to her of Christ, and always have done, just as I think of Him, and as if I expected sympathy from her in my love to Him. It was the same with my darling Ernest. If I required a little self-denial, I said, cheerfully, "This is hard, but doing it for our best Friend sweetens it," and their enthusiasm was pleasant to see. Ernest threw his whole soul into whatever he did, and sometimes when engaged in play would hesitate a little when directed to do something else, such as carrying a message for me, and the like. But if I said, "If you do this cheerfully and pleasantly, my darling, you do it for Jesus, and that will make Him smile upon you," he would invariably yield at once.

Is not this the true, the natural way of linking every little daily act of a child's life with that Divine Love, that Divine Life which gives meaning to all things?

But what do I mean by the vain boast that I have always trained my children thus? Alas! I have done it only at times; for while my theory was sound, my temper of mind was but too often unsound. I was too often impatient with my dear little boy; often my tone was a worldly one; I was often full of eager interest in mere outside things, and forgot that I was living or that my children were living save for the present moment.

It seems now that I have a child in heaven, and am bound to the invisible world by such a tie that I can never again be entirely absorbed by this one.

I fancy my ardent, eager little boy as having some such employments in his new and happy home as he had here. I see him loving Him who took children in His arms and blessed them, with all the warmth of which his nature is capable, and as perhaps employed as one of those messengers whom God sends forth as His ministers. For I cannot think of those active feet, those busy hands as always quiet. Ah, my darling, that I could look in upon you for a moment, a single moment, and catch one of your radiant smiles; just one!

August 4

How full are David's Psalms of the cry of the sufferer! He must have experienced every kind of bodily and mental torture. He gives most vivid illustrations of the wasting, wearing process of disease— for instance, what a contrast is the picture we have of him when he was "ruddy, and withal of a beautiful countenance, and goodly to look to" (1st Samuel 16:12), and the one he paints of himself in after years, when he says, "I may tell all my bones, they look and stare upon me; my days are like a shadow that declineth, and I am withered like grass. I am weary with groaning; all the night make I my bed to swim; I water my couch with my tears. For my soul is full of troubles; and my life draweth near unto the grave" (Psalm 22:17; 102:11; 6:6; 88:3).

And then what wails of anguish are these!

"I am afflicted, and ready to die from my youth up; while I suffer thy terrors I am distracted. Thy wrath lieth hard upon me and thou hast afflicted me with all thy waves. All thy waves and thy billows have gone over me. Lover and friend hast thou put far from me, and mine acquaintance into utter darkness" (Psalm 88:15,7; 42:7; 88:18).

Yet through it all what grateful joy in God, what expressions of living faith and devotion! During my long illness and confinement to my room, the Bible has been almost a new book to me, and I see that God has always dealt with His children as He deals with them now, and that no new thing has befallen me. All these weary days so full of feebleness, these nights so full of unrest, have had their appointed mission to my soul. And perhaps I have had no discipline so salutary as this forced inaction and uselessness, at a time when youth and natural energy continually cried out for room and work.

August 15

I dragged out my drawing materials in a listless way this morning, and began to sketch the beautiful scene from my window. At first I could not feel interested. It seemed as if my hand was crippled and lost its cunning when it unloosed its grasp of little Ernest, and let him go. But I prayed, as I worked, that I might not yield to the inclination to despise and throw away the gift with which God has Himself endowed me. Mother was gratified, and said it refreshed her to see me act like myself once more. Ah, I have been very selfish, and have been far too much absorbed in my sorrow and my illness and my own petty struggles.

August 19

I met today an old friend, Maria Kelly, who is married, it seems, and settled down in this pretty village. She asked so many questions about my little Ernest that I had to tell her the whole story of his precious life, sickness and death. I forced myself to do this quietly, and without any great demand on her sympathies. My reward for the constraint I thus put upon myself was the abrupt question:

"Haven't you grown stoical?"

I felt the angry blood rush through my veins as it has not done in a long time. My pride was wounded to the quick, and those cruel, unjust words still rankle in my heart. This is not as it should be. I am constantly praying that my pride may be humbled, and then when it is attacked, I shrink from the pain the blow causes, and am angry with the hand that inflicts it. It is just so with two or three unkind things Martha has said to me. I can't help brooding over them and feeling stung with their injustice, even while making the most desperate struggle to rise above and forget them. It is well for our fellow creatures that God forgives and excuses them, when we fail to do it, and I can easily fancy that poor Maria Kelly is at this moment dearer in His sight than I am who have taken fire at a chance word.[27] And I can see now, what I wonder I did not see at the time, that God was dealing very kindly and wisely with me when He made Martha overlook my good qualities, of which I suppose I have some, as everybody else has, and call out all my bad ones, since the axe was thus laid at the root of self-love. And it is plain that self-love cannot die without a fearful struggle.

May 26, 1846

How long it is since I have written in my journal! We have had a winter full of cares, perplexities and sicknesses. Mother began it by such a severe attack of inflammatory rheumatism as I could not have supposed she could live through. Her sufferings were dreadful, and I might almost say her patience was, for I often thought it would be less painful to hear her groan and complain, than to witness such heroic fortitude, such sweet docility under God's hand.

I hope I shall never forget the lessons I have learned in her sick-room. Ernest says he never shall cease to rejoice that she lives with us, and that he can watch over her health. He has indeed been like a son to her, and this has been a great solace amidst all her sufferings. Before she was able to leave the room, poor little Una was overcome by one of her ill turns, and is still very feeble. The only way in which she can be diverted is by reading to her, and I have done little else these two months but hold her in my arms, singing little songs and hymns, telling stories and reading what few books I can find that are unexciting, simple, yet entertaining. My precious little darling! She bears the yoke in her youth without a frown, but it is agonizing to see her suffer so. How much easier it would be to bear all her physical infirmities myself! I suppose to those who look on from the outside, we must appear like a most unhappy family, since we hardly get free from one trouble before another steps in. But I see more and more that happiness is not dependent on health or any other outside prosperity. We are at peace with each other and at peace with God; His dealings with us do not perplex or puzzle us, though we do not pretend to understand them. On the other hand, Martha, with absolutely perfect health, with a husband entirely devoted to her, and with every wish gratified, yet seems always burdened with care and dissatisfied. Her servants worry her very life out; she misses the homely household duties to which she has been accustomed; and her conscience stumbles at little things, and overlooks greater ones. It is very interesting, I think, to study different homes, as well as the different characters that form them.

Amelia's little girls are quiet, good children, to whom their father writes what Mr. Underhill and Martha pronounce "beautiful" letters, wherein he always styles himself their "broken-hearted but devoted father." "Devotion," to my mind, involves self-sacrifice, and I cannot reconcile its use, in this case, with the life of ease he leads, while all the care of his children is thrown upon others. But some people; by means of a few such phrases, not only impose upon themselves but upon their friends, and pass for persons of great sensibility.

As I have been confined to the house nearly the whole winter, I have had to derive my spiritual support from books, and as mother gradually recovered, she enjoyed reading Leighton's[28] writings with me, as I knew she would. Dr. Cabot comes to see us very often, but I do not now find it possible to get the instruction from him I used to do. I see that the Christian life must be individual, as the natural character is— and that I cannot be exactly like Dr. Cabot, or exactly like Mrs. Campbell, or exactly like mother, though they all three stimulate and are an inspiration to me. But I see, too, that the great points of similarity in Christ's disciples have always been the same. This is the testimony of all the good books, sermons, hymns, and memoirs I read— that God's ways are infinitely perfect; that we are to love Him for what He is, and therefore equally as much when He afflicts as when He prospers us; that there is no real happiness but in doing and suffering His will, and that this life is but a scene of testing through which we pass to the real life above.

Chapter 21

May 30

Ernest asked me to go with him to see one of his patients, as he often does when there is a lull in the tempest at home. We both feel that as we have so little money of our own to give away, it is a privilege to give what services and what cheering words we can. As I took it for granted that we were going to see some poor old woman, I put up several little packages of tea and sugar, with which Susan Green always keeps me supplied, and added a bottle of my own raspberry vinegar, which, I find, never seems to miss with old people. Ernest drove to the door of an aristocratic-looking house, and helped me to get down in his usual silence.

"It is probably one of the servants we are going to visit," I thought, within myself; "but I am surprised at his bringing me. The family may not approve it."

The next thing I knew I found myself being introduced to a beautiful, brilliant young lady, who sat in a wheel-chair like a queen on a throne in a room full of tasteful ornaments, flowers and birds. Now, I had come away just as I was, when Ernest called me, and that *"was"* means a very plain gingham dress in which I had been darning stockings all the morning. I suppose a saint wouldn't have cared for that, but *I* did, and for a moment stood the picture of confusion, my hands full of oddly shaped parcels, and my face all in a flame.

"My wife, Miss Clifford," I heard Ernest say, and then I caught the curious, puzzled look in her eyes, which said as plainly as words could:

"What *has* the creature brought me?"

"I ask your pardon, Miss Clifford," I said, thinking it best to speak out just the honest truth, "but I supposed the doctor was taking me to see some one of his old women, and so I have brought you a little tea, and a little sugar, and a bottle of raspberry vinegar!"

"How delicious!" she cried. "It really refreshes me to meet with a genuine human being at last! Why didn't you make some stiff, prim speech, instead of telling the truth out and out? I declare I mean to keep all you have brought me, just for the fun of the thing."

This put me at ease, and I forgot all about my dress in a moment.

"I see you are just what the doctor boasted you were," she went on. "But he never would bring you to see me before. I suppose he has told you why I could not go to see you?"

"To tell the truth, he never speaks to me of his patients unless he thinks I can be of use to them."

"I dare say I do not look much like an invalid," she

said; "but here I am, tied to this chair. It is six months since I could bear my own weight upon my feet."

I saw then that though her face was so bright and full of color, her hand was thin and transparent. But what a picture she made as she sat there in her magnificent beauty, relieved by such a background of foliage, flowers and artistic objects!

"I told the doctor the other day that life was nothing but a humbug, and he said he would bring me a remedy against that false notion the next time he came, and you, I suppose, are that remedy," she continued. "Come, begin; I am ready to take any number of doses."

I could only laugh and try to look daggers at Ernest, who sat looking over a magazine, apparently absorbed in its contents.

"Ah!" she cried, nodding her head shrewdly, "I knew you would agree with me."

"Agree with you in calling life a humbug!" I cried, now fairly aroused. "Death itself is not more a reality!"

"I have not tried death yet," she said, more seriously; "but I have tried life twenty-five years, and I know all about it. It is eat, drink, sleep, yawn and be bored. It is what shall I wear, where shall I go, how shall I get rid of the time; it says, 'How do you do? How is your husband? How are your children?'— it means, 'Now I have asked all the conventional questions, and I don't care a fig what their answer may be.' "

"This may be its meaning to some persons," I replied, "for instance, to mere pleasure-seekers. But of course it is interpreted quite differently by others. To some it means nothing but a dull, hopeless struggle with poverty and hardship— and its whole aspect might be changed to them, should those who do not know what to do to get rid of the time, spend their surplus leisure in making this struggle less brutalizing."

"Yes, I have heard such doctrine, and at one time I tried charity myself. I picked up a dozen or so of the dirty little wretches out of the streets, and undertook to clothe and teach them. I might as well have tried to instruct the chairs in my room. Besides the whole house had to be aired after they had gone, and mamma missed two teaspoons and a fork, and was perfectly disgusted with the whole thing. Then I went on to knitting socks for babies, but they only occupied my hands, and my head felt as empty as ever. Mamma took me off on a journey, as she always did when I took to moping, and that diverted me for a while. But after that everything went on in the old way. I got rid of part of the day by changing my dress, and putting on my pretty things— it is a great thing to have a habit of wearing one's ornaments, for instance; and then in the evening one could go to the opera or the theater, or some other place of amusement, after which one could sleep all through the next morning, and so get rid of that. But I had been used to such things all my life, and they had gotten to be about as flat as flat can be. If I had been born a little earlier in the history of the world, I would have gone into a convent; but that sort of thing is out of fashion now."

"The best convent," I said, "for a woman, is the seclusion of her own home. There she may find her vocation and fight her battles, and there she may learn the reality and the earnestness of life."

"Pshaw!" she cried. "Excuse me, however, for saying that; but some of the most brilliant girls I know have settled down into mere married women, and spend their whole time in nursing babies! Think how belittling!"

"Is it more 'belittling' than spending it in dressing, driving, dancing, and the like?"

"Of course it is. I had a friend once who shone like a star in society. She married, and had four children as fast as she could. Well! what was the consequence? She lost her beauty, lost her spirit and animation, lost her youth, and lost her health. The only earthly things she can talk about are teething, dieting and the measles!"

I laughed at this exaggeration, and looked around to see what Ernest thought of such talk. But he had disappeared.

"As you have spoken plainly to me, knowing me to be a wife and a mother, you must allow me to speak plainly in return," I began.

"Oh, speak plainly, by all means! I am quite sick and tired of having truth served up in pink cotton, and scented with lavender."

"Then you will permit me to say, that when you speak so contemptuously of the vocation of maternity, you dishonor, not only the mother who bore you, but the Lord Jesus Himself, who chose to be born of woman, and to be ministered unto by her through a helpless infancy."

Miss Clifford was a little startled.

"How terribly in earnest you are!" she said. "It is plain

that to you, at any rate, life is indeed no humbug."

I thought of my dear ones, of Ernest, of my children, of mother, and of James, and I thought of my love to them and of theirs to me. And I thought of Him who alone gives reality to even such joys as these. My face must have been illuminated by the thought, for she dropped the bantering tone she had used to this point, and asked, with real earnestness: "What is it you know, that I do not know, that makes you so satisfied, while I am so dissatisfied?"

I hesitated before I answered, feeling as I never felt before how ignorant, how unfit to lead others, I really am. Then I said:

"Perhaps you need to know God, to know Christ?"

She looked disappointed and tired. So I came away, first promising, at her request, to go to see her again. I found Ernest just driving up, and told him what had taken place. He listened in his usual silence, and I longed to hear him say whether I had spoken wisely and well.

June 1

I have been to see Miss Clifford again, and made mother go with me. Miss Clifford took a fancy to her at once.

"Ah!" she said, after one glance at the dear, loving face, "nobody need tell me that you are good and kind. But I am a little afraid of good people. I fancy they are always criticizing and expecting me to imitate their perfection."

"Perfection does not demand perfection," was mother's answer. "I would rather be judged by an angel than by a man." And then mother led her on, little by little, and most skillfully, to talk of herself and of her state of health. She is an orphan, and lives in this great, stately house alone with her servants. Until she was laid aside by the state of her health, she lived in the world and of it. Now she is a prisoner, and prisoners have time to think.

"Here I sit," she said, "all day long. I never was fond of staying at home, or of reading, and needle work I absolutely hate. In fact, I do not know how to sew."

"Some such pretty, feminine work might divert you of a few of the long hours of these long days," said mother. "One can't be always reading, you know."

"But a lady came to see me, a Mrs. Goodhue, one of your good sort, I suppose, and she preached me quite a sermon on the employment of time. She said I had a solemn admonition from Providence, and ought to devote myself entirely to religion. I had just begun to be interested in a bit of embroidery, but she frightened me out of it. But I can't bear such dreadfully good people, with faces a mile long."

Mother made her produce the collar, or whatever it was, showed her how to hold her needle and arrange her pattern, and they both got so absorbed in it that I had leisure to look at some of the beautiful things with which the room was full.

"Make the object of your life right," I heard mother say, at last, "and these little details will take care of themselves."

"But I haven't any object," Miss Clifford objected,

"unless it is to get through these tedious days somehow. Before I was taken ill my chief object was to make myself attractive to the people I met. And the easiest way to do that was to dress appropriately and make myself look as attractive as I could."

"I suppose," said mother, "that most girls could say the same. They have an instinctive desire to please, and they take what they conceive to be the shortest and easiest road to that end. It requires no talent, no education, no thought to dress tastefully; the most empty-hearted, frivolous young person can do it, provided she has enough money. Those who can't get the money make up for it by a fearful expenditure of precious time. They plan, they cut, they fit, they rip, they trim till they can appear in society looking exactly like everybody else. They think of nothing, talk of nothing but how this shall be fashioned and that be trimmed; and as to their hair, Satan uses it as his favorite net, and catches them in it every day of their lives."

"But I never cut or trimmed," said Miss Clifford.

"No, because you could afford to have it done for you. But you acknowledge that you spent a great deal of time in dressing because you thought that to be the easiest way of making yourself attractive. But it does not follow that the easiest way is the best way, and sometimes the longest way around is the shortest way home."

"For instance?"

"Well, let us imagine a young lady, living in the world as you say you lived. She has never seriously reflected on any subject one half hour in her life. She has been carried along by the current and let it take her where it would. But at last some influence is brought to bear upon her which leads her to stop to look about her and to think. She finds herself in a world of serious, momentous events. She sees that she cannot live in it, was not meant to live in it forever, and that her whole unknown future depends on *what she is*, not on *how she looks*. She begins to cast about for some plan of life, and this leads—"

"A plan of life?" Miss Clifford asked. "I never heard of that."

"Yet you would smirk at an architect, who, having a noble structure to build, should begin to work on it in a haphazard way, putting in a brick here and a stone there, weaving in straws and sticks if they come to hand, and when asked on what work he was engaged, and what manner of building he intended to erect, would reply he had no plan, but thought something would come of it."

Miss Clifford made no reply. She sat with her head resting on her hand, looking dreamily before her, a truly beautiful, but unconscious picture. I, too, began to reflect, that while I had really aimed to make the most out of life, I had not done it methodically or intelligently.

We are going to try to stay in town this summer. Before now Ernest would not listen to my suggestion of what a savings this would be. He always said this would turn out anything but a savings in the end. But now we have no teething baby; little Raymond is a strong, healthy child, and Una remarkably well for her, and money is so slow to come in and so fast to go out. What discomforts we suffer in the country it would take a book to write down, and here we shall have our own home, as usual. I shall not have to be separated from Ernest, and shall have leisure to devote myself to two very interesting people who must stay in town all the year round, no matter who goes out of it. I mean dear Mrs. Campbell and Miss Clifford, who both attract me, though in such different ways.

Chapter 22

October 8

Well, I had my own way, and I am afraid it has been an unwise one, for though I have enjoyed the leisure afforded by everybody being out of town, and the opportunity it has given me to devote myself to the very sweetest work on earth, the care of my darling little ones, the heat and the stifling atmosphere have been trying for me and for them. My pretty Rose went last May, to bloom in a home of her own, so I thought I would not look for another nurse, but take the whole care of them myself. This would not be much of a task to a strong person, but I am not strong, and a great deal of the time just dressing them and taking them out to walk has exhausted me. Then all the mending and other sewing must be done, and with the over-exertion creeps in the fretful tone, the impatient word. Yet I never can be as impatient with little children as I would be but for the remembrance that I should count it only a joy to minister once more to my darling boy, cost what weariness it might.

But now new cares are at hand, and I have been

searching for a person to whom I can safely trust my children when I am laid aside. Thus far I have had, in this capacity, three different Temptations in human form.

The first, a smart, tidy-looking woman, informed me at the outset that she was perfectly competent to take the whole charge of the children, and would prefer my attending to my own affairs while she attended to hers.

I replied that my affairs lay chiefly in caring for and being with my children; to which she returned that she feared I would not suit her, as she had her own views concerning the training of children. She added, with condescension, that at all events she would expect in any case of difference (of judgment) between us, that I, being the younger and least experienced of the two, would always yield to her. She then went on to give me her views on the subject of nursery management.

"In the first place," she said, "I never pet or fondle children. It makes them babyish and sickly."

"Oh, I see you will not suit me," I cried. "You need go no farther. I consider love the best educator for a little child."

"Indeed, I think I shall suit you perfectly," she replied, nothing daunted. "I have been in the business twenty years, and have always suited wherever I lived. You will be surprised to see how much sewing I shall accomplish, and how quiet I shall keep the children."

"But I don't want them kept quiet," I persisted. "I want them to be as merry and cheerful as crickets, and I care a great deal more to have them amused than to have the sewing done, though that is important, I confess."

"Very well, ma'am, I will sit and rock them each and every hour if you wish it."

"But I don't wish it," I cried, exasperated at the coolness which gave her such an advantage over me. "Let us say no more about it; you do not suit me, and the sooner we part the better. I must be mistress of my own house, and I want no advice in relation to my own children."

"I shall hardly leave you before you will regret parting with me," she returned, in a placid, pitying way.

I was afraid I had not been quite dignified in my interview with this person, with whom I ought to have had no discussion, and my composure was not restored by her shaking hands with me in a patronizing way at parting, and expressing the hope that I would one day "be a green tree in the Paradise of God." Nor was it any too great a consolation to find that she had suggested to my cook that my intellect was not quite sound.

Temptation the second confessed that she knew nothing, but was willing to be taught. Yes, she might be willing, but she could not be taught. She could not see why Herbert should not have everything he chose to cry for, nor why she should not take the children to the kitchens where her friends abode, instead of keeping them out in the air. She could not understand why she must not tell Una every half hour that she was as fair as a lily, and that the little angels in heaven cried for such hair as hers. And there was no rhyme or reason, to her mind, why she could not have her friends visit her nursery, since, as she declared, the cook would hear all her secrets if she received them in the kitchen. Her assurance that she thought me a very nice lady, and that there never were two such children as mine, failed to move my hard heart, and I was thankful when I got her out of the house.

Temptation the third appeared, for a time, the perfection of a nurse. She kept herself and the nursery and the children in most refreshing order; she amused Una when she was more than usually unhealthy with a perfect fund of innocent stories; the work flew from her nimble fingers as if by magic. I boasted everywhere of my good fortune, and sang her praises in Ernest's ears till he believed in her with all his heart.

But one night we were out late; we had been spending the evening at Aunty's, and came in with Ernest's night-key as quietly as possible, in order not to arouse the children. I crept softly to the nursery to see if all was going on well there. Bridget, it seems, had taken the opportunity to wash her clothes in the nursery, and they hung all about the room drying, a hot fire raging for the purpose. In the midst of them, with a candle and prayer-book on a chair, Bridget knelt fast asleep, the candle within an inch of her sleeve. Her assurance when I aroused her that she was not asleep, but merely rapt in devotion, did not soften my hard heart, nor was I moved by the representation that she was a saint, and always wore black on that account. I packed her off in anything but a saintly disposition, and felt that a fourth Temptation would scatter what little grace I still possessed to the four winds. These changes upstairs made discord, too, below. My cook was displeased at so much coming and going, and made the kitchen a sort of a purgatory which I dreaded to enter. At last, when her temper fairly ran away with her, and she became impertinent to the last degree, I said, coolly: "If any *lady* should speak to me in this way I would resent it. But no lady would so far forget herself. And I overlook your rudeness on the ground that you do not know better than to make use of such words."

This capped the climax! She declared that she had never been told before that she was no lady and did not know how to behave, and gave warning of her leaving at once.

I wish I could help running to tell Ernest all these annoyances. It does no good, and only worries him. But how much of a woman's life is made up of such trials and provocations! and how easy it is when on one's knees to bear them aright, and how far easier to bear them wrong when one finds the coal going too fast, the butter out just as one is sitting down to breakfast, the potatoes watery and the bread sour or heavy! And then when one is well nigh desperate, does one's husband fail to say, in bland tones:

"My dear, if you would just *speak* to Bridget, I am sure she would improve."

Oh, that there were indeed magic in a spoken word!

And do what I can, the money Ernest gives me will not hold out. He knows absolutely nothing about that hydra-headed monster, a household. I have had to go back to sewing as furiously as ever. And with the sewing the old pain in the side has come back, and the sharp, quick speech that I hate, and that Ernest hates, and that every-body hates. I groan, being burdened, and am almost weary of my life. And my prayers are all mixed up with worldly thoughts and cares. I am appalled at all the things that have got to be done before winter, and am tempted to cut short my devotions in order to have more time to accomplish what I *must* accomplish.

How have I gotten into this slough?[29] When was it that I came down from the Mount where I had seen the Lord, and came back to make these miserable, petty things as much my business as ever? Oh, these fluctuations in my religious life amaze me! I cannot doubt that I am really God's child; it would be a dishonor to Him to doubt it. I cannot doubt that I have held as real communion with Him as with any earthly friend— and oh, it has been far sweeter!

October 20

I made a parting visit to Mrs. Campbell today, and, as usual, have come away strengthened and refreshed. She said all sorts of kind things to cheer and encourage me, and stimulated me to take up the burden of life cheerfully and patiently, just as it comes. She assures me that these fluc-tuations of feeling will by degrees give place to a calmer life, especially if I avoid, so far as I can do it, all unnecessary work, distraction and hurry. And a few quiet, resting words from her have given me courage to press on toward perfection, no matter how much imperfection I see in myself and others. And now I am waiting for my Father's next gift, and the new cares and labors it will bring with it. I am glad it is not left for me to decide my own lot. I am afraid I could never see precisely the right moment for welcoming a new bird into the nest, dearly as I love the rustle of their wings and the sound of their voices when they do come. And surely *He* knows the right moments who knows all my struggles with a certain sort of poverty, poor health and domestic care. If I could feel that all the time, as I do at this moment, how happy I would always be!

January 16, 1847

This is the tenth anniversary of our wedding-day, and it has been a delightful one. If I were called upon to declare what has been the chief element of my happiness, I would say it was not Ernest's love to me or mine to him, or that I am once more the mother of three children, or that my own dear mother still lives, though I revel in each and all of these. But underneath them all, deeper, stronger than all, lies a peace with God that I can compare to no other joy, which I guard as I would guard hidden treasure, and which must abide even if all other things pass away.

My baby is two months old, and her name is Ethel. The three children together form a beautiful picture which I am never tired of admiring. But they will not give me much time for writing. This little newcomer takes all there is of me. Mother brings me pleasant reports of Miss Clifford, who, under her gentle, wise influence is becoming an earnest Christian, already rejoicing in the Providence that arrested her where it did, and forced her to reflection.

Mother says we ought to study God's providence more than we do, since He has a meaning and a purpose in everything He does.[30] Sometimes I can do this and find it a source of great happiness. Then worldly cares seem *mere* worldly cares, and I forget that His wise, kind hand is in every one of them.

February 5

Helen has been spending the whole day with me, as she often does, helping me with her skillful needle, and with the children, in a very sweet way. I am almost ashamed to indulge in writing down how dearly she seems to love me, and how inclined she is to sit at my feet as a learner at the very moment I am longing to possess her sweet, gentle temper. But one thing puzzles me in her, and that is the difficulty she finds in getting hold of these simple truths her father used to grope after but never found till just as he was passing out of the world. It seems as if God had compensated such turbulent, fiery natures as mine by revealing Himself to them, for the terrible hours of shame and sorrow through which their sins and follies cause them to pass. I suffer far more than Helen does, suffer bitterly, painfully, but I also enjoy tenfold more. For I know whom I have believed, and I cannot doubt that I am truly united to Him. Helen is naturally very reserved, but by degrees she has come to talk with me quite frankly. Today as we sat together in the nursery, little Raymond snatched a toy from Una, who, as usual, yielded to him without a frown. I called him to me; he came reluctantly.

"Raymond, dear," I said, "did you ever see papa snatch anything from me?"

He smiled, and shook his head.

"Well then, until you see him do it to me, never do it to your sister. Men are gentle and polite to women, and little boys should be gentle and polite to little girls."

The children ran off to their play, and Helen said,

"Now how different that is from my mother's management with us! She always made us girls yield to the boys. They would not have thought they could go up to bed unless one of us had gotten a candle for them."

"That, I suppose, is the reason then that Ernest expected me to wait upon him after we were married," I replied. "I was a little stiff about yielding to him, for besides mother's precepts, I was influenced by my father's example. He was so courteous, treating her with as much respect as if she were a queen, and yet with as much love as if she were always a girl. I naturally expected the very same from my husband."

"You must have been disappointed then," she said.

"Yes, I was. It cost me a good many pouts and tears of which I am now ashamed. And Ernest seldom annoys me now with the little neglects that I used to make so much of."

"Sometimes I think there are no 'little' neglects," said Helen. "It takes less than nothing to annoy us."

"And it takes more than everything to please us!" I cried. "But Ernest and I had one stronghold to which we always fled in our troublous times, and that was our love for each other. No matter how he provoked me by his little heedless ways, I *had* to forgive him because I loved him so. And he had to forgive me my faults for the same reason."

"I had no idea husbands and wives loved each other so," said Helen. "I thought they got over it as soon as their cares and troubles came on, and just jogged on together, somehow."

We both laughed and she went on.

"If I thought I could be as happy as you are, I would be tempted to be married myself."

"Ah, I thought your time would come!" I cried.

"Don't ask me any questions," she said, her pretty face growing prettier with a bright, warm glow. "Give me advice instead; for instance, tell me how I can be sure that if I love a man I shall go on loving him through all the wear and tear of married life, and how can I be sure he can and will go on loving me?"

"Well, then, setting aside the fact that you are both lovable and loving, I will say this: Happiness, in other words love, in married life is not a mere accident. When the union has been formed, as most Christian unions are, by God Himself, it is His intention and His will that it shall prove the unspeakable joy of both husband and wife, and become more and more so from year to year. But we are imperfect creatures, wayward and foolish as little children, horribly unreasonable, selfish and willful. We are not capable of enduring the shock of finding at every turn that our idol is made of clay, and that it is prone to tumble off its pedestal and lie in the dust, till we pick it up and set it in its place again. I was struck with Ernest's asking in the very first prayer he offered in my presence, after our marriage, that God would help us love each other; I felt that love was the very foundation on which I was built, and that there was no danger that I would ever fall short in giving to my husband all he wanted, in full measure. But as he went on day after day repeating this prayer, and I naturally made it with him, I came to see that this most precious of earthly blessings had been and must be God's gift, and that while we both looked at it in that light, and felt our dependence on Him for it, we might safely encounter together all the assaults made upon us by the world, the flesh and the devil. I believe we owe it to this constant prayer that we have loved each other so uniformly and with such growing comfort in each other; so that our little discords always have ended in fresh accord, and our love has felt conscious of resting on a rock— and that rock was the will of God."

"It is plain, then," said Helen, "that you and Ernest are sure of one source of happiness as long as long as you live, whatever hardships you may meet with. I thank you so much for what you have said. The fact is you have been brought up to carry religion into everything. But I was not. My mother was as good as she was lovely, but I think she felt, and taught us to feel, that we were to put it on as we did our Sunday clothes, and to wear it, as we did them, carefully and reverently, but with pretty long and serious faces. But you mix everything up so, that when I am with you I never know whether you are most like or unlike other people. And your mother is exactly the same."

"But you forget that it is to Ernest I owe my best ideas

about married life; I don't remember ever talking with my mother or anyone else on the subject. And as to carrying religion into everything, how can one help it if one's religion is a vital part of one's self, not a cloak put on to go to church in and hang up out of the way again until next Sunday?"

Helen laughed. She has the merriest, yet gentlest little laugh one can imagine. I long to know who it is that has been so fortunate as to touch her heart!

March 2

I know now, and glad I am! The sly little puss is purring at this moment in James' arms; at least I suppose she is, as I have discreetly come up to my room and left them to themselves. So it seems I have had all these worries about Lucy for nothing. What made her so fond of James was simply the fact that a friend of his had looked on her with a favorable eye, regarding her as a very proper mother for four or five children who are in need of a shepherd. Yes, Lucy is going to marry a man so much older than herself, that on a pinch he might have been her father. She does it from a sense of duty, she says, and to a nature like hers duty may perhaps suffice, and no cry of the heart have to be stifled in its performance.

We are all so happy in the happiness of James and Helen that we are not in the mood to criticize Lucy's decision. I have a strange and most absurd envy when I think about what a good time they are having at this moment downstairs, while I sit here alone, vainly wishing I could see more of Ernest. Just as if my happiness were not a deeper, more blessed one than theirs, which must be purged of much dross before it will prove itself to be like fine gold. Yes, I suppose I am as happy in my dear, precious husband and children as a wife and mother can be in a fallen world, which must not be a real heaven lest we should love the land we journey through so well as to want to pitch out tents in it forever, and cease to look and long for the home toward which we are bound.

James will be married almost immediately, I suppose, since he is set to sail for Syria early in April. How much a missionary and his wife must be to each other, when, severing themselves from all they have ever loved before, they go forth, hand in hand, not merely to be foreigners in heathen lands, but to be henceforth strangers in their own should they ever return to it!

Helen says, playfully, that she does not have a missionary spirit, and is not at all sure that she shall go with James. But I don't think that he feels very anxious on that point!

March 20

It does one's heart good to see how happy they are! And it does one's heart good to have one's husband set up an opposition to the goings on by behaving like a lover himself.

Chapter 23

It is a great while since I wrote that. *"God has been just as good as ever"* ; I want to say that before I say another word. But He has indeed smitten me very sorely.

While we were in the midst of our rejoicing about James and Helen, and the bright future that seemed opening before them, he came home one day very ill. Ernest happened to be in and attended to him at once. But the disease was, at the very outset, so violent, and raged with such absolute fury, that no remedies had any effect. Everything, even now, seems confused in my mind. It seems as if there was a sudden transition from the most brilliant, joyous health, to a brief but fearful struggle for life, speedily followed by the awful mystery and stillness of death. Is it possible, I still ask myself, that four short days wrought an event whose consequences must run through endless years?— Poor mother! Poor Helen!— When it was all over, I do not know what to say of mother but that she behaved and quieted herself like a weaned child. Her sweet composure awed me; I dared not give way to my own vehement, terrible sorrow; in the presence of this Christ-like patience, all noisy demonstrations seemed profane. I thought no human being was less selfish, more loving than she had been for many years, but the spirit that now took possession of her flowed into her heart and life directly from that great Heart of love, whose depths I had never even begun to sound. There was, therefore, something absolutely divine in her bearing, in the tones of her voice, in the very smile on her face. We could compare its expression to nothing but Stephen, when he, being full of the Holy Ghost, looked up steadfastly to heaven and saw the glory of God, and Jesus standing on the right hand of God (Acts 7:55).

As soon as James was gone Helen came to live in our home; there was never any discussion about it, she came naturally to be one of us. Mother's health, already very frail, gradually failed, and encompassed as I was with cares, I could not be with her constantly. Helen took the place to her of a daughter, and found herself welcomed like one. The atmosphere in which we all lived was one which cannot be described; the love for all of us and for every living thing that flowed in mother's words and tones passed all knowledge. The children's little joys and sorrows interested her exactly as if she was one of themselves; they ran to her with every petty grievance, and every new pleasure. During the time she lived with us she had won many warm friends, particularly among the poor and the suffering. As her strength would no longer allow her to go to them, those who could do so came to her, and I was struck to see she had ceased entirely from giving counsel, and now gave nothing but the most beautiful, tender compassion and sympathy. I saw that she was failing, but flattered myself that her own serenity and our care would prolong her life still for many years. I longed to have my children become old enough to fully appreciate her sanctified character; and I thought she would gradually fade away and be set free,

> *As light winds wandering through groves of bloom,*
> *Detach the delicate blossoms from the tree.*

But God's thoughts are not as our thoughts nor His ways as our ways. Her feeble body began to suffer from the rudest assaults of pain; day and night, night and day, she lived through a martyrdom in which what might have been a lifetime of suffering was concentrated into a few months. To witness these sufferings was like the sundering of joints and marrow, and once, only once, thank God! my faith in Him staggered and reeled to and fro. "How *can* He look down on such agonies?" I cried in my secret soul; "Is this the work of a God of *love*, of *mercy?*" Mother seemed to suspect my thoughts, for she took my hand tenderly in hers and said, with great difficulty:

"Though He slay me, yet will I trust in Him (Job 13:15). He is just as good as ever." And she smiled. I ran away to Ernest, crying. "Oh, is there *nothing* you can do for her?"

"What should a poor mortal do where Christ has done so much, my darling?" he said, taking me in his arms. "Let us stand aside and see the glory of God, with our shoes from off our feet." But he went to her with one more desperate effort to relieve her, yet in vain.

Mrs. Embury, of whom mother was fond, and who is always very kind when we are in trouble, came in just then, and after looking on a moment in tears she said to me: "God knows whom He can trust! He would not lay His hand thus on all His children."

Those few words quieted me. Yes, God knows. And now it is all over. My precious, precious mother has been a saint in heaven more than two years, and has forgotten all the battles she fought on earth, and all her sorrows and all her sufferings in the presence of her Redeemer. She knew that she was going, and the last words she uttered— and they were spoken with somewhat of the playful, quaint manner in which she had spoken all her life, and with her own bright smile— still sound in my ears: "I have given God a great deal of trouble, but He is driving me into His pasture now!"

And then, with her cheek on her hand, she fell asleep, and slept on, till just at sundown she awoke to find herself in the green pasture, the driving all over for ever and ever.

Who by searching can find out God? My dear father entered heaven after a prosperous life by a path in which he was unconscious of a pang, and our beloved James went bright and fresh and untarnished by conflict straight to the Master's feast. But what a long lifetime of bereavement, sorrow, and suffering was my darling mother's pathway to glory! Surely her felicity must be greater than theirs, and the crown she has won by such a struggle must be brighter than the stars! And this crown she is even now, while I sit here choked with tears, casting joyfully at the feet of her Saviour!

My sweet sister, my precious little Helen, still nestles in our hearts and in our home. Martha made one passionate appeal to her to return to her, but Ernest interfered: "Let her stay with Katy," he said. "James would have chosen to have her with the one human being like himself."

Does he then think me, with all my faults, the infirmity of frail health, and the cares and burdens of life weighing upon me, enough like that sparkling, brave boy to be of use and comfort to dear Helen? I take courage at the thought and rouse myself afresh, to bear on with fidelity and patience. My steadfast aim now is to follow in my mother's footsteps; to imitate her cheerfulness, her benevolence, her bright, inspiring ways, and never to rest till in place of my selfish nature I become as full of Christ's love as she became. I am glad she is at last relieved from the knowledge of all my cares, and though I so often *yearn* to throw myself into her arms and pour out my cares and trials into her sympathizing ears, I would not have her back for all the world. She has gotten away from all the turmoil and suffering of life; *let her stay!*

The scenes of sorrow through which we have been passing have brought Ernest nearer to me than ever, and I can see that this varied discipline has softened and sweetened his character. Besides, we have modified each other. Ernest is more demonstrative, more attentive to those little things that make the happiness of married life, and I am less childish, less vehement— I wish I could say less selfish, but here I seem to have come to a standstill. But I do understand Ernest's trials in his profession far better than I did, and can feel and show some sympathy in them. Of course the life of a physician is necessarily one of self-denial, spent as it is amid scenes of suffering and sorrow, which he is often powerless to alleviate. But there is besides the wear and tear of years of poverty; his bills are disputed or allowed to run on year after year unpaid; he is often dismissed because he cannot put himself in the place of Providence and save life, and a truly grateful, generous patient is almost an unknown rarity. I do not speak of these things to complain of them. I suppose they are a necessary part of that whole providential plan by which God molds and fashions and tempers the human soul, just as my petty, but incessant household cares are. If I had nothing to do but love my husband and children and perform for them, without obstacle or hindrance, the sweet ideal duties of wife and mother, how content I would be to live always in this world! But what would become of me if I were not called, in the pursuit of these duties and in contact with real life, to bear "restless nights, ill-health, unwelcome news, the faults of servants, contempt, ingratitude of friends, my own failings, lowness of spirits, the struggle in overcoming my corruption, and a score of kindred trials!"

Bishop Wilson[31] charges us to bear all these things "as unto God," and "with the greatest privacy." How seldom I have met them save as lions in my way, that I would avoid if I could, and how I have tormented my friends by tedious complaints about them! Yet when compared with the great tragedies of suffering I have both witnessed and suffered, how petty they seem!

Our household, deprived of mother's and James' bright presence, now numbers just as many members as it did before they left us. Another angel has flown into it, though not on wings, and I have four darling children, the baby, who can hardly be called a baby now, being nearly two years old. My hands and my heart are full,[32] but two of the children go to school, and that certainly makes my day's work easier.

The little things are happier for having regular employment, and we are so glad to meet each other again after the brief separation! I try to be at home when it is time to expect them, for I love to hear the eager voices ask, in chorus, the moment the door opens: "Is mamma at home?" Helen has taken Daisy to sleep with her, which after so many years of ups and downs at night, now with restless babies, now to answer the bell when Ernest is out, is a great relief to me. Poor Helen! She has never recovered her cheerfulness since James' death. It has crushed her energies and left her very sorrowful. This is partly owing to a soft and tender nature, easily borne down and overwhelmed, partly to what seems an almost constitutional inability to find rest in God's will. She assents to all we say to her about submission, in a sweet, gentle way, but then comes the invariable, mournful wail, "But it was so unexpected! It came so suddenly!" But, I love the little thing, and her love for us all is one of our greatest comforts.

Martha is greatly absorbed in her own household, its

cares and its pleasures. She brings her little Underhills to see us occasionally, when they put my children quite out of countenance by their consciousness of the fine clothes they wear, and their knowledge of the world. Even I find it hard not to feel humiliated in the presence of so much of the sort of wisdom in which I am lacking.

As to Lucy, she is exactly in her sphere: the calm dignity with which she reigns in her husband's house, and the moderation and self-control with which she guides his children, are really instructive. She has a baby of her own, and though it acts just like other babies, and kicks, scratches, pulls and cries when it is washed and dressed, she goes through that process with a serenity and deliberation that I envy with all my might. Her predecessor in the nursery was all nerve and brain, and has left four children made of the same material behind her. But their wild spirits on one day, and their depression and languor on the next, have no visible effect upon her. Her influence is always quieting; she tones down their vehemence with her own calm decision and practical good sense. It is amusing to see her seated among those four little stallions, who love each other in such a distracted way that somebody's feelings are always getting hurt, and somebody always crying. By a sort of magnetic influence she heals these wounds immediately, and finds some ordinary occupation as an antidote to these poetical moods. I confess that I am instructed and reproved whenever I go to see her, and wish I were more like her.

But there is no use in trying to engraft an opposite

nature on one's own. What I am, that I must be, except as God changes me into His own image. And everything brings me back to that, as my supreme desire. I see more and more that I must be myself what I want my children to be, and that I cannot make myself over even for their sakes. This must be His work, and I wonder that it goes on so slowly; that all the disappointments, sorrows, sicknesses I have passed through, have left me still selfish, still full of imperfections!

March 5, 1852

This is the fifth anniversary of James' death. Thinking it all over after I went to bed last night, his sickness, his death, and the weary months that followed for mother, I could not get to sleep till long past midnight. Then Una woke, crying with the earache, and I was up till nearly day-break with her, poor child. I got up weary and depressed, almost ready to faint under the burden of life, and dreading to meet Helen, who is doubly sad on these anniversaries. She came down to breakfast dressed as usual in deep mourning, and looking as spiritless as I felt. The prattle of the children relieved the somber silence maintained by the rest of us, each of whom acted depressingly on the others. How things do flash into one's mind. These words suddenly came into mine, as we sat so gloomily at the table God had spread for us, and which He had enlivened by the four young faces around it—

Why should the children of a King
Go mourning all their days?

Why, indeed? Children of a *King!* I felt grieved that I was so intent on my own sorrows as to lose sight of my relationship to Him. And then I asked myself what I could do to make the day less wearisome and sorrowful to Helen. She came, after a time, with her work to my room. The children took their goodbye kisses and went off to school; Ernest took his, too, and set forth on his day's work, while Daisy played quietly about the room.

"Helen, dear," I ventured at last to begin, "I want you to do me a favor *today*."

"Yes," she said, languidly.

"I want you to go to see Mrs. Campbell. This is the day for her beef-tea, and she will be looking out for one of us."

"You must not ask me to go today," Helen answered.

"I think I must, dear. When other springs of comfort dry up, there is one always left to us. And that, as mother often said, is usefulness."

"I do try to be useful," she said.

"Yes, you are very kind to me and to the children. If you were my own sister you could not do more. But these little duties do not relieve that aching void in your heart which yearns so for relief."

"No," she said, quickly, "I have no such yearning. I just want to settle down as I am now."

"Yes, I suppose that is the natural tendency of sorrow. But there *is* great significance in the prayer for 'a heart at leisure from itself, to soothe and sympathize.'"

"Oh, Katy!" she said, "you don't know, you can't know, how I feel. Until James began to love me so I did not know there was such a love as that in the world. You know our family is different from yours. And it is so delightful to be loved. Or rather it was!"

"Don't say *was*," I said. "You know we all love you dearly, dearly."

"Yes, but not as James did!"

"That is true. It was foolish of me to expect to console you by such suggestions. But to get back to Mrs. Campbell. She will sympathize with you, if you will let her, as very few can, for she has lost both husband and children."

"Ah, but she *had* a husband for a time, at least. It is not as if he were snatched away before they had lived together."

If anybody else had said this I would have felt that it was out of mere perverseness. But dear little Helen is not perverse; she is simply overburdened with sorrow.

"I grant that your *disappointment* was greater than hers," I went on. "But the *affliction* was not. Every day that a husband and wife walk hand in hand together upon earth makes of the two more and more one flesh. The selfish element which at first formed so large a part of their attraction to each other disappears, and the union becomes so pure and beautiful as to form a fitting type of the union of Christ and His church (Ephesians 5:22-33). There is nothing else on earth like it."

Helen sighed.

"I find it hard to believe," she said, "there can be

anything more delicious than the months in which James and I were so happy together."

"Suffering together would have brought you even nearer," I replied. "Dear Helen, I am very sorry for you; I hope you feel that, even when, according to my deficiency, I fall into arguments, as if one could argue a sorrow away!"

"You are so happy," she answered. "Ernest loves you so dearly, and is so proud of you, and you have such lovely children! I ought not to expect you to sympathize perfectly with my loneliness."

"Yes, I am happy," I said, after a pause; "but you must admit, dear, that I have had my sorrows, too. Until you become a mother yourself, you cannot comprehend what a mother can suffer, not merely for herself, in losing her children, but in seeing their sufferings. I think I may say of my happiness that it *rests* on something higher and deeper than even Ernest and my children."

"And what is that?"

"The will of God, the sweet will of God. If He should take them all away, I might still possess a peace which would flow on forever. I know this partly from my own experience and partly from that of others. Mrs. Campbell says that the three months that followed the death of her first child were the happiest she had ever known. Mrs. Wentworth, whose husband was snatched from her almost without warning, and while using expressions of affection for her such as a lover addresses to his bride, said to me, with tears rolling down her cheeks, yet with a smile,

'I thank my God and Saviour that He has not forgotten and passed me by, but has counted me worthy to bear this sorrow for His sake.' And listen to this passage from the life of Wesley,[33] which I happened upon this morning:

"He visited one of his disciples, who was ill in bed, and after having buried seven of her family in six months, had just heard that the eighth, her husband, whom she dearly loved, had been cast away at sea. 'I asked her,' he says, 'do you not fret at any of these things?' She says, with a lovely smile, 'Oh, no! how can I fret at anything which is the will of God? Let Him take all beside, He has given me Himself. I love, I praise Him every moment.' "

"Yes," Helen objected, "I can imagine people saying such things in moments of excitement; but afterwards, they have hours of awful agony."

"They have 'hours of awful agony,' of course. God's grace does not harden our hearts, and make them invincible against suffering, like coats of armor. They can all say, '*Out of the depths* have I cried unto Thee' (Psalm 130:1), and it is they alone who have been down into the depths, and had rich experience of what God could be to His children there, who can utter such testimonials to His honor, as those I have just repeated."

"Katy?" Helen inquired, "do you always submit to God's will?"

"In great things I do," I said. "What grieves me is that I am constantly forgetting to recognize God's hand in the little every-day trials of life, and instead of receiving them as from Him, find fault with the instruments by which He sends them. I can give up my child, my only brother, my darling mother without a word; but to receive every tiresome visitor as sent expressly and directly to weary me by the Master Himself; to meet every negligence on the part of the servants as His choice for me at the moment; to be satisfied and patient when Ernest gets particularly absorbed in his books, because my Father sees that little discipline suitable for me at the time; all this I have not fully learned."

"All you say discourages me," said Helen, in a tone of deep dejection. "Such perfection was only meant for a few favored ones, and I do not dare so much as to aim at it. I am perfectly sure that I must be satisfied with the low state of grace I am in now and always have been."

She was about to leave me, but I caught her hand as she attempted to pass me, and made one more attempt to reach her poor, weary soul.

"But *are* you satisfied, dear Helen?" I asked, as tenderly as I would speak to a little sick child. "Surely you crave happiness, as every human soul does!"

"Yes, I crave it," she replied, "but God has taken it from me."

"He has taken away your earthly happiness, I know, but only to convince you what better things He has in store for you. Let me read you a letter which Dr. Cabot wrote me many years ago, but which has been an almost constant inspiration to me ever since."

She sat down, resumed her work again, and listened

to the letter in silence. As I came to its last sentence the three children rushed in from school, at least the boys did, and threw themselves upon me like men assaulting a fort. I have formed the habit of giving myself entirely to them at the proper moment, and now entered into their frolicsome mood as joyously as if I had never known a sorrow or lost an hour's sleep. At last they went off to their playroom, and Una settled down by my side to amuse Daisy, when Helen began again.

"I would like to read that letter myself," she said, "Meanwhile I want to ask you one question. What *are* you made of that you can turn from one thing to another like lightning? Talking one moment as if life depended on your every word, and then frisking about with those wild boys as if you were a child yourself?"

I saw Una look up curiously, to hear my answer, as I replied,

"I have always aimed at this flexibility. I think a mother, especially, must learn to enter into the happy moods of her children at the very moment when her own heart is sad. And it may be as religious an act for her to romp with them at that time as to pray with them at others."

Helen now went away to her room with Dr. Cabot's letter, which I silently prayed might bless her as it has blessed me. And then a weary, disheartened mood came over me that made me feel that all I had been saying to her was but as sounding brass and a tinkling cymbal, since my life and my professions did not correspond. To this point my consciousness of imperfection has made me hesitate to say much to Helen. Why are we so afraid of those who live under the same roof with us? It must be the conviction that those who daily see us acting in a petty, selfish, trifling way, must find it hard to conceive that our prayers and our desires take a wider and higher aim. Dear little Helen! May the ice once broken remain broken forever.

Chapter 24

Helen returned Dr. Cabot's letter in silence this morning, but, directly after breakfast, set forth to visit Mrs. Campbell, with the little bottle of beef-tea in her hands, which ought to have gone yesterday. I had a busy day before me; the usual Saturday baking and Sunday dinner to oversee, the children's lessons for tomorrow to superintend and hear them repeat, their clean clothes to lay out, and a basket of stockings to mend. My mind was somewhat distracted with these cares, and I found it a little difficult to keep on with my morning devotions in spite of them. But I have learned, at least, to face and fight such distractions, instead of running away from them as I used to do. My faith in prayer, my resort to it, becomes more and more the foundation of my life, and I believe, with one wiser and better than myself, that nothing but prayer stands between my soul and the best gifts of God; in other words, that I can and shall get what I ask for.

I went down into the kitchen, put on my large baking apron, and began my labors; of course the door-bell rang,

and a poor woman was announced. It is very sweet to follow Fenelon's[34] counsel and give oneself to Christ in all
these interruptions; but this time I said, "Oh, dear!" before
I thought. Then I wished I hadn't, and went up, with a
cheerful face, at any rate, to my unwelcome visitor, who
proved to be one of my aggravating poor folks— a great
giant of a woman, in perfect health, and with a husband to
support her if he will. I told her that I could do no more
for her; she answered me rudely, and kept on urging her
claims. I felt ruffled; why should my time be thus frittered
away, I asked myself. At last she went off, abusing me in a
way that chilled my heart. I could only beg God to forgive
her, and return to my work, which I had hardly resumed
when Mrs. Embury sent for a pattern I had promised to
lend her. Off came my apron, and up two pairs of stairs I
ran; after a long search it came to light. Work resumed;
door-bell again. Aunty wanted the children to come to an
early dinner. Going to Aunty's is next to going to Paradise
to them. Everything was now hurry and flurry; I tried to
be patient, and not to fret their temper by undue attention
to nails, ears, and other susceptible parts of the human
frame, but after it was all over, and I had kissed all the
sweet, dear faces goodbye, and returned to the kitchen, I felt
sure that I had not been the perfect mother I want to be in
all these little emergencies— yes, far from it. Bridget had
let the milk I was going to use boil over, and finally burn
up. I was annoyed and irritated, and already tired, and did
not see how I was to get more, as Mary was cleaning the
silver (to be sure, there is not much of it), and had other

extra Saturday work to do. I thought Bridget *might* offer to run to the corner for it, though it isn't her business, but she is not obliging, and seemed as sulky as if I had burned the milk, not she. "After all," I said to myself, "what does it signify, if Ernest gets no dessert? It isn't good for him, and how much precious time is wasted over just this one thing? However, I reflected, that arbitrarily refusing to indulge him in this respect is not exactly my mission as his wife; he is perfectly healthy, and likes his little luxuries as well as other people do. So I humbled my pride and asked Bridget to go for the milk, which she did, in a lofty way of her own. While she was gone the marketing came home, and I had everything to dispose of. Ernest had sent home some apples, which plainly meant, "I want some apple pie, Katy." I looked nervously at the clock, and undertook to gratify him. Mary came down, crying, to say that her mother, who lived in Brooklyn, was very sick; could she go to see her? I looked at the clock once more; told her she could go, of course, as soon as lunch was over; this involved my doing all her absence left undone.

At last I got through with the kitchen, the Sunday dinner being well under way, and ran upstairs to put away the host of little garments the children had left when they took their flight, and to make myself presentable at lunch. Then I began to be uneasy lest Ernest should not be punctual, and Mary be delayed; but he came just as the clock struck one. I ran joyfully to meet him, very glad now that I had something good to give him. We had just gotten through lunch, and I was opening my mouth to tell Mary she could go, when the doorbell rang once more, and Mrs. Fry, of Jersey City, was announced. I told Mary to wait till I found whether she had eaten lunch or not; no, she hadn't; had come to town to see friends off, was half famished, and would I do her the favor, etc., etc. She had a fashionable young lady with her, a stranger to me, as well as a Miss Somebody else, from Albany, whose name I did not catch. I apologized for having finished lunch. Mrs. Fry said all they wanted was a cup of tea and a bit of bread and butter, nothing else, dear; now don't put yourself out.

"Now be bright and animated, and like yourself," she whispered, "for I have brought these girls here on purpose to hear you talk, and they are prepared to fall in love with you on the spot."

This speech sufficed to shut my mouth.

Mary had to get ready for these unexpected guests, whose appetites proved equal to a raid on a good many things besides bread and butter. Mrs. Fry said, after she had devoured nearly half a loaf of cake, that she would really try to eat a morsel more, which Ernest remarked, drily, was a great triumph of mind over matter. As they talked and laughed and ate leisurely on, Mary stood looking the picture of despair. At last I gave her a glance that said she might go, when a new visitor was announced— Mrs. Winthrop, from Brooklyn, one of Ernest's patients a few years ago, when she lived here. She professed herself greatly indebted to him, and said she had come at this hour because she could make sure of seeing him. I tried to excuse him, as I knew he would be thankful to have me do, but no, see him she must ; he was her "pet doctor," he had such "sweet, bedside manners," and "I am such a favorite with him, you know!"

Ernest did not receive his "favorite" with any special warmth; but invited her out to lunch and chivalrously led her to the table we had just left. Just like a man! Poor Mary! she had to fly around and get up what she could; Mrs. Winthrop devoted herself to Ernest with a persistent ignoring of me that I thought rude and unwomanly. She asked if he had read a certain book; he had not; she then said, "I need not ask, then, if Mrs. Elliott has done so? These charming dissipations which she gets up so nicely, must absorb all her time." "No, indeed," replied Ernest. "But she contrives to read the report of all the murders, of which the newspapers are full."

Mrs. Winthrop took this speech literally, drew away her skirts from me, looked at me through her eye-glass, and said, "Is it possible?" At last she departed. Helen came home, and I gave her an account of my morning; she laughed heartily, and it did me good to hear that musical sound once more.

"It is nearly three o'clock," I said, as we at last had restored everything to order, "and this whole day has been frittered away on most insignificant trifles. It isn't living to live so. Who is the better for my being in the world since six o'clock this morning?"

"I am for one," she said, kissing my hot cheeks; "and you have given a great deal of pleasure to several persons. Your and Ernest's hospitality is always graceful. I admire it in you both; and this is one of the little ways, not to be despised, of giving real enjoyment." It was nice of her to say that; it quite refreshed me.

At the dinner table Ernest complimented me on my good housekeeping.

"I was proud of my little wife at lunch," he said.

"And yet you said that outrageous thing about my reading about nothing but murders!" I said.

"Oh, well, you understood it," he said, laughingly.

"But that dreadful Mrs. Winthrop took it literally."

"What do we care for Mrs. Winthrop?" he returned. "If you could have seen the contrast between you two in my eyes!"

After all, one must take life as it comes; its homely details are so mixed up with its sweet charities, and loves, and friendships that one is forced to believe that God has joined them together, and does not desire that they should be put asunder. It is something wonderful that my husband has been satisfied with his wife and his home today; that does me good.

March 30

A stormy day and the children home from school, and no little frolicking and laughing going on. It must be delightful to feel healthy and strong while one's children are young, there is so much to do for them. *I do it;* but no one can tell the effort it costs me. What a contrast there is between their vitality and the weariness under which I suffer! When their noise became intolerable, I proposed to read to them; of course they made ten times as much clamor of pleasure and of course they leaned on me, ground their elbows into my lap, and tired me all out. As I sat with this precious little group about me, Ernest opened the door, looked in, gravely and without a word, and instantly disappeared. I felt uneasy and asked him, this evening, why he looked so. Was I indulging the children too much, or what was it? He took me into his arms and said:

"My precious wife, why will you torment yourself with such fancies? My very heart was yearning over you at that moment, as it did the first time I saw you surrounded by your little class at Sunday-school, years ago, and I was asking myself why God had given me such a wife, and my children such a mother."

Oh, I am glad I have gotten this written down! I will read it over when the sense of my deficiencies overwhelms me, while I ask God why He has given me such a patient, forbearing husband.

April 1

This has been a sad day for our church. Dear Dr. Cabot has gone to his eternal home, and left us as sheep without a shepherd.

His death was sudden at the last, and found us all unprepared for it. But my tears of sorrow are mingled with tears of joy. His heart had long been in heaven, he was ready to go at a moment's warning; never was a soul so constantly and joyously on the wing as his. Poor Mrs.

Cabot! She is left very desolate, for all their children are married and settled at a distance. But she bears this sorrow like one who has long felt herself a pilgrim and a stranger on earth. How strange that we ever forget that we are all such!

April 16

The desolate pilgrimage was not long. Dear Mrs. Cabot was this day laid away by the side of her beloved husband, and it is delightful to think of them as not divided by death, but united by it in a complete and eternal union.

I never saw a husband and wife more tenderly attached to each other, and this is a beautiful close to their long and happy married life. I find it hard not to wish and pray that I may as speedily follow my precious husband, should God call him away first. But it is not for me to choose.

How I shall miss these faithful friends, who, from my youth up, have been my stay and my staff in the house of my pilgrimage! Almost all the disappointments and sorrows of my life have had their Christian sympathy, particularly the daily, wasting solicitude concerning my darling Una, for they too watched for years and years, loving our delicate little flower, and saw it fade and die. Only those who have suffered thus can appreciate the heart-soreness through which, no matter how outwardly cheerful I may be, I am always passing. But what then! Have I not ten thousand times made this my prayer, that in the words of Leighton, "my will might become identical with God's will."

And shall He not take me at my word? Just as I was writing these words, my canary burst forth with a song so joyous that a song was put also into my mouth. Something seemed to say, this captive sings in his cage because it has never known liberty, and cannot regret a lost freedom. So the soul of my child, limited by the restrictions of a feeble body, never having known the gladness of exuberant health, may sing songs that will enliven and cheer. Yes, and does sing them! What should we do without her gentle, loving presence, whose frailty calls forth our most tender affections and whose sweet face makes sunshine in the shadiest places! I am sure that the boys are truly blessed by having a sister always at home to welcome them, and that their best manliness is appealed to by her helplessness.

What this child is to me I cannot tell. And yet, if the skillful and kind Gardener should choose to house this delicate plant before frosts come, should I dare to complain?

Chapter 25

Miss Clifford came to lunch with us on Wednesday. Her remarkable restoration to health has attracted a good deal of attention, and has given Ernest a certain reputation which does not come amiss to him. Not that he is ambitious; a more unworldly man does not live; but his extreme reserve and modesty have obscured the light that is now beginning to shine. We all enjoyed Miss Clifford's visit. She is one of the freshest, most original creatures I ever met with, and kept us all laughing with her quaint speeches, long after every particle of lunch had disappeared from the table. But this changeable nature turns to the serious side of life with marvelous ease and swiftness, as perhaps all sound ones ought to do. I took her up to my room where my work-basket was, and Helen followed, with hers.

"I have brought something to read to you, dear Mrs. Elliott," Miss Clifford began, the moment we had seated ourselves, "which I have just lighted upon, and I am sure you will like. A nobleman writes to Fenelon asking certain questions, and a part of these questions, with the replies, I want to enjoy with you, since they cover a good deal of the ground we have often discussed together":

> "I.— *How shall I offer my purely insignificant actions to God; such as walks, visits made and received, dress, little proprieties, such as washing the hands, etc., the reading of books of history, business with which I am charged for my friends, other amusements, such as shopping, having clothes made, and furniture. I want to have some sort of prayer, or method of offering each of these things to God.*
>
> *Reply— The most insignificant actions cease to be such, and become good as soon as one performs them with the intention of conforming one's self in them to the will of God. They are often better and purer than certain actions which appear more virtuous: first, because they are less of our own choice and more in the order of Providence when one is obliged to perform them; second, because they are simpler and less exposed to vain self-gratification; third, because if one yields to them with moderation, one finds in them more of death to one's inclinations than in certain acts of fervor in which self-love mingles; and finally, because these little occasions occur more frequently, and furnish a secret occasion for continually making every moment profitable.*
>
> *It is not necessary to make great efforts nor acts of great reflection, in order to offer what are called insignificant actions. It is enough to lift the soul one instant to God, to make, a simple offering of it. Everything which God wishes us to do, and which enters into the course of occupation suitable to our position, can and ought to be offered to God; nothing is unworthy of Him but sin. When you feel that an action cannot be offered to God, conclude that it is not appropriate for a Christian; it is at least necessary to suspect it, and seek light*

concerning it. I would not have a special prayer for each of these things, the elevation of the heart at the moment is sufficient.

As for visits, commissions and the like, as there is danger of following one's own taste too much, I would add to this elevating of the heart a prayer for grace to moderate myself and use precaution.

II.— In prayer I cannot keep my mind fixed on God, or I have intervals of time when it drifts elsewhere, and it is often distracted for a long time before I perceive it. I want to find some means of becoming its master.

Reply— Fidelity in following the rules that have been given you, and in recalling your mind every time you perceive its distractions with patience and humility; you deserve nothing better. Is it surprising that recollection is difficult to a man so long dissipated and far from God?

III.— I wish to know if it is best to record, in my journal, the faults and the sins I have committed, in order not to run the risk of forgetting them. I excite in myself to repentance for my faults as much as I can; but I have never felt any real grief on account of them. When I examine myself at night, I see persons far more perfect than I am complain of more sin; but as for me, I seek, and find nothing; and yet it is impossible there should not be many points on which to plead for pardon every day of my life.

Reply— You should examine yourself every night, but simply and briefly. In the disposition to which God has brought you, you will not voluntarily commit any considerable fault without remembering and reproaching yourself for it. As to little faults, scarcely perceived, even if you sometimes forget them, this need not make you uneasy.

As to lively grief on account of your sins, it is not necessary. God gives it when it pleases Him. True and essential conversion of the heart consists in a full will to sacrifice all to God. What I call "full will" is a fixed immovable disposition of the will to resume none of the voluntary affections which may alter the purity of the love to God and to abandon itself to all the crosses which it will perhaps be necessary to bear, in order to accomplish the will of God always and in all things. As to sorrow for sin, when one has it, one ought to return thanks for it; when one perceives it to be lacking, one should humble one's self peacefully before God without trying to excite it by vain efforts.

You find in your self-examination fewer faults than persons more advanced and more perfect do; it is because your interior light is still feeble. It will increase, and the view of your infidelities will increase in proportion. It suffices, without making yourself uneasy, to try to be faithful to the degree of light you possess, and to instruct yourself by reading and meditation. It will not do to try to obstruct the grace that belongs to a more advanced period. It would only serve to trouble and discourage you, and even to exhaust you by continual anxiety; the time that should be spent in loving God would be given to forced returns upon yourself, which secretly nourish self-love.

IV.— In my prayers my mind has difficulty in finding anything to say to God. My heart is not in it, or it is inaccessible to the thoughts of my mind.

Reply— It is not necessary to say much to God. Oftentimes one does not speak much to a friend whom one is delighted to see; one looks at him with pleasure; one speaks certain short words to him which are mere expressions of feeling. The mind has no part in them, or next to none; one keeps repeating the same words. It is not so much a variety of *thoughts that one seeks in intercourse with a friend, as a certain repose and correspondence of heart. It is thus we are with God, who does not despise being our most tender, most cordial, most familiar, most intimate friend. A word, a sigh, a sentiment, says all to God; it is not always necessary to have transports of conscious tenderness; a will all naked and dry, without life, without vivacity, without pleasure, is often purest in the sight of God. In closing, it is necessary to content one's self with giving to Him what He gives it to give, a fervent heart when it is fervent, a heart firm and faithful in its barrenness, when He deprives it of conscious fervor. It does not always depend on you to feel; but it is necessary to wish to feel. Leave it to God to choose to make you feel sometimes, in order to sustain your weakness and infancy in Christian life; sometimes weaning you from that sweet and consoling sentiment which is the milk of babes, in order to humble you, to make you grow, and to make you robust in the violent exercise of faith, by causing you to eat the bread of the strong in the sweat of your brow. Would you only love God according as He will make you take pleasure in loving Him? You would be loving your own tenderness and feeling, fancying that you were loving God. Even while receiving sensible gifts, prepare yourself by pure faith for the time when you might be deprived of them; and you will suddenly succumb if you had only relied on such support.*

I forgot to speak of some practices which may, at the beginning, promote the remembrance of the offering one ought to make to God, of all the ordinary acts of the day.

1. Form the resolution to do so, every morning, and call yourself to account in your self-examination at night.

2. Make no resolutions but for good reasons, either from propriety or the necessity of relaxing the mind, etc. Thus, in accustoming one's self to retrench the useless little by little, one accustoms one's self to offer what is not proper to curtail.

> 3. *Renew one's self in this disposition whenever one is alone, in order to be better prepared to remember it when in company.*
>
> 4. *Whenever one surprises one's self in too great a wastefulness, or in speaking too freely of his neighbor, let him collect himself and offer to God all the rest of the conversation.*
>
> 5. *To flee, with confidence, to God, to act according to His will, when one enters company, or engages in some occupation which may cause one to fall into temptation. The sight of danger ought to warn of the need there is to lift the heart toward Him by one who may be preserved from it."*

We both thanked her as she finished reading, and I begged her to lend me the volume that I might make the above copy.

I hope I have gained some valuable hints from this letter, and that I shall see more plainly than ever that it is a religion of principle that God wants from us, not one of mere feeling.

Helen remarked that she was most struck by the assertion that one cannot forestall the graces that belong to a more advanced period. She said she had assumed that she *ought* to experience all that the most mature Christian did, and that it comforted her to think of God as doing this work for her, making repentance, for instance, a free gift, not a conquest to be won for one's self.

Miss Clifford said that the whole idea of giving one's self to God in such little daily acts as visiting, shopping, and the like, was entirely new to her.

"But imagine," she went on, her beautiful face lighted up with enthusiasm, "what a blessed life that must be, when the base things of this world, and things that are despised, are so many links to the invisible world, and to the things God has chosen!"

"In other words," I said, "the top of the ladder that rests on earth reaches to heaven, and we may ascend it as the angels did in Jacob's dream" (Genesis 28:12).

"And *descend* too, as they did," Helen put in, despondently.

"Now you shall not speak in that tone," cried Miss Clifford. "Let us look at the bright side of life, and believe that God means us to be always ascending, always getting nearer to Himself, always learning something new about Him, always loving Him better and better. To be sure, our souls are sick, and of themselves can't keep 'ever on the wing,' but I have had some delightful thoughts of late from just hearing the title of a book, 'God's method with the maladies of the soul.' It gives one such a conception of the seeming ills of life; to think of Him as our Physician, the ills all *remedies* the deprivations only a wholesome course for our good, the losses all gains. Why, as I study this individual case, and that, see how patiently and persistently He tries now this remedy, now that, and how infallibly He cures the souls that submit to His remedies, I love Him so! I love Him so! And I am so astonished that we are restless under His unerring hand! Think how He has dealt with me. My soul was sick unto death, sick with worldliness, and self-pleasing and folly. There was only one way of making me listen to reason, and that was just the way He took. He snatched me right out of the world and shut me up in one room, crippled, helpless, and alone, and set me to thinking, thinking, thinking, till I saw the emptiness and shallowness of all in which I had hitherto been involved. And then He sent you and your mother to show me the reality of life, and to reveal to me my invisible, unknown Physician. Can I love Him with half my heart? Can I be asking questions as to how much I am to pay towards the debt I owe Him?"

By this time Helen's work had fallen from her hands and tears were in her eyes.

"How I thank you," she said softly, "for what you have said. You have interpreted life to me! You have given me a new conception of my God and Saviour!"

Miss Clifford seemed quenched and humbled by these words; her enthusiasm faded away and she looked at Helen with a disapproving demeanor as she replied: "Don't say that! I never felt so unfit for anything but to sit at the feet of Christ's disciples and learn of them."

Yet I, so many years one of those disciples, had been sitting at her feet, and had learned of her. Never had I so realized the magnitude of the work to be done in this world, nor the power and goodness of Him who has undertaken to do it all. I was glad to be alone, to walk my room singing praises to Him for every instance in which, as my Physician, He had "disappointed my hope and defeated my joy," and given me to drink of the cup of sorrow and bereavement.

May 24

I read to Ernest the extract from Fenelon which has made such an impression on me.

"Every business man, in fact every man leading an active life, ought to read that," he said. "We would have a new order of things as the result. Instead of fancying that our ordinary daily work was one thing and our religion quite another thing, we would transform our acts of drudgery into acts of worship. Instead of going to prayer-meetings to get into a 'good frame,' we would live in a good frame from morning till night, from night till morning, and prayer and praise would be only another form for expressing the love and faith and obedience we had been exercising amidst all the various pressures of business."

"I only wish I had understood this years ago," I said. "I have made prayer too much of a luxury, and have often inwardly chafed and fretted when the care of my children at times, made it utterly impossible to leave them for private devotion— when they have been sick, for instance, or in other similar emergencies. I reasoned this way: 'Here is a special demand on my patience, and I am naturally impatient. I *must* have time to go away and entreat the Lord to equip me for this conflict.' But I see now that the simple act of cheerful acceptance of the duty imposed and the solace and support withdrawn would have united me more fully to Christ than the highest enjoyment of His presence in prayer could."

"Yes, every act of obedience is an act of worship," he said.

"But why don't we learn that sooner? Why do we waste our lives before we learn how to live?"

"I am not sure," he returned, "that we do not learn as fast as we are willing to learn. God does not force instruction upon us, but when we say, as Luther[35] did, 'More light, Lord, more light,' the light comes."

I questioned myself after he had gone as to whether this could be true of me. Is there not in my heart some secret reluctance to know the truth, lest that knowledge should call to a higher and a holier life than I have yet lived?

June 2

I went to see Mrs. Campbell a few days ago, and found, to my great joy, that Helen had just been there, and that they had had a long and earnest conversation together. Mrs. Campbell's health has failed a good deal of late, and it is not likely that we shall have her with us much longer. Her every look and word is precious to me when I think of her as one who is so soon to enter the unseen world, and see our Saviour, and be welcomed home by Him. If it is so delightful to be with those who are on the way to heaven, what would it be to have fellowship with one who had come from that glorious place, and could tell us what it is!

She spoke freely about death, and said Ernest had promised to take complete charge of her funeral, and to see that she was buried by the side of her husband.

"You see, my dear," she added, with a smile, "though I am expecting to be so soon a saint in heaven, I am a human being still, with human weaknesses. What can it really matter where this weary old body is laid away, when I have done with it, and gone and left it forever? And yet I am leaving directions about its disposal!" I said I was glad that she was still human, but that I did not think it a weakness to take thought for the abode in which her soul had dwelt so long. I saw that she was tired and was just preparing to leave, but she held me and would not let me go.

"Yes, I am tired," she said, "but what of that? It is only a question of days now, and all my tired feelings will be over. Then I shall be as young and as fresh as ever, and shall have strength to praise and to love God as I cannot do now. But before I go I want once more to tell you how good He is, how blessed it is to suffer with Him, how infinitely happy He has made me in the very hottest heat of the furnace. It will strengthen you in your trials to recall this my dying testimony. There is no wilderness so dreary but that His love can illuminate it; no desolation so desolate but that He can sweeten it. I *know* what I am saying. It is no delusion. I believe that the highest, purest happiness is known only to those who have learned Christ in sick-rooms, in poverty, in painful suspense and anxiety, amid hardships, and at the open grave."

Yes, the radiant face, worn by sickness and suffering, but radiant still, said in language yet more unspeakably impressive,

"To learn Christ, this is life!"

I came into the busy and noisy streets as one descending from the mount, and on reaching home found my darling Una very ill in Ernest's arms. She had fallen, and injured her head. How I had prayed that God would temper the wind to this shorn lamb, and now she had had such a fall! We watched over her till far into the night, scarcely speaking to each other, but I know by the way in which Ernest held my hand clasped in his that her precious life was in danger. He consented at last to lie down, but Helen stayed with me. What a night it was! God only knows what the human heart can experience in a space of time that men call hours. I went over all the past history of the child, recalling all her sweet looks and words, and my own secret complaints at the delicate health that has cut her off from so many of the pleasures that belong to her age. And the more I thought, the more I clung to her, on whom, frail as she is, I was beginning to lean, and whose influence in our home I could not think of losing without a shudder. Alas, my faith seemed, for a time, to flee, and I could see just what a poor, weak human being is without it. But before daylight crept into my room light from on high streamed into my heart, and I gave even this, my ewe-lamb, away, as my free-will offering to God. Could I refuse Him my child because she was the very apple of my eye? No indeed, then, but let me give to Him, not what I value least, but what I prize and delight in most. Could I not endure heart-sickness for Him who had given His only Son for me! And just as I got to that sweet consent to suffer, He who had only lifted the rod to test my faith laid it down. My darling opened her eyes and looked at us intelligently, and with her own loving smile. But I dared not snatch her and press her to my heart; for her sake I must be outwardly calm at least.

June 6

I am at home with my precious Una, all the rest having gone to church. She lies peacefully on the bed, sadly disfigured, for the time, but Ernest says he apprehends no danger now, and we are a most happy, a most thankful household. The children have all been greatly moved by the events of the last few days, and hover about their sister with great sympathy and tenderness. Where she fell from, or how she fell, no one knows; she remembers nothing about it herself, and it will always remain a mystery.

This is the second time that this beloved child has been returned to us after we had given her away to God.

And as the giving cost us ten-fold more now than it did when she was a feeble baby, so we receive her now as a fresh gift from our loving Father's hand, with ten-fold delight. Ah, we have no excuse for not giving ourselves entirely to Him. He has revealed Himself to us in so many sorrows, and in so many joys; revealed Himself as He does not do unto the world!

Chapter 26

May 13

This has been a Sunday to be held in long remembrance. We were summoned early this morning to Mrs. Campbell, and have seen her joyful release from the fetters that have bound her so long. Her loss to me is irreparable. But I can truly thank God that one more "tired traveler" has had a sweet "welcome home." I can minister no longer to her bodily wants, and listen to her counsels no more, but she has entered as an inspiration into my life, and through all eternity I shall bless God that He gave me that faithful, praying friend. How little they know who languish in what seem useless sick-rooms, or amid the restrictions of frail health, what work they do for Christ by the power of saintly living, and by even fragmentary prayers.

Before her words fade out of my memory I want to write down, from hasty notes made at the time, her answer to some of the last questions I asked her on earth. She had always enjoyed intervals of comparative ease, and it was in one of these that I asked her what she conceived to be the characteristics of an advanced state of grace. She replied, "I think that the mature Christian is always, at all times, and in all circumstances, what he was in his best moments in the progressive stages of his life. There were seasons, all along his journey, when he loved God supremely; when he embraced the cross joyfully and penitently; when he held intimate communion with Christ, and loved his neighbor as himself. But he was always in terror, lest under the force of temptation, all this should give place to deadness and dullness, when he should chafe and rebel in the hour of trial, and judge his fellow-man with a harsh and bitter judgment, and give way to angry, passionate emotions. But these fluctuations cease, after a time, to disturb his peace. Love to Christ becomes the abiding, inmost principle of his life; he loves Him rather for what He is than for what He has done or will do for him individually, and God's honor becomes so dear to him that he feels personally wounded when that is called in question. And the will of God becomes so dear to him that he loves it best when it 'triumphs at his cost.'"

"Once he only prayed at set times and seasons, and idolized good frames and fervent emotions. Now he prays without ceasing, and whether on the mount or down in the depths depends wholly upon his Saviour.

"His old self-confidence has now given place to child-like humility that will not let him take a step alone, and the sweet peace that is now habitual to him, combined with the sense of his own imperfections, fills him with love to his fellow-man. He hears and believes and hopes and endures all things and thinks no evil. The tones of his voice, the very expression of his countenance, become changed, love now controlling where human passions held sway. In short, he is not only a new creature in Jesus Christ, but the habitual and blessed consciousness is that this is so."

These words were spoken deliberately and with reflection.

"You have described my mother, just as she was from the moment her only son, the last of six, was taken from her," I said, at last. "I never before quite understood how that final sorrow weaned her, so to say, from herself, and made her life all love to God and all love to man. But I see it now. Dear Mrs. Campbell, pray for me that I may yet wear her mantle!"

She smiled with a significance that said she had already done so, and then we parted— parted that she might end her pilgrimage and go to her rest— parted that I might pursue mine, I know not how long, nor amid how many cares and sorrows, nor with what weariness and heart-sickness— parted to meet again in the presence of Him we love, with those who have come out of great tribulation, whose robes have been made white in the blood of the Lamb, and who are before the throne of God, and serve Him day and night in His temple, to hunger no more, neither thirst any more, for the Lamb which is in the midst of the throne shall lead them into living fountains of waters; and God shall wipe away all tears from their eyes (Revelation 7:14-17).

May 25

We were talking of Mrs. Campbell, and of her blessed life and blessed death. Helen said it discouraged and troubled her to see and hear such things.

"The last time I saw her when she was able to converse," said she, "I told her that when I reflected on my lack of submission to God's will, I doubted whether I really could be His child. She said, in her gentle, sweet way:

"'Would you venture to resist His will, if you could? Would you really have your dear James back again in this world, if you could?'"

"'I would, I certainly would,' I said.

"She returned, 'I sometimes find it a help, when dull and cramped in my devotions, to say to myself: Suppose Christ should now appear before you, and you could see Him as He appeared to His disciples on earth, what would you say to Him? This brings Him near, and I say what I would say if He were visibly present. I do the same when a new sorrow threatens me. I imagine my Redeemer as coming *personally* to say to me, "For your sake I am a man of sorrows and acquainted with grief; now for My sake give me this child, bear this burden, submit to this loss," Can I refuse Him? Now, dear, He has really come thus to you, and asked you to show your love to Him, your faith in Him, by giving Him the most precious of your treasures. If He were here at this moment, and offered to restore it to you, would you dare to say, "Yea, Lord, I know, far better than Thou dost, what is good for him and good for me; I will have him return to me, cost what it may; in this world of uncertainties and disappointments I shall be sure of happiness in his society, and he will enjoy more here on earth with me than he could enjoy in the companionship of saints and angels and of the Lord Himself in heaven," Could you dare to say this?' Oh, Katy, what straits she drove me into! No, I could not dare to say that!"

"Then, my darling little sister!" I cried, "you will give up this struggle? You will let God do what He will with His own?"

"I *have* to let Him," she replied; "but I submit because I must."

I looked at her gentle, pure face as she uttered these words, and could only marvel at the strong will that had no expression there.

"Tell me," she said, "do you think a real Christian can feel as I do? For my part I doubt it. I doubt everything."

"Doubt everything, but believe in Christ," I said. "Suppose, for argument's sake, you are not a Christian. You can become one now." The color rose in her lovely face; she clasped her hands together in a sort of ecstasy.

"*Yes*" she said, "I *can*."

At last God had sent her the word she wanted.

May 28

Helen came to breakfast this morning in a simple white dress. I had no time to tell the children not to allude to it, so they began in chorus: "Why, Aunty Helen! you have put on a white dress!"

"Why, Aunty, how strange you look!"

"Hurrah! if she don't look like other folks!"

She bore it all with her usual gentleness; or rather with a positive sweetness that captivated them as her negative patience had never done. I said nothing to her, nor did she to me till late in the day, when she came to me, and said:

"Katy, God taught you what to say. All these years I have been tormenting myself with doubts as to whether I could be His child while so unable to say, Thy will be done. If you had said, 'Why, yes, you must be His child, for you professed yourself one a long time ago, and ever since have lived like one,' I would have remained as wretched as ever. As it is, a mountain has been rolled off my heart. Yes, if I was not His child yesterday, I can become one today; if I did not love Him then, I can begin now."

I do not doubt that she *was* His child, yesterday, and last year, and years ago. But let her think what she pleases. A new life is opening before her; I believe it is to be a life of entire devotion to God, and that out of her sorrow there shall spring up a wondrous joy.

September 2, Sweet Briar Farm

Ernest spent Sunday with us, and I have just driven him to the station, and seen him safely off. Things have prospered with us to such a degree that he has been extravagant enough to give me the use, for the summer, of a beautiful little pony and an antiquated vehicle, and I have learned to drive. To be sure I broke one of the shafts of the poor old thing the first time I ventured forth alone, and the other day nearly upset my cargo of children in a pond where I was silly enough to undertake to water my horse. But Ernest, as usual, had patience with me, and begged me to spend as much time as possible in driving about with the children. It is a new experience, and I enjoy it quite as much as he hoped I would. Helen is not with us; she has spent the whole summer with Martha; for Martha, poor thing, is suffering terribly from rheumatism and is almost entirely helpless. I am so sorry for her, after so many years of vigorous health, how hard it must be to endure this pain. With this drawback, we have had a delightful summer; not one sick day, nor one sick night. With no baby to keep me awake, I sleep straight through, as Raymond says, and wake in the morning refreshed and cheerful. We shall have to go home soon; how cruel it seems to bring up children in a great city! Yet what can be done about it? Wherever there are men and women there must be children; what a howling wilderness either city or country would be without them!

The only drawback on my felicity is the separation from Ernest, which become more painful every year to us both. God has blessed our married life; it has had it waves and its billows, but, thanks be unto Him, it has at last settled down into a calm sea of untroubled peace. While I was secretly upbraiding my dear husband for giving so much attention to his profession as to neglect me and my children, he was becoming, every day, more the ideal of a physician, cool, calm, thoughtful, studious, ready to sacrifice his life at any moment in the interests of humanity. How often I have mistaken his preoccupied air for indifference; how many times I have inwardly accused him of coldness, when his whole heart and soul were filled with the grave problem of life, aye, and of death likewise.

But we understand each other now, and I am sure that God dealt wisely and kindly with us when He brought together two such opposite natures. No man of my vehement nature could have borne with me as Ernest has done, and if he had married a woman as calm, as undemonstrative as himself what a strange home his would have been for the nurture of little children? But the heart was in him, and only wanted to be awakened, and my life has called forth music from his. Ah, there are no partings and meetings now that leave discords in the remembrance, no neglected birthdays, no forgotten courtesies. It is beautiful to see the thoughtful brow relax in the presence of wife and children, and to know that ours is, at last, the happy home I so long sighed for. Is the change all in Ernest? Is it not possible that I have grown more reasonable, less childish and aggravating?

We are at a farmhouse. Everything is plain, but neat and nice. I asked Mrs. Brown, our hostess, the other day, if she did not envy me my four little pets; she smiled, said they were the best children she ever saw, and that it was fine to have a family if you have means to start them in the world; for her part, she lived from hand to mouth as it was, and was sure she could never stand the worry and care of a house full of young ones.

"But the worry and care is only half the story," I said. "The other half is pure joy and delight."

"Perhaps so, to people that are well-to-do," she replied; "but to poor folks, driven to death as we are, it's another thing. I was telling him yesterday what a mercy it was that there weren't any young ones around to get under my feet, and I could take city boarders, and help work off the mortgage on the farm."

"And what did your husband say to that?"

"Well, he said we were young and hearty, and there was not such a great hurry about the mortgage, and that he'd give his right hand to have a couple of boys like yours."

"Well?"

"Why, I said, supposing we had a couple of boys, they wouldn't be like yours, dressed to look genteel and to have their genteel ways; but a pair of wild colts, into everything, tearing their clothes off their backs, and wasting money faster than we could earn. He said, 'twasn't the clothes, 'twas the flesh and blood he wanted, and 'twasn't no use to argufy about it; a man that hadn't got any children wasn't mor'n half a man. 'Well,' says I, 'supposing you had a pack of 'em, what have you got to give 'em?' 'Jest exactly what my father and mother gave me,' says he; 'two hands to earn their bread with, and a welcome you could have heard from Dan to Beersheba.[36]'"

"I like to hear that!" I said. "And I hope many such welcomes will resound in this house. Suppose money does come in while little goes out; suppose you get possession of the whole farm; what then? Who will enjoy it with you? Who will you leave it to when you die? And in your old age who will care for you?"

"You seem awful earnest," she said.

"Yes, I am in earnest. I want to see little children adorning every home, as flowers adorn every meadow and every wayside. I want to see them welcomed to the homes they enter, to see their parents grow less and less selfish, and more and more loving, because they have come. I want to see God's precious gifts accepted, not frowned upon and refused."

Mr. Brown came in, so I could say no more. But my heart warmed towards him, as I looked at his frank, good-humored face, and I would have been glad to give him the right hand of fellowship. As it was, I could only say a word or two about the beauty of his farm, and the scenery of this whole region.

"Yes," he said, gratified that I appreciated his fields and groves, "it *is* an awfully pretty laying farm. Part of it was her father's, and part of it was my father's; there ain't another like it in the country. As to the scenery, I don't know as I ever looked at it; city folks talk a good deal about it, but they've nothing to do but look around." Walter came trotting in on two bare, white feet, and with his shoes in his hand. He had had his nap, felt as bright and fresh as he looked rosy, and I did not wonder at Mr. Brown's snatching him up and clasping his sunburnt arms about the little fellow, and pressing him against the warm heart that yearned for nestlings of its own.

September 23

Home again, and full of the thousand cares that follow the summer and precede the winter. But let mothers and wives fret as they will, they enjoy these labors of love, and would feel lost without them. For what amount of leisure, ease, and comfort would I exchange husband and children and this busy home?

Martha is better, and Helen has come back to us. I don't know how we have lived without her so long. Her life seems necessary to the completion of every one of ours. Some others have fancied it necessary to the completion of theirs, but she has not agreed with them. We are glad enough to keep her, and yet I hope the day will come when she, so worthy of it, will taste the sweet joys of wifehood and motherhood.

January 1, 1853

It is not always so easy to practice, as it is to preach. I can see in my wisdom forty reasons for having four children and no more. The comfort of sleeping in peace, of having a little time to read, and to keep on with my music; strength with which to look after Ernest's poor people when they are sick; and, to tell the truth, strength to be bright and fresh and lovable to him— all these little joys have been growing ever precious to me, and now I must give them up. I want to do it cheerfully and without a frown. But I find I love to have my own way, and that at the very moment I was asking God to appoint my work for me, I was secretly marking it out for myself. It is mortifying to find my will less in harmony with His than I thought it was, and that I want to prescribe to Him how I shall spend the time, and the health and the strength which are His, not mine. But I will not rest till this struggle is over; till I can say with a *smile*, "Not my will! Not my will! But Thine!"

We have been, this winter, one of the happiest families on earth. Our love to each other, Ernest's and mine, though not perfect— nothing on earth is— has grown less selfish, more Christ-like; it has been sanctified by prayer and by the sorrows we have borne together. Then the children have been healthy and happy, and the source of almost unmitigated joy and comfort. And Helen's presence in this home, her sisterly affection, her patience with the children and her influence over them, is a benediction for which I cannot be thankful enough. How delightful it is to have a sister! I think it is not often the case that true sisters have such perfect Christian sympathy with each other as we have. Ever since the day she ceased to torment herself with the fear that she was not a child of God, and laid aside the somber garments she had worn so long, she has had a peace that has hardly known a cloud. She says, in a note written to me about the time:

> "*I want you to know, my darling sister, that the despondency that made my affliction so hard to bear fled before those words of yours, which, as I have already told you, God taught you to speak. I do not know whether I was really His child, at the time, or not. I had certainly had an experience very different from yours; prayer had never been much more to me than a duty; and I had never felt the sweetness of that harmony between God and the human soul that I now know*

can take away all the bitterness from the cup of sorrow. I knew— who can help knowing it that reads God's word?— that He required submission from His children and that His children gave it, no matter what it cost. The Bible is full of beautiful expressions of it; so are our hymns; so are the written lives of all good men and good women; and I have seen it in you, my dear Katy, at the very moment you were accusing yourself of the lack of it. Entire oneness of the will with the Divine Will seem to me to be the law and the gospel of the Christian life; and this evidence of a renewed nature I found lacking in myself. At any moment during the three years following James's death I would have snatched him away from God, if I could; I was miserably lonely and desolate without him, not merely because he had been so much to me, but because his loss revealed to me the distance between Christ and my soul. All I could do was to go on praying, year after year, in a dreary, hopeless way, that I might learn to say, as David did, 'I opened not my mouth because Thou didst it' (Ps. 39:9). When you suggested that instead of trying to find out whether I had loved God I should begin to love Him now, light broke in upon my soul; I gave myself to Him that instant and as soon as I could get away by myself I fell upon my knees and gave myself up to the sense of His sovereignty for the first time in my life. Then, too, I looked at my 'light affliction,' and at the 'weight of glory' (2nd Cor. 4:17) side by side, and thanked Him that through the one He had revealed to me the other. Katy, I know the human heart is deceitful above all things, but I think it would be a dishonor to God to doubt that He then revealed Himself to me as He does not do to the world, and that the sweet peace I then found in yielding to Him will be more or less mine so long as I live. Oh, if all sufferers could learn what I have learned! that every broken heart could be healed as mine has been healed! My precious sister, cannot we make this one part of our mission on earth, to pray for every sorrow-stricken soul, and whenever we have influence

*over such, to lead it to honor God by instant obedience to His
will, whatever that may be? I have dishonored Him by years
of rebellious, carefully-nursed sorrow; I want to honor Him
now by years of resignation and grateful joy."*

Reading this letter over in my present mood has done
me good. More beautiful faith in God than Helen's I have
never seen; let me have it, too. May this prayer, which, under
the inspiration of the moment, I can offer without a misgiving, become the habitual, deep-seated desire of my soul:

*"Bring into captivity every thought to the obedience of
Christ. Take what I cannot give— my heart, body,
thoughts, time, abilities, money, health, strength, nights,
days, youth, age, and spend them in Thy service, O my
crucified Master, Redeemer, God. Oh, let not these be mere
words! Whom have I in heaven but Thee? And there is no
one upon the earth that I desire in comparison to Thee.
My heart is athirst for God, for the living God. When shall
I come and appear before God?"*

Chapter 27

August 1

I have just written to Mrs. Brown to know whether she will take us for the rest of the summer. A certain little man, not a very old little man, either, has kept us in town till now. Since he has come, we are all very glad of him, though he came on his own invitation, brought no wardrobe with him, does not pay for his board, never speaks a word, takes no notice of us, and wants more waiting on than any one else in the house. The children are full of delicious curiosity about him, and overwhelm him with presents of the most heterogeneous character.

August 9, Sweet Briar Farm

We got there this afternoon, bag and baggage. I had not said a word to Mrs. Brown about the addition to our family circle, knowing she had plenty of room, and as we alighted from the carriage, I snatched my baby from his nurse's arms and ran gayly up the walk with him in mine. "If this splendid fellow doesn't convert her nothing will," I said to myself. At that instant what should I see but Mrs. Brown, running to meet me with a boy in her arms exactly like Mr. Brown, only not quite six feet long, and not yet sun-burnt.

"There!" I cried, holding up my little old man.

"There!" said she, holding up hers.

We laughed till we cried; she took my baby and I took hers; after looking at him I liked mine better than ever; after looking at mine she was perfectly satisfied with hers.

We got into the house at last; that is to say, we mothers did; the children darted through it and out of the door that led to the fields and woods, and vanished in the twinkling of an eye.

Mrs. Brown had always been a pretty woman, with bright eyes, shining, well-kept hair, and a color in her cheeks like the rose which had given its name to her farm. But there was now a new beauty in her face; the mysterious and sacred sufferings and joys of maternity had given it thought and feeling.

"I had no idea I would be so fond of a baby," she said, kissing it, whenever she stopped to put in a comma; "but I don't know how I ever got along without one. He's off at work nearly the whole day, and when I had gotten through with mine, and had put on my afternoon dress, and was ready to sit down, you can't think how lonesome it was. But now, by the time I am dressed, baby is ready to go out to get the air; he knows the minute he sees me bring out his little hat that he is going to see his father, and he's awful fond of his father. Though that isn't so strange, either, for his father's awful fond of him. All his little ways are so pretty, and he never cries unless he's hungry or tired. Tell mother a pretty story now; yes, mother hears, bless his little heart!"

Then when Mr. Brown came home to his supper, his face was a sight to see, as he caught sight of me at my open window, and came to it with the child's white arms clinging to his neck, looking as happy and as bashful as a girl.

"You see she must needs go to quartering this bouncing young one on to me," he said, "as if I didn't have to work hard enough before. Well, maybe he'll get his feed off the farm; we'll see what we can do."

"Mamma," Una whispered, as he went off with his facsimile, to kiss it rapturously, behind a woodpile, "do you think Mrs. Brown's baby *very* pretty?"

Which was so mild a way of suggesting the fact of the case, that I kissed her without trying to hide my amusement.

August 10

After being cooped up in town so large a part of the summer, the children are nearly wild with delight at being in the country once more. Even our timid Una skips about with a buoyancy I have never seen in her; she never has her ill turns when out of the city, and I wish, for her sake, that we could always live here. As to Raymond and Walter, I never pretend to see them except at their meals and their bedtime; they just live out of doors, following the men at their work, asking all sorts of absurd questions, which Mr. Brown reports to me every night, with shouts of delighted laughter. Two gay and gladsome boys they are; really good without being priggish; I don't think I could stand that. People ask me how it happens that my children are all so promptly obedient and so happy. As if it were by *chance* that some parents have such children, or *chance* that some have not! I am afraid it is only too true, as some one has remarked, that 'this is the age of obedient parents!'[37] What then will be the future of their children? How can they yield to God who have never been taught to yield to human authority? And how well fitted will they be to rule their own households who have never learned to rule themselves?

August 31

This has been one of those cold, dismal, rainy days which are not infrequent during the month of August. So the children have been obliged to give up the open air, of which they are so fond, and fall back upon what entertainment could be found within the house. I have read to them the little journal I kept during the whole life of the brother I am not willing they should forget. His quaint and perceptive sayings were delicious to them; the history of his first steps, and his first words sounded to them like a fairy tale. And the story of his last steps, his last words on earth, had for them such a tender charm, that there was a cry of disappointment from them all, when I closed the little book, and told them we would have to wait till we got to heaven before we could know anything more about his precious life.

How thankful I am that I kept this journal, and that I have almost as charming ones about most of my other children! What I speedily forgot amid the pressure of cares and of new events is safely written down, and will be the source of endless pleasure to them long after the hand that wrote has ceased from its labors, and lies inactive and at rest. Ah, it is a blessed thing to be a mother!

September 1

This baby of mine is certainly the sweetest and best I ever had. I feel an inexpressible tenderness for it which I cannot quite explain to myself, for I have loved them all dearly, most dearly. Perhaps it is so with all mothers; perhaps they all grow more loving, more forbearing, more patient as they grow older, and yearn over these helpless little ones with an ever-increasing, yet chastened delight. One cannot help sheltering their tender infancy, who will so soon pass forth to fight the battle of life, each one waging an invisible warfare against invisible foes. How thankfully we would fight it for them, if we might!

September 20

The mornings and evenings are very cool now, while in the middle of the day it is quite hot. Ernest comes to see us very often, under the pretense that he can't trust me with so young a baby! He is so tender and thoughtful, and spoils me so, that this world is very bright to me; I am a little jealous of it; I don't want to be so happy in Ernest, or in my children, as to forget for one instant that I am a pilgrim and a stranger on earth.

Evening

There is no danger that I shall. Ernest suddenly made his appearance tonight, and in a great burst of distress quite unlike anything I ever saw in him, revealed to me that he had been feeling the greatest anxiety about me ever since the baby came. It is all nonsense. I cough, to be sure; but that it is obviously due to the varying temperature we always have at this season. I shall get over it as soon as we get home, I dare say.

But suppose I should not; what then? *Could* I leave this precious little flock, uncared for, untended? Have I faith to believe that if God calls me away from them, it will be in love to them? I do not know. The thought of getting away from the sin that still so easily besets me, is very delightful, and I have enjoyed so many, many such foretastes of the bliss of heaven that I know I should be happy there; but then, my children, all of them under twelve years old! I will not choose, I dare not.

My married life has been a beautiful one. It is true that sin and folly, and sickness and sorrow, have marred its perfection, but it has been adorned by a love which has never faltered. My faults have never alienated Ernest; his faults, for like other human beings he has them, have never overcome my love to him. This has been the gift of God in answer to our constant prayer, that whatever other bereavement we might have to suffer, we might never be bereft of this benediction. It has been the glad secret of a happy marriage, and I wish I could teach it to every human being who enters upon a state that must bring with it the depth of misery, or life's most sacred and mysterious joy.

October 6

Ernest has let me stay here to see the autumnal foliage in its ravishing beauty for the first, perhaps for the last, time. The woods and fields and groves are lighting up my very soul! It seems as if autumn had caught the inspiration and the glow of summer, had hidden its floral beauty, its gorgeous sunsets and its bow of promise in its heart of hearts, and was now flashing it forth upon the world with a lavish and opulent hand. I can hardly tear myself away, and return to the prose of city life. But Ernest has come for us, and is eager to get us home before colder weather. I laugh at his anxiety about his old wife. Why need he fancy that this trifling cough is not to give way as it often has done before? Dear Ernest! I never knew that he loved me so.

October 31

Ernest's fear that he had let me stay too long in the country does not seem to be justified. We went so late that I wanted to indulge the children by staying late. So we have only just gotten home. I feel about as healthy as usual; it is true I have a little soreness around the chest, but it does not signify anything.

I never was so happy in my husband and children, in other words, in my *home* as I am now. Life looks very attractive. I am *glad* that I am going to get well.

But Ernest watches me carefully, and wants me, as a precautionary measure, to give up music, writing, sewing and painting— the very things that occupy me!— and lead an idle, useless life, for a time. I cannot refuse what he asks so tenderly, and as a personal favor to himself. Yet I should like to fill the few remaining pages of my Journal; I never like to leave things incomplete.

June 1, 1858

I wrote that seven years ago, little dreaming how long it would be before I would use a pen. Seven happy years ago!

I suppose that some who have known what my outward life has been during this period would think of me as a mere object of pity. There has certainly been suffering and deprivation enough to justify the sympathy of my dear husband and children, and the large circle of friends who have rallied about us. How little we knew we had so many precious ones!

God has dealt very tenderly with me. I was not stricken down by sudden disease, nor were the things I delighted in all taken away at once. There was a gradual loss of strength and gradual increase of suffering, and it was only by degrees that I was asked to give up the employments in which I delighted, my household duties, my visits to the sick and suffering, the society of beloved friends. Perhaps Ernest perceived and felt my deprivations sooner than I did; his sympathy always seemed to out-run my disappointments. When I compare him, as he is now, with what he was when I first knew him, I bless God for all the precious lessons He has taught him at my cost. There is a tenacity and persistence about his love for me that has made these years almost as wearisome to him as they have been to me. As for myself, if I had been told what I was to learn through these lengthy sufferings, I am afraid I would have shrunk back in terror, and so have lost all the sweet lessons God proposed to teach me. As it is, He has led me on, step by step, answering my prayers in His own way; I cannot bear to have a single human being doubt that it has been a perfect way. I love and adore it *just as it is*.

Perhaps the suspense has been one of the most trying features of my case. Just as I have unclasped my hand from my dear Ernest's; just as I have let go of my almost frantic hold of my darling children; just as heaven opened before me, and I fancied my weariness over and my wanderings done; just then almost every alarming symptom would disappear, and life recall me from the threshold of heaven itself. Thus I have been emptied from vessel to vessel, till I have learned that he only is truly happy who has no longer a choice of his own, and lies passive in God's hand.

Even now no one can foretell the issue of this sickness. We live a day at a time, not knowing what shall be on the morrow. But whether I live or die, my happiness is secure, and so, I believe, is that of my beloved ones. This is a true picture of our home:

A sick-room full of the suffering that ravages the body, but cannot touch the soul. A worn, wasting mother ministered unto by a devoted, saintly husband and by unselfish, Christian children. Some of the peace of God, if not all of it, shines in every face, is heard in every tone. It is a home that typifies and foreshadows the home that is perfect and eternal.

Our dear Helen has been given us for this emergency. Is it not strange that seeing our domestic life would have awakened in her some yearnings for a home and a heart and children of her own. She has said that there was a weary point in her life when she made up her mind that she was never to know these joys. But she accepted her lot gracefully. I do not know any other word that describes so well the beautiful offering she made of her life, first to God, and then to us. He accepted it, and has given her all the cares and responsibilities of domestic life, without the transcendent joys that sustain the wife and the mother. She has been all in all to our children, and God has been all in all to her. And she is happy in His service and in our love.

June 13

It took me nearly two weeks to write the above, at intervals, as my strength allowed. Ernest has consented to my finishing this volume, of which so few pages yet remain.

And he let me see a dear old friend who came all the way from my native town to see me— Dr. Eaton, our family physician as long as I could remember. He is of an advanced age, but full of vigor, his eye bright, and with a healthful glow on his cheek. But he says he is waiting and longing for his summons home. About that home we had a delightful talk together that did my very heart good. Then he made me tell him about this long sickness and the years of frail health and some of the sorrows through which I had toiled.

"Ah, these lovely children are explained now," he said.

"Do you really think," I asked, "that it has been *good* for my children to have a feeble, afflicted mother?"

"Yes, I really think so. A disciplined mother— disciplined children."

This comforting thought is one of the last drops in a cup of contentment already full.

June 20

Another Sunday, and all are at church except my darling Una, who keeps watch over her mother. These Sundays, when I have had them each alone in turn, have been blessed days to them and to me. Surely this is some compensation for what they lose in me of health and vigor. I know the state of each soul as far as it can be known, and have every reason to believe that my children all love my Saviour and are trying to live for Him. I have learned, at last, not to despise the day of small things, to cherish the most tender blossom, and to expect my dear ones to be imperfect before they become perfect Christians.

Una is a sweet, composed young girl, now eighteen years old, and what can I say more of the love her brothers bear to her, than this: they *never tease her*. She has long ceased asking why she must have delicate health when so many others of her age are full of physical life and vigor, but stands in her lot and place, doing what she can, suffering what she must, with a meekness that makes her lovely in my eyes, and that I am sure unites her closely to Christ.

June 27

It was Raymond's turn to stay with me today. He opened his heart to me more freely than he had ever done before.

"Mamma," he began, "if papa is willing, I have made up my mind— that is to say if I ever get decently good— to go on a mission."

I said, playfully: "And mamma's consent is not to be asked?"

"No," he said, getting hold of what there is left of my hand, "I know you wouldn't say a word. Don't you remember telling me once, when I was a little boy, that I might go and be welcome?"

"And don't you remember," I returned, "that you cried for joy, and then relieved your mind still farther, by walking on your hands, with your feet in the air?"

We both laughed heartily, at this remembrance, and

then I said: "My dear boy, you know your father's plan for you?"

"Yes, I know he expects me to study with him, and take his place in the world."

"And it is a very important place."

His countenance fell, as he fancied I was not entering heartily into his wishes.

"Dear Raymond," I went on, "I gave you to God long before you gave yourself to Him. If He can make you useful in your own, or in other lands, I bless His name. Whether I live to see you a man, or not, I hope you will work in the Lord's vineyard wherever He calls. I never asked anything for you but usefulness, in all my prayers for you; never once. His eyes filled with tears; he kissed me, and walked away to the window, to compose himself. My poor, dear, lovable, loving boy! He has all his mother's trials and struggles to contend with; but what does it matter if they bring him the same peace?

June 30

Everybody wonders to see me once more interested in my long-closed Journal, and becoming able to see the dear friends from whom I have been, in a measure, cut off. We cannot ask the meaning of this remarkable increase of strength.

I have no wish to choose. But I have come to the last page of my Journal, and living or dying, shall write in this volume no more. It closes upon a life of much childishness and great sinfulness, whose record makes me blush with shame, but I no longer need to relieve my heart with seeking sympathy in its unconscious pages, nor do I believe it good to go on analyzing it as I have done. I have had large experiences of both joy and sorrow; I have seen the nakedness and the emptiness, and I have seen the beauty and sweetness of life. What I have to say now, let me say to Jesus. What time and strength I used to spend in writing here, let me now spend in praying for all men, for all sufferers, for all who are out of the way, for all whom I love. And their name is Legion, for I love everybody.

Yes, I love everybody! That crowning joy has come to me at last. Christ is in my soul; He is mine; I am as conscious of it as that my husband and children are mine; and His Spirit flows forth from mine in the calm peace of a river, whose banks are green with grass, and glad with flowers. If I die it will be to leave a wearied and worn body, and a sinful soul, to go joyfully to be with Christ, to be weary and to sin no more. If I live, I shall find much blessed work to do for Him. So living or dying, I shall be the Lord's.

But I wish, oh, how earnestly, that whether I go or stay, I could inspire some lives with the joy that is now mine. For many years I have been rich in faith; rich in an unfaltering confidence that I was beloved of my God and Saviour. But something was missing; I was always groping for a mysterious grace the lack of which made me often sorrowful in the very midst of my most sacred joy, imperfect when I most longed for perfection. It was that *personal love to Christ* of which my precious mother so often spoke to me, which she often urged me to seek upon my knees. If I had known then, as I know now, what this priceless treasure could be to a sinful human soul, I would have sold all that I had to buy the field in which it lay hidden. But not till I was shut up to prayer and to the study of God's word by the loss of earthly joys, sickness destroying the flavor of them all, did I begin to penetrate the mystery that is learned under the cross. And wondrous as it is, how simple is this mystery! To love Christ, and to know that I love Him— this is all!

And when I entered upon the sacred yet oft-times homely duties of married life, if this love had been mine, how would that life have been transfigured! The petty faults of my husband under which I chafed would not have moved me; I would have welcomed Martha and her father to my home and made them happy there; I would have had no conflicts with my servants, shown no irritability to my children. For it would not have been I who spoke and acted, but Christ who lived in me.

Alas! I have had less than seven years in which to atone for a sinful, wasted past, and to live a new and a Christ-like life. If I am to have yet more, thanks be to Him who has given me the victory, that Life will be Love. Not the love that rests merely in the contemplation and adoration of its object; but the love that gladdens, sweetens and comforts other lives. To this end let me close with these words:

O gift of gifts! O grace of faith!
My God! how can it be
That Thou, who hast discerning love,
Shouldst give that gift to me?

How many hearts thou mightst have had
More innocent than mine!
How many souls more worthy far
Of that sweet touch of Thine?

Ah, grace! into unlikeliest hearts
It is thy boast to come;
The glory of Thy light to find
In darkest spots a home.

Oh, happy, happy that I am!
If thou canst be, O faith,
The treasure that thou art in life,
What wilt thou be in death?[38]

{Dear reader, as you conclude this book, ask yourself if
this gift of gifts is yours. May you be led to step heavenward
as the day draws near to the glorious return of Jesus Christ,
the Lord of heaven and earth.}

Endnotes

1   Thomas à Kempis (1380-1471), was a German mystic, whose writings were loved by Mrs. Prentiss. In the memoirs of Edward Payson, the author's beloved father, the following excerpt of a letter to a young pastor describes his deep affection for the devotional writings of Thomas: "The books which I have found most useful to me are (Jonathan) Edwards' Works, (David) Brainerd's Life, (John) Newton's Letters, (John) Owens' Treatises on *Indwelling Sin, Mortification of Sin in Believers*, and *Psalm 130* [see Volume 6 of Owen's writings by Banner of Truth Trust] and Thomas à Kempis' *Imitation of Christ*, especially translated by Payne. If you have never read Thomas à Kempis, I beg you to acquire it. Some things you will not like; but, for spirituality and weanedness from the world, I know of nothing equal to it." (*The Complete Works of Edward Payson*, Vol. 1, p. 251, Sprinkle Publications).

2   Henry Martyn (1781-1812) was an Anglican missionary to India, who translated the New Testament into Hindustani. His Journals remain among the classics of English devotional literature.

3   Robert Pollok (1798-1827) was a gifted Scottish poet.

4   Sit Walter Scott (1771-1832) was a Scottish novelist and poet.

5   To "stanch" is to stop the blood flowing from a wound.

6   *Heaven— A World of Love*, by Jonathan Edwards is a beautiful, biblical discussion of what heaven will be like for its inhabitants. Available through Calvary Press.

7   Consumption was the progressive wasting away of the body; especially that form accompanying pulmonary phthisis and associated with coughing, spitting up blood, hectic fever, etc. This was very common in that day.

8   Jeremy Taylor (1613-1667) was an Anglican bishop and writer

born and educated at Cambridge. His books *Holy Living* and *Holy Dying* are among his most notable works.

9   Richard Baxter (1615-1691) was one of the greatest of the Puritan divines. His writings continue to touch the hearts of multitudes. Baxter subtitled *The Saints Everlasting Rest* as *A Treatise on the Blessed State of the Saints, in their Enjoyment of God in Heaven.* It is intended to help us fix our attention upon heavenly realities in the midst of this perishing world.

10   An aromatic plant common in the south of Europe. It is related to Lavander, and yields an oil used in medicines and perfumes.

11   The expression "to be kept in leading strings" means to be placated or treated as a child, as leading strings is a reference to a state of infancy, dependence, or to be under the guidance of others.

12   William Potts Dewees (1768-1841) was an American physician who wrote, *Treatise on the Physical and Medical Treatment of Children* in 1825. It became a popular book with parents in the mid-nineteenth century.

13   Dorcas is the godly woman described in Acts chapter 9 whom the Apostle Peter raised from the dead. She was known for her good and kind deeds.

14   Blancmange is a white, sweet, pudding-like dessert made from various ingredients, including cornstarch, gelatine, almond milk, vanilla, and rum and shaped in a mold. It was a very plain and ordinary dessert of the day.

15   Beef-tea is strong beef broth used especially for the sick.

16   A cudgel is a heavy stick used primarily as a weapon, and "to take up cudgels for" is to engage in a contest on behalf of someone or something else.

17   A fender is a screen used to prevent coals or sparks from escaping a fireplace.

18   These words accurately express the deepest longing of the author, especially seen in her popular hymn, *More Love to Thee, O Christ.*

19   To be "a cumberer of the ground" is to be useless and burdensome. This very expression is from the parable of the barren fig tree in Luke 13:7.

20   The expression "The King of Terrors" is taken from Job 18:14 where Bildad describes the state of the wicked before the grave. Death is also personified in Scripture in places such as Isaiah 28:15, Psalm 49:14,15, and Hebrews 2:15.

21   Caroline Fry (1787-1846) was a godly woman who suffered much. She wrote, among other helpful books, *Christ our Example.*

22   Jonathan Edwards (1703-1758), was the greatest philosopher and theologian of America's history. His deep writings had a profound influence upon Elizabeth Prentiss, and are still gratefully read today by many Christians.

23   The expression "a pelican in the wilderness" is one of desolation, drawn from Psalm 102:6. Of this imagery Spurgeon says, "a mournful and even hideous object, the very image of desolation." (The Treasury of David, Vol. 2)

24   This German phrase— "den Jammer und das Elend der Welt" is drawn from a popular German story, it means "the misery and the distress of the world."

25   This is a direct quote from John Bunyan's classic work *The Pilgrim's Progress.* These are the very words which Hopeful spoke to Christian as they were both crossing The River of Death. Our author was a great lover of this masterpiece of the Christian life, and allusions to it are found scattered throughout this book. In a letter to a friend she once said, "You ask if I revel in *The Pilgrim's Progress*— Yes, I do. I think it is an *amazing* book." One of her greatest pleasures during her only trip to England was her visit to the grave of "The Tinker of Bedford", as Bunyan was affectionately known. To obtain a copy of *The Pilgrim's Progress,* contact Calvary Press.

26   The phrase "on sufferance" means to merely tolerate something.

27   The phrase "to take fire" meant to begin to burn with emotion; i.e. to fly into a passion.

28   Robert Leighton (1611-1684) was a graduate of Edinburgh University, and the Archbishop of Glasgow, Scotland. Among his many devotional writings is the classic commentary on 1st Peter, of which Spurgeon declared— "We scarcely need to commend this truly heavenly work... it is a favorite with all spiritual men." Mrs. Prentiss, in a letter to a dear friend, once wrote: "I am re-reading Archbishop Leighton on 1st Peter; I wonder if you like it as much as my husband and I do!" (*An Obedient and Patient Faith*, available through Calvary Press Publishing)

29   The Slough of Despond was a pit into which Christian fell after first setting out for the celestial city in *The Pilgrim's Progress*. It represents a place of deep discouragement for a weary pilgrim.

30   Providence has been defined as— God's most holy, wise and powerful preserving and governing all His creatures and all their actions. One of the finest works on this grand theme is *The Mystery of Providence*, by John Flavel.

31   Daniel Wilson (1778-1858) was an Anglican Bishop in India.

32   This very expression was used by our author describing the circumstances surrounding her writing of this book. Upon the tragic death of her dear sister-in-law, she sacrificially cared for her nephew, Francis. "Many a page of *Stepping Heavenward* was written with this child in her arms; and perhaps that is one secret of its power." (*More Love To Thee*, p. 237, available through Calvary Press Publishing)

33   John Wesley (1703-1791) was the founder of Methodism, whose tireless evangelistic labors were centered mainly in Great Britain and America. Although used by God, some of his methods and theology were found wanting.

34   Francis Fenelon (1651-1715) was a French mystic. Mrs. Prentiss found much helpful counsel in his writings, as seen in these words of her husband: "Her delight in his writings dated back more than a quarter of a century, and continued, unabated, to the end of her days. She regarded him with a sort of personal affection and reverence... What attracted her to Fenelon was not his doctrine of salvation— she found it better taught by Bunyan and Leighton— it

was (rather) his marvelous knowledge of the human heart, his keen insight into the proper workings of nature and grace, his deep spiritual wisdom, and the sweet mystic tone of his piety." (*More Love To Thee*, pp. 319f, available through Calvary Press Publishing)

35   Martin Luther (1483-1546), the great German Reformer, was raised up by the Lord to bring God's people back to a commitment to the Bible alone as their source of authority, the doctrine known as *Sola Scriptura*. The little prayer being quoted sums up his child-like faith and dependence upon his Heavenly Father for heavenly wisdom, in the right interpretation of His all-sufficient Word. It is the same attitude expressed in Scripture itself in Psalm 119:18.

36   The phrase "from Dan to Bersheeba" became a proverbial expression meaning— from one end of a territory to its farthest extremity. Dan was the northern-most tribe in the land of Israel, and Beersheba was its southern-most city (see Judges 20:1; 2nd Samuel 24:2; 1st Kings 4:25).

37   The expression "obedient parents" refers to the common evil of children being in complete control of their parents, as if parents are to be obedient to their children's desires. Contact Calvary Press to obtain outstanding books on biblical parenting.

38   Fittingly, the words of the hymn which Mrs. Prentiss selected to close this glorious book, were sung at her funeral in August of 1878 in Dorset, Vermont. The words were written by the English hymn writer Frederick Faber (1814-1863) whose poems were often used to comfort and encourage her heart.

A History of the Book

by George L. Prentiss

By the time STEPPING HEAVENWARD first appeared, Mrs. Prentiss had become known already by her *Little Susy's Six Birthdays* and other books for children, as also by *The Flower of the Family*, and a succession of volumes for youth of both sexes; but in *Stepping Heavenward* she struck a higher and stronger note. In this work she aimed to help and to cheer all her readers, whether old or young, in the hard struggle of life. She composed the larger part of it in the winter and spring of 1867-8 while absorbed in caring for a little motherless nephew who died shortly after. Referring especially to this part, she once said to a friend, "Every word of that book was a prayer, and seemed to come of itself. I never knew how it was written, for my heart and hands were full of something else." On going to Dorset for the summer she carried the manuscript with her, but in no mood to finish it. In a letter dated August 3, she said: "I feel now as if I should never write any more. Book-making looks formidable." I begged her to take the story up again, and two gifted Christian ladies, then sojourning in Dorset, joined their persuasion to mine. Several years later, one of them, Miss E. A. Warner, wrote to me:

Do you remember coming into the parlor one morning where Miss Hannah Lyman and I were sitting by ourselves, and telling us that your wife was writing a story but had become so discouraged she threatened to throw it aside as not worth finishing? "I like it myself," you added, "it really seems to me one of the best things she has ever written, and I am trying to get her to read it to you and see what you think of it. The next morning she came to our room with a little green box in her hand, saying, with her merry laugh, "Now you've got to do penance for your sins, you wicked women!" and, sitting down by the window, while we took our sewing, she began to read to us in manuscript the work which was destined to touch and strengthen so many hearts— "which," to use the words of another, "has become a part of the soul-history of many thousands of Christian women, young and old, at home and abroad." It was a rare treat to listen to it, with comments from her interspersed, some of them droll and witty, others full of profound religious feeling. Now and then, as we queried if something was not improbable or unnatural, she would give us bits of history from her own experience or that of her friends, going to show that stranger things had occurred in real life. I need not say we insisted on its being finished, feeling sure it would do great good; though I must confess that I do not think either of us, much as we enjoyed it, was fully aware of its great merits. She went on with her work, occasionally reading to us what she had added. In those days she always spoke of it as her "Katy book," no other title having been given to it. But one morning she came to the breakfast table with her face all lighted up. "I've got a name for my book," she exclaimed, "it came to me while I was lying awake last night. You know Wordsworth's Stepping Westward? I am going to call it "Stepping Heavenward;" don't you like it? I do." We all felt it was exactly the right name, and she added, "I think I will put in Wordworth's poem as a preface."

The work was first printed as a serial in "The Advance" of Chicago. As it drew to a close Mr. J.B.T. Marsh, one of the editors, wrote to her:

You will notice that the story is completed this week. I wish it could have continued six months longer. I have several times been on the point of writing you to express my own personal satisfaction and to acquaint you with the great unanimity and volume of praise of it, which has reached us from our readers. I do not think anything since the time of The National Era and Uncle Tom's Cabin has been more heartily received. We have had hundreds of letters of which the expression has been: "We quarrel to see who shall have the first reading of the story." I think if you should ever come West my wife would overturn almost any stone for the sake of welcoming you to the hospitality of our cottage on the Lake Michigan shore.

When issued in book form its reception surpassed all expectation. Notwithstanding the favor it met with in "The Advance," Mrs. Prentiss had still great misgiving about its success— a misgiving that constantly haunted her while engaged in writing it. But all doubt on the subject was soon dispelled. *Stepping Heavenward* seemed to meet so many real, deep, inarticulate cravings in such a multitude of hearts, that the response to it was instant and general.

Others of Mrs. Prentiss' books were enjoyed, praised, laughed over; but this one was taken by timid hands into secret places, pored over by eyes dim with tears, and its lesson prayed out at many a Jabbok. It was one of those books which sorrowing women read to each other, and which lured many a bustling Martha from the fretting of her care-cumbered life to ponder the new lesson of rest in toil. It was one of those books of which people kept a lending copy, that they might enjoy the uninterrupted companionship of their own.

The circulation of *Stepping Heavenward* was very large. In this country not less, probably, than a hundred and fifty thousand copies have been sold; while abroad, where it was not copyrighted, the sale is estimated to have reached a much larger number of copies perhaps half a million. Four leading houses in Great Britain republished the work. It was translated into German, French, Norwegian, Swedish, Italian, and I know not what other languages. The German version long ago passed into the sixth edition. Baron Tauchnitz, the celebrated Leipsic publisher, inserted it also in his noted *Collection of British Authors*. In a letter asking my permission to do so, he praised the work in very high terms. Indeed, the testimonials to its power and beauty from beyond the sea were even more striking than those at home. Men and women known the world over as scholars and authors or for their high culture, social position and leadership in the service of God and humanity, expressed their admiration without stint. One of them, said to have been an eminent German theologian, used this language respecting it: "Already many a good, noble gift, rich in blessing, is come to us from North America; but we do not hesitate to designate *Stepping Heavenward* as the best among all from there which we have ever seen."

An interesting chapter might be written about the different translations of *Stepping Heavenward*. I will refer to one of them, the German version. It was made by an invalid lady of Göttingen, and led to a correspondence, which has not yet ceased. Her letters, overflowing with grateful affection and giving details respecting the successive editions of the work, the welcome it received into thousands of German homes and it great usefulness, have been running on now for nearly thirty years.

The Secret of Its Influence

Stepping Heavenward, while deeply religious, is wholly free from formulas. Every page bears the stamp of earnest conviction. The tone throughout is honest, sympathetic and full of good cheer. No false or jarring notes are struck. All is natural and true to life. The "one human heart" beating in the bosom of the race and, more or less feebly, in its humblest members, is depicted with a skill, fidelity, and gentleness and soothing touch, which could come only of deep personal experience and the keenest observation. If the lessons taught by the story are at times painful, they are yet sweet, inspiring and fresh as a summer breeze. No discouraging, still less gloomy or pessimistic sentence can be found in the entire volume. *Stepping*

Heavenward is its dominant, animating, ever-recurring thought as well as its aim and name. And this is largely the secret of its influence. This, too, explains the fact, attested by innumerable witnesses, that the book is almost equally adapted and dear to all classes and conditions of readers who aspire to a life in harmony with the holy will of God. I say "almost equally adapted and dear;" for I cannot forget that it was written expressly to give aid and comfort to women, both young and old— more especially to suffering wives and mothers— hard-pressed by the terrible cares and battles of life. If I may judge by the letters in which they poured out to the author their feelings of grateful love and admiration *Stepping Heavenward* was better adapted and dearer to them than it could possibly be to men. Mrs. Prentiss used to say, laughingly, that she did not understand men and could not write for them.

The letters referred to came from all parts of this country, from Europe and even from the ends of the earth; and they were written by persons belonging to every class in society. Among them was one which Mrs. Prentiss specially prized. It was written on coarse, brown grocery paper by a poor crippled boy in the interior of Pennsylvania and led to a correspondence that continued for years. The book was read with equal delight by persons not only of all classes from a queen to a poor negro woman, but of all nationalities and creed; by Protestants and Roman Catholics, by Calvinists, Arminians, High Churchmen, Evangelicals, Quakers and Unitarians. It had that touch of nature which makes the whole world akin. Thousands of its readers appeared to think their own case was described, so plainly did they see themselves mirrored in its pages. The number of Katys, Katy's mothers, Marthas, Mrs. Campbells, Dr. Cabots, Dr. Elliots, both son and father, who were positively identified as originals of these characters, was a marvel. The questions put to her on this point in letters and conversation greatly amused Mrs. Prentiss, especially the questions relating to Katy. She ridiculed the suggestion that she herself had sat as the model for Katy. "Everybody is asking (she wrote to her daughter, then in Germany) if I meant in Katy to describe myself. The next book I write I'll make my heroine black and everybody will say, 'Oh, there you are again, black to the life!'"

Nevertheless, she and Katy *were* astonishingly alike. Who that knew her well could fail to see it at every turn. In depicting Katy she was, unconsciously no doubt, drawing a most life-like picture of herself. As for example in such passages as this: "Why need I throw my whole soul into whatever I do? Why can't I make so much as an apron for little Ernest without the ardor and eagerness of a soldier marching to battle? I wonder if people of my temperament ever get toned down and learn to take life coolly?" At all events, if there had been no Elizabeth Prentiss I feel quite sure the Katy of *Stepping Heavenward* would have been impossible.

In planning and writing *Stepping Heavenward,* she seemed to have no thought whatever of pecuniary profit or of reputation. "Even Satan never ventured to suggest that I write for money," she once said. Nor had literary ambition, so far as I could perceive, anything to do with her books. Once written and published she rarely alluded to them, or cared to hear them mentioned. "Mr. R. (she wrote to her daughter in Germany) has sent me a letter from a man in Nice, whose wife wants to translate Katy into French. I sent word they might translate it into Hottentot for all me." But if the message was to the effect that some poor, bed-ridden old woman, or a sorrow-stricken young mother, had found comfort in one of her books, it would send a thrill of joy through her whole frame. "Much of my experience of life (she wrote to a friend, not long before her death) has cost me a great price and I wish to use it for strengthening and comforting other souls."

If the whole secret of the charm of *Stepping Heavenward* were told, it would be needful to point out the literary, as well as the practical and religious sources of its power. All through the volume, from the poem of Wordsworth at its beginning to the hymn of Faber at its close, one sees constant indications of familiarity with the best literature. Mrs. Prentiss was not only a great reader, but, like her father, she possessed a wonderful faculty for absorbing and assimilating what she read, whether in English, French or German. Her taste was very broad; and she could pass from Bunyan, Baxter, Leighton, Fenelon, Tauler and Tholuck, George Herbert, Keble and Manning, to Sir Walter Scott, Goethe, Victor Hugo, Dickens, Irving, Longfellow, Hawthorne and Mrs. Stowe, without the slightest jar or sense of incongruity. Everything genuine and truthful; everything that taught her a new lesson in the study of human nature, interested her deeply and passed readily into her own style and thought.

The letters Mrs. Prentiss received thanking her for *Stepping Heavenward*, along with those that have reached me since her death, form a very beautiful tribute to her memory. One, addressed to her, arrived from London a few days before her last illness. It was written by a young wife and mother closely related to two of the most honored families in England, and sought counsel in regard to a certain question of duty that had grown out of special domestic trials. *Stepping Heavenward*, the writer said, had formed an era in her religious life; she had read it through *from fifty to sixty times*; it had its place by the side of her Bible; and no words could express the good it had done her, or the comfort she had derived from its pages.

Here is an extract from a letter to me written by a distinguished Methodist divine of the Northwest:

> *In a letter from my daughter, who is the wife of a missionary in China, she speaks of sending a part of Sunday afternoon in reading Stepping Heavenward, and adds, "This must be at least the twelfth time I have read it through." She is a cultivated and devout Christian, fully occupied in studying, teaching, translating and a hundred other things; and yet finds time to read and re-read again and again her favorite book.*

Here is an extract from a recent letter of Mrs. John R. Mott, describing a visit to a girls' school in Shanghai:

> *The school is the only attempt I know of to reach the daughters of the highest classes. The principal is Miss Laura*

> Haygood, a sister of Bishop Haygood of the Southern Meth-odist Church. The school is Anglo-Chinese, English being a great attraction in a port. The principal is a very strong, womanly and Christian character and the conduct of the school is thoroughly Christian. There were, I think, about thirty girls in the school when I was there, but it has been growing rapidly since. They were naturally the most attrac-tive girls I saw in China. Some of them were beautiful in person, dress, manners, and, best of all, Christian character. It was such a satisfaction to be able to talk to them in En-glish. A smile went round when I asked the question as to their favorite book, aside from the Bible, and the answer, "Stepping Heavenward" left no doubt on the subject. The teachers also told me that Stepping Heavenward had a re-markable influence among them and that they talked and wrote of it as of no other book.

Testimonies like these have been so numerous that if printed they would form a large volume. Here is an extract from a letter from Old England that comes even while I am writing:

> My mother, who has been staying with me, says that among the last books she read aloud to my father was Step-ping Heavenward, and that they both enjoyed it exceedingly. Your mother wrote it, did she not?"

The father who had just passed away was that admi-rable Christian man and eminent theologian, Professor A.B. Bruce of Scotland.

The interest of the Chinese girls in *Stepping Heav-enward* surprised me at first not a little, notwithstanding that, "More Love to Thee, O Christ," as I had been told, was a special favorite in the native churches. The hymn is so simple and so spiritual that is equally adapted to the expression of religious feeling and aspiration everywhere and among all races; but the story is occidental, modern and even American in style of thought, in manners, and in local coloring. The reason why these bright Chinese girls were so delighted with it can be found only in the Christ-like spirit and the deep knowledge of human nature which mark the book. The inspiration of gospel faith and hope and love is no more a thing of place and race than is sunshine, or the air we breath. That is why the New Testament and the story of the Cross may become as precious, and to all intents and purposes as intelligible also, to a poor Hottentot as to the greatest scholar, scientist, philosopher or theologian in Christendom. The foolishness of God is wiser than men. If we understood better what penitence, prayer and saving grace really mean, according to the Scriptures, we should, perhaps, cease being puzzled to find such spiritual unity amid the most grotesque and repulsive diversities of human condition.

It has been to me a solace and joy, ever since the departure of its author, to give away copies of *Stepping Heavenward* far and near, and then to note the happy influence of the book. Of course every book, even the Bible itself, is powerless to bring light and strength into an unwilling soul; but where there is any real interest in religious things, any sincere desire for spiritual counsel and help, *Stepping Heavenward,* I have found, always brings with it a benediction, especially where relief is most sorely needed. What Dr. Vincent said in his memorial address more than a score of years ago, may be said with equal truth today:

> *I am sure that hers is, in an eminent degree, the bless-*
> *ing of them that were ready to perish. Weary, overtaxed*
> *mother, misunderstood and unappreciated wives, servants,*
> *pale seamstresses, delicate women forced to live in an at-*
> *mosphere of drunkenness and coarse brutality, widows and*
> *orphans in the bitterness of their bereavement, mothers with*
> *their tears dropping over empty cradles— to thousands of*
> *such she was a messenger from heaven.*

And not only, I may add, to thousands of such was she a messenger from heaven, but to thousands also whose path in life was full of sunshine and flowers, did she bring the same message, teaching them that in prosperity as well as in adversity our supreme felicity is in loving God and doing his blessed will as He has made it known to us in Jesus Christ. This lesson of lessons runs, like a golden thread, through *Stepping Heavenward,* and all the rest of Mrs. Prentiss' writings. It is, indeed, only another version, varied in form and by story, of the sublime answer given to the first question in the old Catechism: *What is the Chief End of Man? Man's Chief End is TO GLORIFY GOD AND TO ENJOY HIM FOREVER.*

New York, New York
Christmas Day, 1899.

*Recommended Other Reading
Available Through Calvary Press...*

More Love To Thee
The Life and Letters
of Elizabeth Prentiss

George Lewis Prentiss
Preface by Elisabeth Elliot

So many of our readers have sought to find this book, that Calvary Press felt a need to bring it back into print. In this biography and collection of letters, you are not only introduced to Elizabeth Prentiss, but through her husband's sweet recollections and her own words you begin to feel as if you know her personally. If *Stepping Heavenward* tugged on your heart, then get to know the dear Christian woman who penned it using aspects of her own life's experiences as the basis for much of the story. Elisabeth Elliot writes in her Preface... "Reading Christian biographies has had an immeasurable influence in my life and spiritual growth. *More Love To Thee* reveals the character of a woman who loved God and earnestly sought to help others to love Him."

Ask about other titles in

The Prentiss Series

by Calvary Press!

The Heart of Anger
Lou Priolo

Do you have an angry child? Do you know someone who does? Did you know that parents often unknowingly provoke their children to the point of anger? This is a manual for parents seeking to correct or prevent the development of those angry responses which characterize what the Bible calls "an angry man." Children can easily habituate themselves to think, act, and be motivated with anger— especially if parents do not have the biblical knowledge and wisdom to prevent or intervene to correct such problems of the heart. These pages contain the practical help and real hope for all those facing these vital concerns. Says Jay Adams, "The Church in general will be in Lou's debt for writing it. It is a book whose time has come."

Shepherding A Child's Heart
Tedd Tripp

Pastor John MacArthur writes: "With the plethora of material on parenting and the family, it is distressing to see how few are genuinely biblical. Here is a refreshing exception. Tedd Tripp offers solid, trustworthy, biblical help for parents. If you're looking for the right perspective and practical help on the divine plan for parenting, you won't find a more excellent guide." In an age when the subject of child-rearing is often intertwined with notions of pop-psychology this book will become your definitive guide to a bible based understanding of the parent's role and responsibilities. A landmar book on this subject. If you are a parent or anticipate being one or are involved with children as an educator or caretaker let this be the one book you own if none else.

Heaven— A World of Love
Jonathan Edwards

John Piper, author of *Delighting God* writes: "I believe with all my heart that in order to be useful in this world we must fall in love with another world. In order to transform this world for the glory of Christ we must be saturated with the glory and wisdom of another world. In order to be changed from one degree of glory to another now we must hope fully in the grace that is about to be revealed to us soon. In order to be the light of the world we must put our torch in the flame of heaven. In all of this, Jonathan Edwards is our great helper and *Heaven— A World of Love* is one of his greatest feasts."

"Edwards gives us a taste of heaven that is savoring to the soul."

—Dr. R.C. Sproul, author, Chairman of Ligonier Ministries.

A History of the Work of Redemption
Jonathan Edwards

This monumental work is a fascinating, scholarly analysis of the history of God's work of redeeming His people. Edwards lays out for us a grand overview of how God has crafted the events of this world, as seen in scripture, for the sole purpose of preparing the world for Christ's appearance, His accomplishment of redemption, and the glorious spread of the Gospel thereafter. Your understanding of scripture and the sovereignty of God will forever be changed, you will look at the Old Testament with new eyes as you appreciate it's redemptive history. If you wish to know the Bible in some depth you must become familiar with this work, certainly no pastor or Bible teacher should be without it in their library. Available now for the first time in many years as a stand-alone book.

From Forgiven to Forgiving
Jay Adams

Without a doubt, this is the best book on biblical forgiveness available today. An attractive and affordable soft-cover edition, it is destined to become a classic work on this subject. A must for the library of the pastor, professional counselor and lay person alike. We've grown up learning many popular misconceptions about forgiveness from our parents, society and even our churches. The mission of Dr. Jay Adams is to challenge us through the scriptures to understand the issues of forgiveness and to experience the power of forgiveness— as God intended. This book has been greatly used by God and will continue to be instrumental in the saving of marriages, friendships, church memberships, and any relationship where issues of forgiveness have not been dealt with properly. An excellent book to use for group study or a church Sunday school study.

The Person and Work of the Holy Spirit
Benjamin B. Warfield

In our present day the person and the work of the Holy Spirit is too often misunderstood. Whole denominations hold to and promote unscriptural doctrines concerning God's Spirit and His operation in the lives of Christians today. So how can one know with certainty the character and the ways and means by which the Holy Spirit works in the Church of God? Would it not be by seeking our answer from God Himself? In this volume, are assembled for the first time anywhere the completeworks of Benjamin B. Warfield regarding the Holy Spirit. The sermons, articles and book reviews contained in this book will instruct you and challenge you to know the Holy Spirit as He has revealed Himself— through the scriptures.

An Obedient & Patient Faith

An Exposition of 1st Peter
by Robert Leighton

This classic commentary has been considered by many to be the most valuable single commentary on scripture ever written. Spurgeon considered it a "heavenly work...a favorite with all spiritual men." The depth of First Peter is glorious and the depth and thoroughness by which Leighton exposits and explains it is fantastic. In an age when the study of Theology was the universal and highest pursuit, Leighton was preeminent.

Within these pages lies a banquet of precious and delightful truths to be savored, every page is full of the flavor and aroma of deep piety and judicious instruction. No student of the scriptures should be without this invaluable commentary.

From Religion to Christ
Peter Jeffery

Under the cover of a dark night, a gray-haired Jewish Rabbi approached a much younger man to inquire about matters which were deeply troubling him. That conversation between Nicodemus and Jesus of Nazareth has intrigued God's people for the past two millennia. In this book, we are taken back to that night's conversation and are shown how the words Jesus spoke to Nicodemus on a Jerusalem hillside some two thousand years past are essential to our salvation today. The author is deeply concerned that millions of people are just like Nicodemus was that night— religious, but not redeemed by God. A careful and prayerful reading of this book can be used of God to open the eyes of many to see clearly that their religion is empty and vain, but salvation can and will be found in Jesus Christ alone.

The Duties of Church Members to their Pastors

John Angell James

together in one volume with—

A Plea to Pray for Pastors

Gardner Spring

In *The Duties of Church Members to their Pastors*, J.A. James sets forth nine specific duties which the members of the church owe their pastors. If they are carefully followed, the church of Christ will be greatly enriched and will stand ready for divine blessing.

Pastor John MacArthur writes, "*A Plea to Pray for Pastors* is excerpted from Gardiner Spring's excellent book, The Power of the Pulpit. It is nearly 200 years old, but its message is as fresh and relevant as the day it was written. My own heart echoes this plea.

---

for a complete catalog of all our offerings,

please be sure to call us at 1-800-789-8175

or visit our new website:

www.calvarypress.com

The Mission of Calvary Press

The ministry of Calvary Press is firmly committed to printing quality Christian literature relevant to the dire needs of the church and the world at the close of the 20th century. We unashamedly stand upon the foundation stones of the Reformation of the 16th century— Scripture alone, Faith alone, Grace alone, Christ alone, and God's Glory alone!

Our prayer for this new ministry is found in two portions taken from the Psalms: "And let the beauty of the LORD our God be upon us, And establish the work of our hands for us; Yes, establish the work of our hands." (Psalm 90:17)

Calvary Press is thankful to anyone who has a burden for sound doctrine and literature such as that published by this ministry. If you would like to help our efforts by making a donation to this ministry we would greatly appreciate it. Calvary Press is a not-for-profit ministry of Grace Reformed Baptist Church of Long Island, N.Y., all donations will be recognized with a tax-deductible receipt. Thank You in advance for any assistance you would seek to give us in our labors.

**For more information about
the ministry of Calvary Press
please call us toll-free
at 1 (800) 789-8175**